DIY URBANISM IN AFRICA

Africa Now

Africa Now is published by Zed Books in association with the internationally respected Nordic Africa Institute. Featuring high-quality, cutting-edge research from leading academics, the series addresses the big issues confronting Africa today. Accessible but in-depth, and wide-ranging in its scope, Africa Now engages with the critical political, economic, sociological and development debates affecting the continent, shedding new light on pressing concerns.

Nordic Africa Institute

The Nordic Africa Institute (Nordiska Afrikainstitutet) is a centre for research, documentation and information on modern Africa. Based in Uppsala, Sweden, the Institute is dedicated to providing timely, critical and alternative research and analysis of Africa and to co-operation with African researchers. As a hub and a meeting place for a growing field of research and analysis the Institute strives to put knowledge of African issues within reach for scholars, policy makers, politicians, media, students and the general public. www.nai.uu.se

Forthcoming titles
Titles already published

Cecilia Navarra and Cristina Udelsmann Rodrigues (eds), *Transformations of Rural Spaces in Mozambique*

Diana Højlund Madsen (eds), *Gendered Institutions and Women's Political Representation in Africa*

Jesper Bjarnesen and Simon Turner, *Invisibility in African Displacements*

Fantu Cheru and Cyril Obi (eds), *The Rise of China and India in Africa*

Ilda Lindell (ed.), *Africa's Informal Workers*

Iman Hashim and Dorte Thorsen, *Child Migration in Africa*

Prosper B. Matondi, Kjell Havnevik and Atakilte Beyene (eds), *Biofuels, Land Grabbing and Food Security in Africa*

Cyril Obi and Siri Aas Rustad (eds), *Oil and Insurgency in the Niger Delta*

Mats Utas (ed.), *African Conflicts and Informal Power*

Prosper B. Matondi, *Zimbabwe's Fast Track Land Reform*

Maria Eriksson Baaz and Maria Stern, *Sexual Violence as a Weapon of War?*

DIY URBANISM IN AFRICA

Politics and Practice

Stephen Marr and Patience Mususa

LONDON · NEW YORK · OXFORD · NEW DELHI · SYDNEY

THE NORDIC
AFRICA INSTITUTE
NORDISKA AFRIKAINSTITUTET

ZED Books
Bloomsbury Publishing Plc
50 Bedford Square, London, WC1B 3DP, UK
1385 Broadway, New York, NY 10018, USA
29 Earlsfort Terrace, Dublin 2, Ireland

BLOOMSBURY and Zed Books are trademarks of Bloomsbury Publishing Plc

First published in Great Britain 2024 in association with the Nordic Africa Institute,
PO Box 1703, SE-751 47 Uppsala, Sweden

Series design by Alice Marwick
Cover image © Victoria Okoye

A catalogue record for this book is available from the British Library.

Library of Congress Cataloging-in-Publication Data
Names: Marr, Stephen, editor. | Mususa, Patience, editor.
Title: DIY urbanism in Africa: politics and practice/Stephen Marr and Patience Mususa.
Other titles: Do-it-yourself urbanism in Africa | Africa now (Zed Books)
Description: London; New York: Zed, 2023. | Series: Africa now |
"First published in Great Britain 2023 in association with the Nordic Africa
Institute"–Title page verso. | Includes bibliographical references and index. |
Contents: Introduction: Do-it-yourself Urbanism in Africa's Cities/Patience Mususa
and Stephen Marr – Comparative DIY Urbanisms: Reflections on a Concept's Pasts, Presents and Futures/Stephen
Marr – The Makeshift City and Do-it-yourself (DIY) Urbanism/Martin J. Murray – Reflections on the DIY Paradigm
and Urban Living in Nigeria / Mohamed-Bello Yunusa – DIY Urbanism in an African Context and its
Potential as a Collaborative Placemaking Tool for Bridging Africa's Urban Infrastructure Deficit/Mathias
Agbo Jr. – Political Economy of Community-Led Security Provisioning in Urban Africa/Victor Adetula –
The Politics of Urban Insecurity: Hybrid relations and party dominance in Lagos/Nigeria, Henrik Angerbrandt –
"'Accra We De"y': Precarious Histories, Creative Place-Making, and Reimagined Futures in Urban Ghana /
Jennifer Hart – Everyday spatial practices and production of urban commons in Accra, Ghana/Victoria Okoye –
Learning from DIY urbanism: Lessons from Freetown/Federico Monica – DIY Urbanism as Ecotopia: The
Case of the Green Camp Gallery in Durban, South Africa/Antje Daniel – Disability and Urbanism in Malawi/
Jonathan Makuwira – The Biopolitics of Do-it-yourself Urbanism on the Zambian Copperbelt/Patience
Mususa – Conclusion: DIY Urbanism as Politics of Interruption/Stephen Marr and Patience Mususa.
Identifiers: LCCN 2023008147 (print) | LCCN 2023008148 (ebook) | ISBN 9781786999023
(paperback) | ISBN 9781786999016 (hardback) | ISBN 9781786999061 (epub) |
ISBN 9781786999030 (pdf) | ISBN 9781350237537
Subjects: LCSH: Sociology, Urban–Africa. | Cities and towns–Africa–Social conditions. |
Civic improvement–Africa.
Classification: LCC HT169.A35 D59 2023 (print) |
LCC HT169.A35 (ebook) | DDC 307.76096–dc23/eng/20230221
LC record available at https://lccn.loc.gov/2023008147
LC ebook record available at https://lccn.loc.gov/2023008148

ISBN: HB: 978-1-7869-9901-6
         PB: 978-1-7869-9902-3
         ePDF: 978-1-7869-9903-0
         eBook: 978-1-7869-9906-1

Series: Africa Now

Typeset by Integra Software Services Pvt. Ltd.

To find out more about our authors and books visit www.bloomsbury.com
and sign up for our newsletters.

CONTENTS

FIGURES

CONTRIBUTORS

Victor Adetula, Department of Political Science, University of Jos, Nigeria
Victor Adetula is Professor of International Relations & Development Studies at
the University of Jos (Nigeria). He was previously Head of Research at the Nordic
Africa Institute until 2020. He has over three decades of working experience in
academic and policy research, on topics such as democracy and governance and
peace and conflict. He was Claude Ake Visiting Professor in the Department
of Peace & Conflict Research, University of Uppsala (2013), and previously
Head of Africa & Regional Integration Department at the Nigerian Institute of
International Affairs, Lagos (2012), and Nelson Mandela Visiting Professor in the
Centre for International Studies, Jawaharlal Nehru University, New Delhi (2011).

Mathias Agbo Jr, Independent Researcher
Mathias Agbo Jr is an independent sustainability and adaptation researcher and
built environment designer. He runs a design and sustainability consultancy in
Abuja, Nigeria. He has over fourteen years of experience as a designer, project
manager and independent researcher and writer. He has published essays and peer-
reviewed papers on African architecture, urbanism, sustainability and adaptation
design; his bylines have appeared in numerous publications around the world. He
has collaborated with and consulted for several private clients and organizations
like the UNDP, Nigeria's Office of the Vice-President, the American University of
Nigeria and North-East Humanitarian Hub.

Henrik Angerbrandt, Swedish National Council for Crime Prevention
During the time of this research, Henrik Angerbrandt was at the Department
of Peace and Conflict Research, Uppsala University. He has published works on
democratization, ethnic conflict and political violence with a geographical focus
on Africa and has done extensive fieldwork in Nigeria. This work was supported
by the Swedish Research Council [grant number 2016-05833]. He is now at the
Swedish National Council for Crime Prevention.

Antje Daniel, Department of Development Studies, University of Vienna, Austria
Antje Daniel is a social scientist in social movement studies, political sociology,
gender and future/utopia at the Department of Development Studies, University of
Vienna. She is also an associated researcher at the Friedrich-Alexander University
Erlangen-Nürnberg and the Centre for Social Change, University of Johannesburg.
In her recent research, she analyses environmental movements in Europe, South
Africa as well as protests against urbanization, for education and democracy.

Jennifer Hart, Department of History, Virginia Tech University, USA
Jennifer Hart is Associate Professor and Chair of the Department of History at Virginia Tech University. A scholar of technology, infrastructure, space and development, Hart is the author of *Ghana on the Go: African Mobility in the Age of Motor Transportation* (2016) as well as *Making an African City: Technopolitics and the Infrastructure of Everyday Life in Colonial Accra* (2024). Hart directs the digital humanities project Accra Wala (www.accrawala.com).

Jonathan J. Makuwira, Department of Development Studies, Malawi University of Science and Technology, Malawi
Jonathan Makuwira is Professor of Development Studies and the current Deputy Vice Chancellor of Malawi University of Science and Technology (MUST). He is a Research Associate in the Department of Development Studies at Nelson Mandela University (NMU), South Africa, where he taught between 2014 and 2017. He is also a Visiting Fellow at Airlangga University, Indonesia. He is the author and co-editor of over forty-five journal articles and thirty book chapters including *Rethinking Multilateralism in Foreign Aid: Beyond the Neoliberal Hegemony* (2020), and *Non-Governmental Development Organisations and the Poverty Reduction Agenda: The Moral Crusaders* (Routledge).

Stephen Marr, Department of Global Political Studies, Malmö University, Sweden
Stephen Marr is Senior Lecturer in the Department of Global Political Studies at Malmö University. Marr's current research interrogates issues of climate adaptation, DIY urbanism and equitable/just sustainable urban development in African cities and the post-industrial American Midwest. He is now at work on a comparative project that emplaces Detroit in conversation with sub-Saharan African cities.

Federico Monica, PhD, Università di Parma, Italy
Federico Monica is an Italian architect and a PhD in urban planning, specialized in the analysis of urban areas and informal settlements in sub-Saharan Africa. He is a consultant for NGOs and international agencies on issues related to urban development, participatory planning and slum upgrading, he developed projects and researches in fifteen different African countries. He is the founder and project manager of Taxibrousse studio, a consulting firm for international development and the founder of Placemarks, a firm specialized in the assessment of satellite imagery. He is the author of several publications about urban development and informality in sub-Saharan Africa.

Martin J. Murray, Professor of Urban Planning, Taubman College, and Adjunct Professor, Department of African-American and African Studies, University of Michigan, USA
Martin Murray is a tenured full professor of the Taubman College urban planning faculty. He is also Adjunct Professor, Department of Afroamerican and African Studies, University of Michigan. His current research engages the fields of urban

studies and planning, global urbanism, cultural geography, distressed urbanism, development, historical sociology and African studies. He has published two books on global urbanism: *The Urbanism of Exception: The Dynamics of Global City Building in the Twenty First Century* (2016) and *Many Urbanisms: Divergent Trajectories of Global City Building* (2022). His most recent book is titled *Infrastructures of Security: Technologies of Risk Management in Johannesburg (2022).*

Patience Mususa, The Nordic Africa Institute, Uppsala, Sweden
Patience Mususa is Senior Researcher at the Nordic Africa Institute, Uppsala. Her research interests cover mining, welfare and urbanization with a regional focus on southern central Africa. Patience is author of the monograph *There Used to Be Order: Life on the Copperbelt after the Privatisation of the Zambia Consolidated Copper Mines (2021).*

Victoria Ogoegbunam Okoye, Institute of Geography, University of Edinburgh, UK
Victoria Ogoegbunam Okoye is Lecturer in Black Geographies at the University of Edinburgh. Her work interrogates spatial experience and place through collaborative, arts-based approaches and an attention to everyday spatial practices in urban West African contexts. Victoria has a PhD in Urban Studies and Planning from the University of Sheffield.

Mohammed-Bello Yunusa, Department of Urban and Regional Planning, Ahmadu Bello University, Nigeria
Mohammed-Bello Yunusa is Professor of Urban Development and Management in the Department of Urban and Regional Planning, Ahmadu Bello University, Zaria. He holds degrees in Sociology (1979), Urban and Regional Planning (1982) and Geography (1992) from Ahmadu Bello University, Zaria.

ACKNOWLEDGEMENTS

This collection would not have been possible without the support of several institutions and funding bodies. The Nordic Africa Institute, along with the Institute for Urban Research and the Department of Global Political Studies at Malmö University, provided funding, administrative resources and a stimulating environment in which to work. The Sultan Maccido Institute for Peace, Leadership and Development Studies at the University of Abuja hosted the initial workshop that resulted in many of the ideas and papers presented in the volume. We are particularly grateful for the support of an Initiation Grant from the Swedish Foundation for International Cooperation in Research and Higher Education (STINT) and a subsequent grant from the Swedish Research Council for Sustainable Development (FORMAS grant no. 2017-01980). Our editorial team, Nick Wolterman and Olivia Dellow, at Bloomsbury, Zed Books, as well as Victoria Engstrand Neascu and Henrik Alfredsson at the Nordic Africa Institute, have professionally guided us through the publication process.

Many thanks to the volume's contributors, who have patiently seen this collection develop during exceptional and challenging times. We are appreciative of your continued support, enthusiasm, and, not to mention, your innovative and insightful essays. We would also like to thank the reviewers who provided critical feedback on the book, along with all the individuals in various forums, workshops and conferences who engaged with, and commented on, the themes of the book. We are especially grateful to Ken Barlow for the excellent copyediting across each of the book's chapters. Finally, it's worth mentioning that this book has been in process for as long Steve's now five-year-old daughter, Elli, has been alive; and although there remains a severe lack of dragons, dinosaurs and kittens in this volume, Papa will endeavour to do better next time!

With much gratitude,
Stephen Marr and Patience Mususa

INTRODUCTION: DO-IT-YOURSELF URBANISM IN AFRICA'S CITIES

Patience Mususa and Stephen Marr

In what ways are African residents making and managing their cities?

Drawing on cases from across sub-Saharan Africa, this collection explores the practical and political processes African residents are engaging in when it comes to organizing and navigating their lives in the city. Encompassed within this investigation are theoretical discussions that engage with the historical and comparative aspects of do-it-yourself (DIY) urbanism, as well as a variety of case studies that examine, among other things, the organization of urban security and experiments in sustainability, welfare, housing and urban management. The book engages with DIY urbanism as a form of auto-construction that includes both 'makeshift' urban infrastructure – such as housing, trading sites and coastal flood defences – and the organization of health, leisure and security services. Alberto Corsin Jimenez (2017) urges us to think of this as a method of city-making, whereby urban residents are not only doing things individually but with others (Jimenez, 2017: 453). It thus becomes a vehicle for experiential systems of knowledge-making to utilize whatever resources, networks and skill are available to fulfil urban societal needs and hopes (Jimenez, 2017: 452). It can also be seen as a resident-driven place-making process shaped by contextual possibilities and constraints – for example, historical, economic, landscape, ecological and/ or socio-cultural factors. In this regard, it is also experimental, driving urban residents towards a constant weaving of knowledge strands in an attempt to cobble together a life (Pieterse, 2011).

The book opens with a series of chapters – by Stephen Marr, Martin Murray, Mohammed-Bello Yunusa and Mathias Agbo Jr – that debate and reflect on DIY urbanism, asking such questions as: What is DIY urbanism exactly? How has it been formulated in the past and how is it being formulated now? And what the possibilities of it in relation to understanding and shaping urban processes? The following chapters explore DIY urbanism through case studies focussed on subjects that range from how services, infrastructure and trade are organized to the impact of colonialism on contemporary infrastructure and urban governance;

from how DIY urbanism can revitalize ideas for more sustainable urban futures to issues of social inclusivity in the city.

Several of the case studies provide insights into how the practice and politics of place-making interact in situations of minimal or subverted bureaucratic intervention. In doing so, the book engages with questions previously raised by Denise Lawrence and Setha Low (1990) on the ways in which the urban built form is produced and how it in turn shapes experiences. Specifically, the chapters by Jennifer Hart, Jonathan Makuwira and Patience Mususa ask how urban residents are making the city and urban life, thereby (re)shaping their political subjectivities; how agency and power is constituted within unequal urban settings; and how intersectional issues – such as class, disability and gender – and historical legacies impact DIY urbanism processes.

Utilizing examples from a variety of African cities, the chapters explore the ways in which DIY activities inform the relationship between the state, its actors and citizens/residents. They also tackle the contradictions and complexities arising from a normative understanding of DIY urbanism as a progressive tool for urban making and management. Such tensions – for example, in how services such as security and welfare are organized – are frequently apparent in the case studies presented, and go some way to responding to the question raised by Donovan Finn and Gordon Douglas (2019) as to whether there is a dark side to DIY urbanism. In this introduction, therefore, we ask: What kinds of political agency does DIY urbanism produce? Specifically, does it lean towards more collective actions that produce common shared spaces and goods; towards more individualistic or libertarian actions; or does it fall somewhere in between? How is the practice of place-making approached by urban residents? What forms of knowledge are required and how are they acquired? What organizational structures are being created as urban residents mobilize their efforts towards making their cities? How do residents, and these institutions, interact with the state and other more formal bureaucratic structures? And finally, is it reasonable to expect African city residents to continue as the primary makers and organizers of their cities and welfare? Cristina Udelsmann Rodrigues (2022), writing on Angola and Mozambique, poses the question of what the state's role is in a context of climate crisis. Similarly, in this book's conclusion we reflect on the future of urban politics in a context of widening inequality and polarization, and probe what the limits of DIY urbanism might be in the face of global challenge and crisis.

DIY urbanism in Africa

Over half of Africa's residents live in informal settlements (UN-Habitat, 2022: 81), with the majority of such residents having to provision their own infrastructure and services. Thus, much of the continent's city infrastructure – including housing, roads, drains and services such as water – is created and run by residents via interactions with public authorities and private actors. All this occurs amid a context in which decades of neoliberal policies have reconfigured the role of the state. For many of the continent's countries, this reconfiguration entailed shifting away from the post-independence role of developmental state tasked with meeting the infrastructural and service needs of populations emerging from repressive colonial rule. Economic decline in postcolonial Africa, catalysed initially in the 1970s by an oil crisis and debt distress, then exacerbated by the ideology of free markets and deregulation pushed by the World Bank and IMF, resulted in the role of the state in many of Africa's countries becoming steadily diminished by the 1980s (Mkandawire, 2001). With countries focussed on how to pay back growing debt, they turned their attention to how they could attract private sector investment into their economies, including for infrastructure. However, countries in general have consistently struggled to attract investment for infrastructure projects oriented towards public services such as water and sanitation (Annamraju, Calaguas and Gutierrez, 2001). Where investment has occurred, it has largely been related to large-scale extractive industries such as mining, where housing, physical infrastructure and services have been required to attract high-skilled labour to often remote locations (Kesselring, 2017). As in the case for the luxury housing projects emerging across Africa's cities, which draw in both international and local investments, the tendency is towards enclave development (Murray, 2015; Myers, 2016). The state in this context thus becomes a facilitator for capital investment, and increasingly a partner to it through public–private partnerships (see Pitcher, 2018). To attract capital, the state must strive for good governance and the rule of law, which entails robust mechanisms to protect property rights. As Adebayo Olukoshi (2004) argues, however, this does not necessarily translate into increased investment.

Meanwhile, the intermittent and occasionally protracted austerity policies instituted by (and on) many African countries in the name of 'fiscal discipline' have meant little social spending on services and infrastructure, despite some governments desiring a more developmental role. The limited space for the public sector, coupled with state industry privatizations aimed at paving the way for the private sector, has also expanded the sphere of precarious informal work due to retrenchments and casualized labour (Fraser and Lungu, 2007; Mususa, 2021).

In addition, the softening of regulatory frameworks has opened space for increased land speculation, which has, among other factors, led to growth in gated housing estates for Africa's wealthy and middle classes. At the same time, the urban poor – having been priced out of affordable land and marginalized by state bureaucracies that favour large-scale capital investments – must trespass on and occupy land for their housing and livelihood activities. Even these land occupations are often organized by brokers connected to ruling parties (Boone, 2011; Chitonge and Mfune, 2015). The brokers sell to small-scale developers, who in turn rent property to those on the urban peripheries. These dynamics have led to a distinctly unequal and fragmented urban landscape, with state actors utilizing repressive measures to manage increasingly restive urban populations (Potts, 2006; Bond, 2019).

The spread of contextually situated neoliberalism in Africa's countries has seen a concomitant growth in democratic aspirations (Harris and Hern, 2019; Mattes, 2019), with civil society mobilization having flourished since the collapse of the Soviet Union (Munalula, Kanyamunya and Kanenga, 2018: 18). The paucity of state welfare or social protection, however, means that the residents of Africa's cities struggle for rights or a voice, pushing them to adopt an entrepreneurial disposition in order to make a life for themselves. This gives both a practical and political bent to what residents do when it comes to making and organizing their lives. It also rewrites the relationship between the state and its citizens: in its retreat from the provision of services and infrastructure, the state gives tacit consent for residents to do things themselves. At the same time, a tension is created: the state does not relinquish its managerial role. This blurs the line between where the responsibilities of the state and its citizens lie in relation to each other – a gap that leaves room for interpretation and contestation. For example, why should citizens comply with the rule of law when the state does not meet its obligations? Or vice versa, how can the state meet its obligations when its citizens do not comply with the rule of law? The space between these perspectives is where the politics of the urban are being negotiated and created.

DIY urbanism in Africa's cities is thus also a product of the laissez-faire approach of governments that have devolved their responsibilities not only to corporate entities but also to individuals and groups. An outcome of this is multiple/alternate nodes of governance that either complement the state and its actors (when interests are aligned) or compete against it.

Engaging with DIY urbanism

DIY urbanism as we approach it in this book is not a category or system of fixed urban practice. Rather, it is a tool we use to explore varying self-driven urban initiatives and processes. We draw from Garth Myers (2020), who has made a case for centring relationality in order to explore how urban residents utilize various resources, including their own labour and social networks, to make urban infrastructures and institutions.

The complex and hybrid nature of the governance arrangements that emerge around DIY activities also cast light on how agency is being deployed in these processes, as well as the relational dynamics of DIY urban processes. Urban residents are engaging individually and collectively across a range of activities and environments, with their actions co-mingling self-interest and altruism. The 'do-it-yourself' in these urbanisms may thus connote a self-reliance that seeks independence from unequal or exploitative structures rather than a freedom that seeks to pursue individual self-interest. It is within these aspects that the political implications of DIY urbanism may be gleaned. For example, in this collection Martin Murray points to the reactionary character of DIY urbanism in order to highlight its 'popular' dimensions, which contradict formal urban governance. This popular aspect plays out both practically and politically, with Victoria Okoye, Federico Monica, Mathias Agbo Jr. and Antje Daniels highlighting in their chapters DIY urbanism's creative and improvisational aspects in this regard.

The openness to experimentation in DIY urbanism points to a particular aspect of its potential: imagining Africa's urban futures. In her case study of a self-organized eco-utopian settlement in Durban, South Africa, Antje Daniels points to the possibilities of building more sustainable urban futures through doing by dreaming and responding to the challenges of the global climate catastrophe. Daniels's argues that the provisional nature of the materials used to make the eco-village's infrastructure is political, in that it shows the possibility for recycling. Her chapter thus highlights the judicious way in which Africa's 'makeshift' cities are made, while pointing to the ways in which residents learn to see what can be reused. Such an approach requires an ongoing situational awareness on the part of urban residents, who must be attentive to whatever networks and resources can be drawn upon in organizing and making their lives in the city.

Mathias Agbo Jr. makes a case for how the relational aspects of DIY urbanism could be adopted for more collaborative planning processes in cities such as Lagos, Nigeria. Agbo Jr. argues that the collaborative potential underlying DIY urban efforts in Africa are undergirded by African communitarian ideals, such as the philosophy of 'ubuntu'. When urban residents get together to create and maintain collective urban infrastructures, these actions are indicative of a mutual recognition and belonging characteristic to African urban experiences. This has significant potential when it comes to mobilizing the state to reshape cities together with their residents.

In his case study on Freetown, Sierra Leone, Federico Monica describes how coastal residents have created flood defences, thus demonstrating civic engagement for climate resilience and indicating the politics of conviviality that arise out of collective action. A politics of conviviality requires that urban residents are attentive not only to the opportunities that lie within their environment, but also to the risks. Like residents of other cities living in vulnerable landscapes, they face both the threat of environmental disasters and the threat of relocation due to health and safety. Thus, in activities such as the creation and maintenance of infrastructures like flood defence systems, residents demonstrate how they can respond and adapt to risks – if only they had adequate support and resources. To mitigate the threat of relocation, they cultivate relationships not only in the places they reside, but across the city and, in order to legitimate their actions, with authorities.

Victoria Okoye points to how the purloining of trading spaces in Accra, Ghana, can be seen as a process of recreating a commons. This is a not an unfamiliar situation across African cities and indicates how potentially socially thick spaces mobilized for economic activity can transform understandings of space, opening then up to wider publics.

Is DIY urbanism progressive?

While the previous section points to the progressive aspects and potential of DIY urbanism, the question remains as to whether it can mobilize a more inclusive democratic urban politics in situations of widening inequality and social fragmentation. As a form of direct civic participation or direct action, DIY urbanism is perceived as democratizing the process of who gets to shape the city.

It involves wider participation in Africa's cities, where this is the primary mode of making the urban, and urban planners have attempted to engage with it as a way of making their planning process more inclusive. Thus, the participatory aspects of DIY urbanism have been celebrated as means of marginalized urban communities getting their concerns heard. This is regarded as a resource not merely for building a just urban society, but establishing coalitions and consensus across varying urban interest groups – be this for housing rights, climate justice or tackling inequality.

Though participatory urban governance has generated a significant urban toolkit (Hamdi, 2014; Watson and Siame, 2018), placing it at the forefront on how urban planners engage with underrepresented voices, it has been nevertheless criticized for depoliticizing contentious issues, such as high inequality, and muting the voices of marginalized urban residents. Scholars have also pointed to bureaucratic participatory processes co-opting critical voices or redirecting them to less contested issues.

In their respective case studies on DIY security provisioning in Africa, Victor Adetula and Henrik Angerbrandt show how these processes of co-optation occur. Both chapters describe a form of DIY urbanism in which wealthy elites draw on a weak regulatory context to capture the state and co-opt grassroots politics and concerns for their own ends. This points to the predatory aspects of DIY, in which processes of mutual support are captured for an exclusive politics – for example, community policing becoming vigilante groups for political elites. This highlights the somewhat libertarian streak that can underlie self-provisioning activities. The ability of the urban elite to effectively 'privatize' their own DIY urban activities and influence the state towards their interests results in a patchwork of wealthy enclaves in Africa's urban areas, underscoring urban inequalities. These enclaves work counter to the processes of commoning (see Victoria Okoye's chapter) that less wealthy urban residents engage in to get by. Thus, two currents are co-mingling to shape Africa's DIY urbanisms: a commoning that engages in trespass to make shared place and infrastructures; and an enclaving that involves privatizing place, services and infrastructures.

The complex political terrains that these forms of urban politics generate require a kind of 'divining' (Devisch, 1996) of the urban – what Mohammed-Bello Yunusa refers to in this collection as a form of 'hacking'. 'Hacking' the city involves tapping into multiple knowledge systems shaped by past and present, with Yunusa pointing out that this form of getting to know the city is informed not just by what is learnt within the urban, but by rural modes of life and practices. It is these aspects of the rural within the city that postcolonial governments have sought to constrain. In her chapter, Jennifer Hart directs us to at how colonial government in Africa governed colonial subjects, deploying what she describes as a kind of 'managerial politics' – and how this has continuities into the present. In doing so, she points to a bureaucratic urban governance that seeks to confine, sanitize and hide the visibly self-provisioned aspects of the city, instead favouring a modernist ideal that serves the interests of wealthy urban residents. Consequently, Africa's cities end up serving the interests of capital and heightening urban inequality.

Nevertheless, the state and other actors are continually investigating how they can tap into the resource base generated by DIY urban activities. Despite the fragmented nature of DIY urbanism, the resource base – including labour and materials – are integrated into wider socio-political and ecological systems. This makes it possible for the state and others to collect rents from self-provisioning processes. For example, in Lusaka, Zambia, having failed to provide reliable access to clean water, the state collects rent from those who have sunk their own wells to draw water from the city's underground aquifers. While this tax acknowledges the collective use of resources such as water, and points to its public utility, it also reflects that the state has relinquished provision of services to the private sector, further individualizing shared resources. These logics play well with rent-seeking capital, and are reflected in the morphing of neighbourhood security groups into large-scale privatized security firms operating not only at a local level, but – as Victor Adetula shows in his chapter – an international level.

DIY organization structures

The possibility that DIY urbanism processes may be subverted for less democratic and inclusive politics highlights the need to investigate the societal organizations and institutions created by residents of African cities. The authors of this collection highlight the importance of a relational approach to getting things done, whether individually or in groups. This involves mobilizing existing networks and being attentive to those that can potentially be created. Given that relationships are material as well as social, involving exchange of labour and resources – including their repurposing or recycling – residents must be attuned to the energies of place, the social phenomena that catalyse social action, and the landscape's affordances.

This synergistic aspect of DIY urbanism practice highlights the temporalities of city-making's organizational structures in Africa. Relationships in these settings are both durable and opportunistic, with their terms subject to change as those interacting seek accommodation within a shifting terrain of interests. A weak regulatory state structure that struggles to codify practice means that residents operate within and around a pliable administrative structure.

Filip De Boeck and Marie Plissart (2014), writing on Kinshasa, Democratic Republic of Congo, have pointed to the opacity of the institutions that mediate social action in African cities, which also leads to a fragmented, illusory view of what makes these cities work. What constitutes community in such settings can be described, we would argue, in terms of fractals rather than wholes. City residents with multiple, sometimes nesting and/or intersecting, interests are coming together to organize various services and infrastructure. While this makes the urban work as a system, its complexity means it is difficult to map or pick apart. When urban residents make their cities, they are also mobilizing political voice and interests. How is power mediated in these processes? When state actors – such as municipal planners – engage or try to reorganize these DIY initiatives, who do they consider the primary stakeholders? This collection shows that those who try to mediate DIY urban processes face a complex task due to the hybrid and distributed power networks that emerge around them. Planners wanting to intervene in the city encounter political currents that pull in several directions, often requiring powerbrokers to manage and attempt to align interests. It is in these processes that marginalized urban residents, dependent on the organizational structures they have created, can direct such interventions towards securing their legitimacy within the city. DIY urbanism can thus become a vehicle for securing urban tenure and pushing for socio-economic rights, as Hestia Victor (2019) outlines in relation to the self-provisioning efforts of residents of Marikana, a mining town in South Africa – something Victor aptly describes as 'DIY formalization'. These actions, argues Victor (2019), sustain not only livelihoods, but political life.

Everyday life, and its attempts to fill service and infrastructure gaps, creates a political terrain characterized by struggle for a decent living and rights to the city. Urban residents attempt to upgrade their living conditions, a practice that is not only reflective of protracted austerity and the laissez-faire state, but is, as Jennifer Hart shows in this collection, a legacy of extractive colonialism. Services and infrastructure, where they are provided, tend to be skewed towards the urban elite (Carmody and Owusu, 2016). Increasingly, the trend towards gated estates is embedding a libertarian logic to African urbanism, with the wealthy going it alone and creating decentralized private services for themselves. Political connections that favour them when it comes to access to state land, as well as processes of state capture, make these forms of DIY urbanism more akin to a rogue politics whereby the wealthy subvert the operation of the state to favour capital, and in its interests work to suppress the majority from retrofitting their own urban places (or at least keep them at the peripheries).

At the heart of these endeavours are diverse understandings of voluntarism, which are being mobilized towards self-interested individual and collective efforts. As the chapters in this collection show, the multiplicity of DIY urban actions described are failing to cohere into any broad-based political push for the (re) establishment of comprehensive state welfare. Though the interests of urban residents may intersect in having access to decent services and infrastructure, the underlying dynamics of DIY practices and the organizational structures emerging around them tend towards the local.

The question of how far the networks of urban constituents organizing their own services and physical infrastructures extend is inextricably bound up with the question of the degree to which DIY urbanism can be considered local. Networks of international land and housing movements, such as Slum Dwellers International, point to how global networks can sustain both a political and practical impetus when calling attention to the precarious urban situations city residents around the world must contend with. However, we argue that the transnational organizing of DIY urban mobilization is likely smoother than that within the state, which faces demands to deliver by virtue of its obligations to citizens. Even so, both transnational and local associational arrangements around DIY efforts proliferate.

In exploring the spatialization of voluntary action in Europe and North America, Nicholas Fye and Christine Mulligan (2003) argue that this tendency towards localization affects efforts aimed at creating a broader, inclusive understanding of citizenship. This, Fye and Mulligan (2003) note, is also down to the different kinds of organizational structures that mobilize voluntary action. For example, some organizational structures may work, or seek to work, quite closely with the state; some may be more formalized in their approach; some may be larger than others; and some may renumerate aspects of voluntary labour (Fye and Mulligan, 2003: 398). The case studies in this collection highlight the diversity of associational arrangements when it comes to mobilizing the provisioning of services and infrastructure in Africa's cities.

Conclusion

This collection brings together urban geographers, political scientists, anthropologists, historians, architects and development studies scholars to engage with the processes that are currently making Africa's cities. In doing so, we seek to free Africa's urban dynamics from a regional silo and place them in conversation with other contexts where similar processes of urban place-making are in play, either due to state retreat or a push for experimentation and alternatives (Douglas, 2014; Kinder, 2016; Myers, 2020). Thus, though the focus of this collection is Africa's cities, we heed the call by various scholars to treat this lens as a stepping stone towards thinking on wider global processes (Parnell and Pieterse, 2016; Robinson, 2016; Myers, 2020) – for example, how cities are organized, governed and materialized in different contexts, be it Lagos or Detroit (Marr, 2016). In shying away from describing DIY urbanism as a particular category of the urban, therefore, we collectively explore its utility as an analytical frame for understanding how – in this case – Africa's cities are made and organized.

Chapter 1

COMPARATIVE DIY URBANISMS: REFLECTIONS ON A CONCEPT'S PASTS, PRESENTS AND FUTURES

Stephen Marr

Introduction

The growth of cities around the globe poses a dramatic challenge to how scholars think about urban environments. Rapid urbanization absent of an industrial base or growing economy; a lack of recognizable or stable public sphere(s) and space(s); state institutions unable to provide basic services; an urban landscape characterized by improvised shanties and precarious infrastructures – such are the new realities of contemporary urban conceptualization(s). Even so, dominant thinking on the making, meaning and spatialities of contemporary cities often fails to reflect these shifting on-the-ground realities,[1] with Austin Zeiderman observing that long-standing urban exemplars increasingly resemble 'anachronistic bygones' (Zeiderman, 2008: 23; see also Harrison, 2006: 320). Meanwhile, Jennifer Robinson, in an important essay (2002) that sparked wider reappraisal of the geographies of urban theory, notes that the emphasis on global/world cities neglects all but the most significant nodes in the transnational market and information economy. The difficulty is not merely, however, that particular cities have been elevated over others as icons of urbanity in the late twentieth and now twenty-first centuries, but that this approach ignores – if not outright effaces – ('ordinary') cities elsewhere in the world (Robinson, 2002: 535).

Conventional conceptualizations of the city drastically limit our ability to envision new urban futures or landscapes beyond sites described/prescribed as ideal-type standards. Although these teleological imaginaries allow us to think in terms of a coming convergence between different locations, progression is always conceived as devolution downwards: New York might turn into Lagos but Lagos will never turn into New York (Zeiderman, 2008: 29). Amin and Graham thus argue for the need to move beyond approaches that promote an ideal-type vision or hold up a single example as encapsulating all that is the city (common tropes include: New York, Victorian London, Los Angeles, Dubai) (1997: 411).

The following chapter expands on ideas first presented in an earlier essay (Marr, 2016).

Multiplicity is therefore a worthy normative and conceptual goal not only in terms of providing diverse analytical frames for thinking about the physicality and aesthetics of cities, but for making sense of the do-it-yourself (DIY) practices, processes and politics initiated by those occupying a city's spaces. Matthew Gandy notes that instead of interpreting African cities as being somehow deformed or 'anomalous', they should be understood as a 'fundamental dimension to the global experience of urbanization' (2006: 374). Similarly, Philip Harrison adopts a more hopeful and holistic lens, asserting that rather than

> seeing Africa as an incomplete or deteriorated example of modernity, we might focus on how Africa, and its many different parts, is – through the resourceful responses of its residents to conditions of vulnerability – in the process of becoming something new that is both part and separate from Western modernity.
>
> (2006: 323)

At the same time, it is unclear to what extent we can identify emancipation in the daily improvisations African urban residents perform in order to mitigate their everyday vulnerabilities.[2] This scepticism, echoed in Pieterse's discussion of African urban development trajectories, is a reminder that in the rush to avoid Africa-bashing stereotypes, we should not overlook the problems confronting African cities. Perhaps the most consequential of these is a daily life 'profoundly sutured by structural and symbolic violence. This suggests that the focus on cityness, on the inventiveness of survivalist practices and the worldliness of African cities, is first and foremost a story about terror' (Pieterse, 2010: 213). To this you can add violence, uncertainty and perpetual vulnerability, but also resiliency, optimism and creativity.

The aforementioned themes of multiplicity – the comparative linkages between and across the Global North and South, along with urban citizens' everyday lives, praxes and work – weigh heavily on this chapter's engagement with DIY urbanism in Africa's cities and elsewhere. Significant questions undergirding the discussion include: Is DIY urbanism one thing, or many? Who can manifest DIY urbanism and under what conditions? Is DIY urbanism better understood as evidence of resistance to domination or acquiescence to it?[3] Does DIY urbanism have a future in global urban environments, or, more dramatically, is it *the* future of urban development over the coming decades? Conversely, does DIY urbanism have a past, and if so, what might these histories tell us about present-day DIY urbanism(s)?

In this chapter, I approach these questions by emphasizing the final one – specifically, I seek to place earlier debates about the relationship between the individual and the modern metropolises of the early-to-mid-twentieth century in conversation with contemporary theorists of the (African) city. The aims of this effort are two-fold. First, I hope to identify common threads between seemingly divergent intellectual traditions and geographies, which traditionally have remained silo-ed from one another. To acknowledge this continuity is to demonstrate that DIY urbanism is neither limited to the present moment, nor something that can be pigeon-holed as emblematic of cities in Africa or the Global South more broadly. Second, playing these diverse authors, localities and concepts off one another illuminates both the commonalities and differences that exist across intellectual, temporal and spatial geographies, thereby undermining the artificial binaries that delineate urban theories of the North from those of the South. In addressing these issues, the chapter serves as an invitation to rethink the terrainical possibilities of urban theory making. We begin with AbdouMaliq Simone.

Turbulence, time, transience: Urban theory in Africa and elsewhere

AbdouMaliq Simone's work over the past two decades (e.g. 2004a, 2006, 2018) provides some conceptual purchase with which to begin making sense of the two conflicting trends outlined above. In *City Life from Jakarta to Dakar*, Simone (2010a) argues that his goal is not to romanticize life in the periphery, but to examine the granular details of city life in order to understand what is actually happening on the ground. Such a focus sheds light on what people do in the city and with each other, while illuminating how these (non-)relationships impact the individual, state institutions – where and when they are present – and the making of the city itself (Simone, 2010a: 38). Tracing the movements, collisions, fissures, intersections, projections, anticipations and/or near misses that take place both in cities' internal spaces and between far-flung metropoles grants insight into the relationships present/active within the localized spaces of cities,[4] as well as how these networks extend over and through space. These stories and rhythmic maps give African urbanity some measure of verticality, enabling its co-presence on the global urban stage rather than accentuating its exceptionality. A key lesson of Simone's work relevant here is that expectation of urbanization functioning as 'the key to social integration probably doesn't mean much anymore, even as a popular myth. The spaces and objects of urban life are increasingly used as ways of making highly particularistic claims and solidifying zones of disengagement' (2010a: 314–15).

The claim that an end has come to the era of the city as generator of cohesion via the aggregation of disparate parts – to the extent that this was ever actually the case – is a rebuke to Western-oriented urban theory's basic assumptions (from Ebenezer Howard to Communitarian theory to Jane Jacobs to New Urbanism to Habermas's notion of the communicative public sphere). Such assumptions continue, however, to persist in the literature and public discourse. A 2011 cover story in the *Atlantic*, for example, extoled the virtues of building skyscrapers to facilitate urban social cohesion in cities that are growing outwards rather than upwards, claiming that, 'Cities are ultimately about the connections between people, and structures … make those connections possible' (Glaeser, 2011). Skyscrapers, in this telling, have an important role to play in cities where rapid horizontal expansion threatens these objectives.

The above assertion dovetails with Lewis Mumford's argument that the city functions as both 'container' and 'magnet'. For Mumford, although the spatial makeup of a city is important, it is ultimately secondary to what actually occurs within its boundaries: namely, how city spaces facilitate interactions directed towards some collective purpose. In a 1937 piece, Mumford depicts the city as an ongoing, ceaseless drama in which residents act.[5] Here, the city is a

> theatre of social action, and an aesthetic symbol of collective unity. The city fosters art and is art: the city creates theatre and is the theatre. It is in the city, the city as theatre, that man's more purposive activities are focused, and work out, through conflicting and cooperating personalities, events, groups into more significant culminations.
>
> (Mumford, 2003: 94)

In his epic work, *The City in History*, published a quarter century later, Mumford further distils the essence of the city: as a stage in which the full array of human actions and characters are gathered, with the city most aptly described as a venue in which 'significant conversations' are made possible (1989: 116). Mumford goes on to note that failed cities are those whose spaces are permeated by an 'absence of dialogue' or in which one only hears the 'equally loud sound of a chorus uttering the same words in cowed if complacent conformity' (1989: 117–18).

If Mumford's vision is at all analogous to the variable urban conditions found in Africa, how might we account for Simone's contention that the city as engine of social integration is an anachronism? Although reliant on different vocabularies and urban topographies, perhaps the ideas that both Simone and Mumford engage with are not so far apart after all. Conceiving of the African city as a theatre, underscored by the everyday practices and machinations necessary to cope with, even create, the city, requires us to think of these dynamics as an improvisational drama with minimal script or obvious narrative arc. Here, roles are as mutable as they are ambiguous. Embedded in circumstances that Simone characterizes as an 'economy of anticipation', residents generally operate without clear knowledge, often unable to predict what might happen next, or why. These individuated uncertainties replace the shared intelligibility of common purpose(s) made possible by 'more significant conversations'. Carrying the point further, it may be more accurate to view the city not so much as a theatre in which residents participate in an ongoing city-wide drama, but rather the location for as many dramas as there are residents. In conditions of extreme vulnerability and uncertainty – of visibility and invisibility – there is no guarantee that people will play by the same rules or work to the same (even bare outline of a) script, as larger-scale collective/shared projects become increasingly difficult to carry out or sustain. Individual dramas may intersect for a time, only to dissipate under the dictates of the next improvisation. All this is to suggest the possibility of a DIY approach that is not just about striving, coping and getting by in daily life, but functions as a form of self-actualization or becoming.

Baudelaire and Benjamin in Africa

Everyday urban life in Africa is suffused with disorientations, incubating and reflecting a situation in which no one knows who can do what with whom and why. Time is compressed into a series of discrete presents – a sort of 'temporal myopia' (Bindé, 2000: 52) – in which the past loses relevancy and the future is little more than the horizon immediately ahead (apart from such long-term dreams as 'making it big' or getting away from 'here'). As such, residents of African cities are faced with a number of seemingly unique conundrums. Widening the field of vision, however, reveals that similar apprehensions are/were apparent under vastly different circumstances, histories and geographies. Charles Baudelaire, for instance – whose writings on Paris have seen him credited as one of the epochal ethnographers of early modernity – articulated a definition of 'modernity' that emphasizes both the fragmentary and the durable: 'By modernity, I mean the ephemeral, the fugitive, the contingent, the half of at whose other half is the eternal and immutable' (Baudelaire, 1995: 13). These two themes – how to decipher the interplay of the transitory in modernity, while making room for a past in which an anchor can be cast – have come to dominate writing about modernity over the past 150 years.

Marshall Berman and Richard Sennett – two influential chroniclers – identify problems that have become exacerbated in the African context. First, consider the turbulence of urban life. Berman describes the cross-cutting currents of modernity as a 'paradoxical unity, a unity of disunity: it pours us all into a maelstrom of perpetual disintegration and renewal, of struggle and contradiction, of ambiguity and anguish' (1982: 15). Writing of the urban setting confronting new arrivals to Victorian London, Sennett gives a sense of the dilemma facing people trying to make sense of the unfamiliar: 'How are these people going to make sense of each other? They are cut loose, … On what terms are they to judge their communication with each other, to what knowledge, to what parallels in past experience does one appeal in dealing with a motley mass?' (1976: 16). The problem of what to do is, however, not simply one of too many people confined within a particular location – this difficulty has been present since the earliest urban accumulations and is resolved over time through the creation of new rituals, codes and statuses. Compounding the problem in modern urbanity is the fact that, despite the important stabilizing role the past offers, people now have only the most tenuous grasp on past and present, cast adrift as they are in contemporary life's whirlwind of 'perpetual becoming' (Berman, 1982). At its best, this perpetual motion affords moments of heroism or adventure amid the collisions that occur from one discrete moment to the next. Here, as the 'multitudes of solitudes make up the modern city come together in a new kind of encounter, to make a *people*' (Berman's italics), city residents are destined to be 'be born again and again out of the street's inner contradictions' (Berman, 1982: 164). More often than not, however, the erosion of the past and subsequent obliteration of a shared 'public geography' creates a profound sense of unease, while simultaneously chipping away at public space (Sennett, 1976: 41, 14–15). Thus, for Berman and others, an ability to cope with the contradictions, paradoxes and possibilities of (urban) modernity is contingent on being able to engage the past.

The question, then, is what sort of engagement with the past is possible, and what form should it take? Berman, Baudelaire and Sennett suggest there is something durable and comforting about the past that allows people to – in tethering themselves to its remembrance – make a 'home in the maelstrom' of modernity (Berman, 1982). These sentiments echo Devisch's evocative description of Kinshasa's villagization, in which residents rehabilitate the virtues of the past in order to withstand the failings of the present (1995: 595). Whether it is making a 'home' or 'nesting' – the term Devisch uses to describe villagization – there is an ongoing process of embeddedness at work. Walter Benjamin, however, offers a different take on how the past is used that speaks to some of the issues raised by Simone regarding mobility and ephemerality. This isn't to say that Benjamin does not allow for the past's reverberations to seep into the present in a durable coupling. One observer notes that in Benjamin's writing on urban forms and experiences, 'something obsolete and yet essential survives in the inexorable transformations of the city' (Demetz, 1978: xxix), while another urban scholar points to his view that the importance of objects' critical-political function is found in their ability to prompt new ideas of the future (Kohn, 2009: 6). Along these lines, in his writings on Paris, Benjamin notes:

> From this epoch [the nineteenth century] stem the arcades and interiors, the exhibitions and panoramas. They are residues of a dream world. The realization of dream elements in waking is the textbook example of dialectical thinking. For this reason dialectical thinking is the organ of historical awakening. Each epoch not only dreams the next, but also, in dreaming, strives toward the moment of awakening.
>
> (1978: 162)

For Benjamin, then, the past carries within it – at least potentially – the means of emancipation, the possibilities of utopia.

Like a medieval mystic, Benjamin divined the meaning of past junk and relics as a means of reinvigorating the present. Hannah Arendt called him a 'pearl diver' bringing these artefacts into the 'world of the living' (1968: 51), while Peter Demetz asserts, 'the ancients may have been "reading" the torn guts of animals, starry skies, dances, runes and hieroglyphs, [while] Benjamin in an age without magic, continues to "read" things, cities, and social institutions as if they were sacred texts' (1978, xxii). Essential to these tasks is constant, disorienting movement through the city. Though the most well-known of Benjamin's archetypes is the *flaneur* – channelled through the figure and writings of Baudelaire – it is his more personal, epigrammatic writings on the experience of the city that speak to the issues at stake here. While Benjamin argues that the *flaneur*, at home in a crowd, regards the city as being as comfortable as a 'living room' (1978: 152), he equates his own experience of walking the streets of Berlin with a 'sabotage' of 'social existence' (1978: 11). Here, movement through the city – particularly in terms of encounters with illicit spaces, such as doorways occupied by sex workers or bars haunted by criminals – means constant passage through thresholds 'not only social but topographical'. Noting this, Benjamin goes on to ask:

> But is it really a crossing, is it not, rather, an obstinate and voluptuous hovering on the brink, a hesitation that has its most cogent motive in the circumstance that

beyond this frontier lies nothingness? But the places are countless in the great cities where one stands on the edge of the void, and the whores in the doorways of tenement blocks and on the less sonorous asphalt of railway platforms are like the household goddesses in this cult of nothingness.

(1978: 11)

These discontinuous spaces and moments where a person stands on the edge of something, or nothing, is for Benjamin – and Baudelaire before him – a crucial aspect of the urban experience. Within them, an individual 'plunges into the crowd as into a reservoir of electric energy[,] circumscribing the experience of shock' (Baudelaire, quoted in Benjamin, 1968: 175), while a gambler becomes a heroic figure, making do under conditions in which experience cannot be accrued and lives are lived moment to moment, dice roll to dice roll (Benjamin, 1968: 178–80).

Surviving the city's sensorium(s) as you pass through it requires heightened, trained senses and a highly refined ability to appraise your surroundings. Benjamin quotes Baudelaire's description of a series of artistic renderings of prostitutes: 'Her eyes, like those of a wild animal, are fixed on the distant horizon; they have the restlessness of a wild animal ..., but sometimes also the animal's tense vigilance' (Benjamin, 1968: 191). High levels of attunement, of being ready, of preparedness, of improvisations – all to take advantage of an opportunity that may or may not come – are precisely the skills crucial to the practice of everyday life in urban Africa. George Packer illustrates the point via the following anecdote from Lagos:

In Lagos, everyone is a striver. I once saw a woman navigating across several lanes of traffic with her small boy in town, and the expression on her face was one I came to think of as typically Lagosian: a look hard, closed, and unsmiling, yet quick and shrewd, taking in everything, ready to ward off an obstacle or seize a chance.

(Packer, 2006)

Writing of the Surrealist understanding of the city – for them, Paris – Benjamin observes, '[t]here, too, are crossroads where ghostly signals flash from the traffic, and inconceivable analogies and connections between events are the order of the day' (1978: 182). The trick in the African city, and perhaps elsewhere, is to evaluate these signals – oscillations between the visible and invisible city – to the best degree possible.

In the context of the African city, two points concerning confusion and movement are relevant. Despite Mumford and Sennett's privileging of cities as venues for conversation and collective goal achievement within which cohesive public geographies/imaginaries can be forged, realities on the ground can make these processes difficult to realize. As Amin and Graham note, rather than regarding the city as being governed according to a uniform standard that everyone is aware of and understands, it is best considered as accommodating a 'co-presence' of multiple spaces, networks and times (1997: 417). Yet, even the notion of 'co-presence' doesn't fully capture the confusions present in the city and alluded to by Benjamin. In his study of the Zambian Copperbelt, James Ferguson goes further, asserting: '[c]ities are noisy. Signification, in the socially complex and culturally plural conditions of the modern metropolis, is complicated and messy, sometimes it simply fails' (1999: 207). For this reason, it is problematic to believe – as those who emphasize collective imaginaries, urban theatres or the importance of communicative action might – in conceptually pure frameworks of meanings known and accepted by most (Ferguson, 1999: 207). Communications only half understood, or not understand at all, become a central feature of the conduct and experience of the city.[6] People thus act not because they are certain of something – though that might be the case – but rather on the basis of mixed messages. Partial understandings can, however, be an asset in the framework proffered by Simone, as within the fragmentary symbolic/cultural/social space of the city, recombining people, objects or ideas into new or unexpected forms offers an essential means of making use of the city.

These confusions not only reflect a discursive muddle but are symptoms of the discordant space(s) of urban modernity in Africa. Mbembe and Nuttall observe that it is not just a matter of Africa experiencing high rates of change, but that 'it is also that uncertainty and turbulence, instability and unpredictability, and rapid, chronic, and multidirectional shifts are the social forms taken, in many instances, by daily experience' (2004: 349). Amidst the city's formlessness, for residents must make sense of its fissures and 'leaks' (Mbembe and Nuttall, 2004: 354) through techniques 'tactile, allegorical, and onomatopoeic … [in the service of] a compositional process that is theatrical and marked by polyphonic dissonances' (Mbembe, 2004: 400). Disjointed and 'kaleidoscopic', the Paris of Baudelaire and Berlin of Benjamin intersect with the contemporary African metropolis.

Movement, exposure, subterfuge: The DIY performance of everyday urban life

Within these fragmentary gaps and borderlands, what is it people do with each other? Moreover, how do they do it and under what circumstances? We will address these questions in two ways: first, through consideration of movement and projection, and, second, through the role of publicness and exposure in the performance of the city. Indeed, in Mbembe and Nuttall's definition of city-ness, these processes play a central role:

> a city is not simply a string of infrastructures, technologies and legal entities, however networked they are. It also comprises actual people, images and architectural forms, footprints and memories; the city is a place of manifold rhythms, a world of sounds, private freedom, pleasures, and sensations.
>
> (2004: 360)

What appears crucial in this account are the rhythms of the city and the movements they facilitate. Diouf (2003), meanwhile, points to the longer-term structural processes – namely the institutional, economic and state failures of the post-colonial era – driving the performance of everyday urban life, particularly among youth culture. My intention here, though, is not to focus on the making and meaning of historical trajectories, but to detail their consequences in terms of the life of the city. For example, Devisch's (1995) narrative of Kinshasa's inability to uphold the promises of modernity and urbanization notes that people have increasingly come to terms with the fact that regardless of their actions they are unlikely to be capable of changing their circumstances. For most people, daily life in the city is simply a matter of getting by amid 'spaces of transit' where 'anonymity and mixing appear to overwhelm any semblance of personal relations and obliterate any ethical point of reference. Rather, one goes there to both "seize a stroke of luck" and "deflect any misfortune" away from oneself and onto another' (Devisch, 1995: 611). This hustling, moving around, trying to make do, encapsulates much of what happens in urban Africa's large cities.

Consider Simone's notion of 'people as infrastructure'. The concept 'emphasises economic collaborations among residents seemingly marginalised from and immiserated by urban life', while also tracking the seemingly arbitrary intersections and collisions that draw together residents 'engaged in complex combinations of objects, spaces, persons and practices' (Simone, 2004b: 407–8). These conditions necessarily require patience and mobility, a sustained vigilance tracking the activities of others across the city. African cities, Simone suggests, become sites of intensified decision-making in which no one really *knows* anything – producing situations in which 'experimentation is necessary, but not everything is to be experimented with' (Simone, 2010b: 135). Although an external observer such as Rem Koolhaas may depict Lagos – the ideal-type model of African urban modernity – as a site of adventure and exploration, for the individuals who live there the city is a tableau of discordant parts in need of assembly: a puzzle to solve, a game to win. To move through the city is to attempt to access, discern, grasp the 'fugitive materials' floating in the urban ether (Simone, 2010b: 143). The flotsam is fleeting, and if you aren't present to take advantage of it, then someone else well. More than that, however, individuals living these spaces of transit must – akin to Benjamin's discussion of the collector or the pearl diver – not only collect these bits of debris, but also make sense of them.

Not only does the city attract human migrants from elsewhere, it finds 'washed up' on its shores fragmentary ways of doing things now long dissociated from their original uses. These bits and pieces of discourses, things, signs and expressions are assembled into personal projects of survival and ways of dealing with one another (Simone, 2010b: 144). It is, then, a matter of taking what is out there and embarking on a reclamation project that combines objects, people and ideas in ways that perhaps don't always appear to make sense. In such a way, new ways of becoming are made possible and new ways of getting by – or even better, getting out – are invented.

Through mobility and encounters with the fleeting and fugitive it is possible to defamiliarize the city, and in doing so appropriate its spaces, things and inhabitants in unexpected ways. In the apocalyptic city described by de Boeck, in which the line between what is real and what is not has disappeared, in which there is a pervasive feeling that what is there isn't really there or is not what matters most, this becomes perhaps the only reasonable course of action (2005: 28–9). While I can only hint at it here, the rationally delirious encounter with the city, its objects and its occupants has fascinating parallels to earlier avant-garde critiques of urban capitalism and alienation – specifically, Situationist notions of *detournement*, where objects became open-ended and can be put to use in ways not originally intended, or the *derive*, where individuals move through the city excavating a 'poetic geography' from which an emancipatory everyday can be constructed (Russell, 2002: 201–2). Though the Situationists offered an artistic critique of the city premised on a sense of play, which sits awkwardly with the motivations of urban Africans operating under conditions of extreme marginality, the similarities in terms of fluid movement and defamiliarized spaces are intriguing.[7]

Ideally, as Simone observes:

> the challenge for popular culture is how to maintain spaces where diverse actors and ways of doing things can intersect, but in practices that enable the intersection to generate new imaginations rather than simply being another occasion where people 'feed off' the resources and energies of others.

(2010a: 320)

Incubating sites of innovation is important, since – as Simone notes – the 'new' stands out, with others jumping on its bandwagon until the next 'new' thing is discovered. Two vignettes from my fieldwork in Gaborone stand out in this context. During my time working as a participant observer/ethnographer in Gaborone's Main Mall – the original downtown square (more like a rectangle) ringed by government buildings, shops and offices dating back to the late 1960s – one of the things that puzzled me was the sheer numbers of people selling mobile phone scratch cards. A few vendors had regular stalls set up offering phones for use if you didn't have a cell phone or enough Pula to afford the full cost of a scratch card. Most others, though, just sold the cards – along with newspapers, sweets and individual cigarettes – at various stands or 'shops'. Others still walked the Mall and its surrounding areas with cardboard trays, cards protruding from slits. The question I had on being confronted by this oversaturated scratch card economy was how anybody could possibly make enough money to make it worthwhile given that, with most of the proceeds going back up the chain to distributers and wholesalers, the sellers usually made only a fraction of the sale cost. Moreover, why did everyone attach themselves to the idea and keep doing it? At the time, most responses I got to my question of 'why?' seemed unsatisfactory: it was just what people with few other options did. In the context of Simone's story of movement and the 'new', though, perhaps this attitude makes more sense. Earlier in the 2000s, at the start of the cell phone boom, entrepreneurs probably could earn enough to make it worthwhile. Amid limited options or innovations, however, more and more people jumped on the bandwagon despite recognizing its dwindling utility as an income generator. It was, simply put, better than doing nothing.

The second anecdote also occurred in the Mall.[8] Early in my fieldwork, when I could still be considered a bit of mystery – an outsider who just seemed to hang around every day and write things in notebooks – a guy in his mid-twenties called me over to where he was sitting. Excited by someone actively seeking me out to talk, I went straight over. After introducing myself, he asked me where I was from. The United States, I replied. He then proceeded to tell me a bit about his background, his education, the difficulty of finding work, all of which culminated in him asking me to give him an idea. I was confused – an idea for what? An idea for a business, for something to do. What kind of business? It didn't really matter – just something that he could do. Not really understanding what this conversation was about, or what he was getting at, I told him that if I had a good idea for a business, I would probably be doing it myself. The conversation wound down quickly after that. In the years since, I've often thought about what happened. Here was a guy who saw in me something unfamiliar, out of the ordinary, I was a person who had 'washed up' on the shores of the city and in doing so injected something new into the environment. Thus, engaging me as a 'fugitive material' was a means by which something new might be created. Maybe I was part of a network this individual could access, or carried within me some insight or kernel of information that could be recombined with other variables or things he knew. Or maybe not. Regardless, he *had* to ask, to seize this moment when something innovative – the 'next big thing' – was possible.

Moreover, the anecdote further illustrates a second kind of projective movement or mobility that forms a significant component of DIY urban praxis – rather than being a matter of horizontal transit through the city, it indicates a verticality whereby it becomes possible to project yourself 'out there' and away from 'here'. This is, perhaps, the obverse of Ferguson's description of 'abjection', which, over and above individuals being deemed inconsequential according to the dictates of global capitalism, connotes an active ejection downward (1999: 236). Instead, we can speak of the possibility and form of a mobility that – even if in most instances it is relegated to spaces of fantasy and imagination, or to ideas and plots that never quite take off – reaches upwards, outwards. Indeed, considered within this framework, it becomes possible to interpret the countless marriage proposals and requests to be taken 'back to America' that I received during my time in Botswana, almost always from people I'd never previously met, didn't know, and would never see again. These propositions became so commonplace that I developed a rote response detailing visa difficulties and offices at the American Embassy they should contact – information that, no doubt, most of them were already familiar with. Regardless, according to this framing, I was the wild card; and in an era in which speculative casino capitalism was the norm, and narratives of rapid accumulation and its disappearance widely told, it made sense to gamble by asking, since nothing was risked in doing so.[9]

Even if I couldn't offer a literal ticket out of Gaborone, people still held a desire to be connected vertically to an 'out there' in even mundane instances. One final field note: I took a student friend of mine out to lunch at Nando's one summer day at the popular mall close to the University of Botswana. Summers in Botswana can be unbearably hot, particularly around midday when the sun is shining brightest, so I suggested that we sit inside in order to enjoy the shade and air conditioning. My friend, however, refused, asking how anyone would know we were eating at Nando's if we sat inside, unseen by those on the street outside. It wasn't just a matter of showing off the disposable income it took to have lunch there, it was the fact of having people bear witness to the occasion – that while you might not have the money to spend at Nando's, you had access to people and networks from elsewhere who did.

The above examples dovetail with the notion of urban mobility as projection discussed by others. Mbembe and Nuttall describe an Africa 'fundamentally in contact with an elsewhere[s]' (2004: 351). Building on this assertion, Simone suggests that while there is some degree of commitment to the locality, ultimately,

> African cities are platforms for people to engage with processes and territories
> that bear a marked sense of exteriority ... Cities straddle not only internal and
> external divides and national and regional boundaries, but also a wide range of
> terrain and geography, both real and imaginary.
>
> (2004b: 425)

Simone further notes that, as a result, Africans are increasingly located in 'half-built environments – i.e. under developed, over-used, fragmented and often make-shift urban infrastructures' (2003: 21). Perhaps they are also 'half-built' as people, constantly on the lookout for something else, something new, ready to move at a moment's notice.

At their core then, neither mobility as physical movement nor as imaginative projection can be separated from the need for public exposure. Livelihoods – from scratch card vending to seeking out 'ideas' – depend on individuals' connecting the dots from their encounters in the city in order to create as expansive a network as possible, thereby cultivating 'cross-cutting interdependencies and [to bring] together people and things that on the surface would not seem to fit' (Simone, 2010b: 136). Existing as a magnet or node for the 'fugitive materials' that wash ashore in the city requires considerable trickery and expertise, as, though you must be as visible as possible, you must also obscure what it is you are doing:

> The task is to find ways to situate yourself so one can assess what is happening –
> who talks to whom, who is visiting whose house, who is riding in the same car,
> who is trading or doing business together [or who is lunching at Nando's] –
> without drawing attention to oneself, without constituting a threat.
>
> (Simone, 2004b: 426–7)

The need for constant visibility twinned with obfuscation calls into question, for example, the taken-for-granted notion that clearly delineated public/private realms are necessary.[10] The dictates of exposure in urban Africa, immersed in dense networks and landscapes, offer an alternative way of thinking about Foucault's warning of panoptic space and surveillance: here, it may be the case that being-in-the-panopticon is less a problem than how well you make use of the visibilities and vantage points it offers.

Some concluding thoughts: DIY urbanisms in Africa and elsewhere

Over the course of the preceding pages, I have tried to draw attention to some of the primary trajectories in both 'Western' and 'African' urban theory. One of my intentions here has been to reconceive African cities as central to the experience of urban modernity, rather than simply functioning as urban templates of cities gone haywire, their dysfunctionality or 'feral'-ity (Norton, 2003) demonstrating just how short they fall of the idealized Western urban model. Second, I have outlined how DIY urbanism(s) across diverse temporal and geographic spans demonstrate points of convergence or overlap. It bears repeating that these findings are not simply of academic or theoretical interest. Indeed, as Achille Mbembe suggests, the story of contemporary cities in Africa has significant bearing on how we conceive of, or engage, their 'Northern' counterparts:

> If there is anything the history of the metropolitan form in Africa brings to the critique of modern urbanism it is that the metropolis is neither a finite nor a static form. In fact, it is almost always a site of excess, of hysteria and exclusions. The metropolis, just like the modern city, reveals itself first and foremost through the discontinuities, its provisionality and fugitiveness, its superfluousness. Particularly in Africa, the blurring of the distinctions between what is public and what is private, the transformation and deformation of inherited urban shapes, is one of the ways by which urban citizens generate meaning and memory.
>
> (2004: 404)

Emplacing Africa within these broader trends points to a way forward when it comes to thinking about urban practices amid pervasive precarity, one that acknowledges the diverse expertise(s) required for their navigation. However, while elevating these perspectives – as a sort of normalization – is both significant and necessary, it is only part of the story. Indeed, significant questions remain under-answered.

For instance, the DIY actions/engagements described above focus largely on small or micro-events, or individual achievements illuminating practices useful for managing everyday life. The emphasis on the individual urban resident potentially obscures the broader political implications of these endeavours. What kind of politics is produced, if any? Is it emblematic of an anarchic *onomatopoeic* scattershot urban praxis with little discernible rhyme or reason, or do these small actions accrete into something larger? Or, perhaps, do these ephemeral moments point to alternative forms of participatory democratic politics undertaken by vulnerable urban individuals? If it is the latter, then we should be thinking through how these seemingly disparate actions and encounters may be stitched together in ways that concretize new collective norms, values and publics. In other words, how might we shift the 'yourself' in DIY to 'ourselves'? What might this 'do-it-together' look like and how might it be brought into being?

At the same time, in terms of thinking about DIY as indicative of liberation or resistance, we ought not get starry-eyed at its emancipatory potential. While individual or even community DIY practices can no doubt engender cooperation, they may just as easily prompt competition and/or conflict. Indeed, in urban localities that play host to innumerable DIY practices, friction – occasionally productive – often seems an inevitable outcome. Furthermore, DIY urbanisms occur under the auspices of global economic machinery impervious to hyper-localized mutations or perturbations, meaning that even if new spaces and practices of politics are inaugurated, larger dynamics of inequality, exclusion and marginality remain unaffected – at least in the short term. In the long-game horizon of the counter-hegemonic war of position, however, such outcomes matter at the margins. These concluding reflections point out an inherent ambiguity in how we ought to approach the making, meaning and significance of DIY urbanism practices and politics. It is therefore important to accept these multiplicities, and in turn the analytical and empirical challenges they pose to practitioners, policymakers and scholars alike.

Notes

1 Consider, for example, the ongoing debates on the postpolitical city, which are still very much embedded in the conventional Western-dominated representations of the city (see Beveridge and Koch, 2017; Swyngedouw, 2009, 2017).
2 Or in Mumbai (Appadurai, 2000) or Sao Paolo (Biehl, 2005).
3 Marr and Mususa address this question more fully in the concluding chapter to this volume.
4 Though, of course, it is not always – if ever – clear where a localized space begins and ends.
5 Mumford's original essay appeared in a 1937 issue of *The Architectural Record*.
6 See Ferguson's chapter 'Asia in miniature' in *Expectations of Modernity* (1999) for a full – and exceptional – account of how this works in practice.
7 Although Simone doesn't make this explicit connection, the chapter 'Reclaiming black urbanism: Inventive methods for engaging urban fields from Dakar to Jakarta' in *City Life from Jakarta to Dakar* (2010a) offers similar insights.
8 This account and subsequent analysis is drawn from Marr (2016: 15).
9 See Devisch's article on Kinshasa (1995), particularly the section about the rise of the lottery and pyramid schemes in the early 1990s; also Comaroff and Comaroff (2000).
10 As articulated in Hanna Arendt's influential book, *The Human Condition*.

Chapter 2

THE MAKESHIFT CITY AND DO-IT-YOURSELF (DIY) URBANISM

Martin Murray

Generally speaking, cities do not develop in accordance with pre-arranged plans or grand visionary schemes. Rather, they emerge in fits and starts, changing in response to a variety of social pressures and unforeseen circumstances. In short, cities are physical manifestations of cooperation and competition, rivalry and conflict, innovation and creativity – a swirl of factors shaped by competing interests, values and ideologies.

Powerful social forces rooted in private property and marketplace bargaining power function as the principal mechanisms behind city building. However, these social forces do not operate in a vacuum – rather, the urban landscape is the complex outcome of top-down technical, legal and logistical expertise wielded by city officials, real estate developers, property owners, urban planners and engineers, in tandem with bottom-up grassroots efforts at place-making. In terms of the latter, these unauthorized efforts at reshaping the urban environment – whether planned or spontaneous, deliberate or accidental – have called attention to the often unplanned and contingent qualities of city building (see Gandy, 2006; Gillick, 2017).

DIY urbanism: Scope and breadth

Sometimes called 'guerrilla urbanism', 'tactical urbanism' or 'everyday urbanism', these unsanctioned interventions into the urban social fabric form part of a wider 'do-it-yourself' (DIY) impulse, whereby urban residents take it upon themselves to engage in activities that are beyond the purview of private property owners, city officials and planning experts due to a lack of capacity, collective will or legal sanction to act (Finn, 2014a: 381). The concept of DIY urbanism captures the bottom-up, often *ad hoc* nature of these interventions, which are directed at satisfying a variety of needs and goals, and operate across a fluid spectrum of legality. As such, DIY urbanism shares with such ideas as 'rogue urbanism', 'vernacular urbanism' and 'makeshift urbanism' a common orientation appropriating and transforming local urban space. Though often merely playful and temporary, DIY interventions are nonetheless frequently innovative, sophisticated and enlightening. Given that they take place outside of official sanction, DIY actions represent a critical challenge for formal planning regulations, urban governance and management systems, acting as a spontaneous 'make-do urbanism' that potentially threatens municipal authorities in much the same way that unauthorized squatting challenges the rights of private property. Despite their creativity and innovative tactics, DIY practices almost always violate planning orthodoxies (which are bound by conformity to existing rules and regulations), bypassing the formal processes and bureaucratic procedures put in place to ensure law and order (Finn, 2014a: 381–2). As such, bottom-up local initiatives operating outside official sanction raise thorny questions related to lawful action and legitimacy (Pegago, 2014).

In its common usage, DIY urbanism encompasses a variety of interventions, ranging from 'self-made' spaces, temporary installations, events and improvisational 'self-help' activities – all of which vary greatly in terms of duration, location, scale and scope. DIY urbanism is at once spontaneous and disruptive, yet planned and deliberate. Activities falling under the rubric of DIY urbanism range from small-scale, individual, clandestine acts of defiance to large-scale, collective, visible actions that take place outside of official sanction and formal endorsement (Finn, 2014a, 2014b).

Put broadly, these bottom-up alterations to the urban social fabric encompass a wide variety of interventions: from extra-legal challenges to state authority to small-scale acts of artistic self-expression; from unauthorized appropriation of under-utilized properties to whimsical temporary interventions – such as public-place beautification – that are largely non-threatening to existing power structures (see Marshall, Duvall and Main, 2016). From graffiti vandalism to mural art, impromptu encampments in out-of-the-way places to kerbside trading, the unauthorized appropriation and alteration of the built environment is a permanent feature of everyday life in the 'makeshift city' (Douglas, 2014: 5; see also Vasudevan, 2015). The variegated nature of these unsanctioned modifications ensures they 'do not constitute a singular, totalizing vision' for grassroots urban activism or for making permanent improvements (Taley, 2015: 138). In this sense, given it can take so many forms, the concept of DIY urbanism cannot claim to have a single unambiguous meaning or identity.

The two faces of DIY urbanism

For the most part, what distinguishes the DIY approach is its direct opposition to top-down, expert-driven, capital-intensive, rule-governed, bureaucratically sanctioned interventions of the kind commonly associated with conventional urban planning approaches.[1] Whereas conventional urban planning interventions largely consist of standardized regulatory frameworks, procedural complexity and rule-governed decision-making, DIY urbanism stems from grassroots decision-making, local engagement and participation, all of which are guided by improvisational practices of experimentation (Deslandes, 2013: 218).

DIY urbanism – along with such related terms as 'rogue' or 'guerrilla' urbanism – is oriented towards small-scale, incremental, grassroots interventions aimed at satisfying basic needs and making immediate improvements in urban environments (Hou, 2010; Pieterse, 2013). On closer inspection, however, the notions denoted by these terms lack clarity or precision. Thus, in the absence of an agreed-upon definition, a great deal of ambiguity arises in their meaning and use. Essentially, DIY urbanism is a rather nebulous term that cannot be reduced to a single universal meaning, but rather functions as an 'umbrella concept' encompassing a variety of normative and procedural principles guiding 'bottom-up' engagement and popular participation in everyday urban life (Talen, 2015).

Borrowing loosely from Mara Ferreri, it can be said that DIY urbanism 'is a complex composite imaginary, which draws upon and is constituted by often radically different and contrasting practices and positions' (2015: 181). These distinctive and at times highly incompatible genealogies and uses constitute a central component of the concept's allure. In short, DIY urbanism 'appears to be a floating signifier capable of encompassing a wide variety of activities and of fitting a broad spectrum of urban discursive frameworks' (Ferreri, 2015: 181).

Along with such conceptualizations as 'temporary urbanism' and 'trial-and-error urbanism', DIY urbanism has sometimes been framed as a living laboratory for experimental ideas geared towards temporary projects, the possible benefits of which include enhanced urban vitality, aesthetic beautification, improved security and nourishing creative energies (see Bishop and Williams, 2012; Dovey, 2014; Gamez and Sorensen, 2014; Fabian and Samson, 2016; Marshall, Duvall and Main, 2016). Seen in this light, DIY urbanism assumes somewhat playful, ludic characteristics – an inventive expression of such positive values as 'pioneering enterprise, social commitment, [and] a spirit of adaptation' (Dovey, 2014: 261–2). Framed in this manner, the endorsement of *ad hoc*, 'pop-up' interventions in the urban landscape's physical fabric represents 'a call to understand the city as a place under constant revision with room to move and space for the unexpected; where temporary opportunities are taken with high levels of creative community engagement and design collaboration' (Dovey, 2014: 261–2). Advocates of this kind of DIY urbanism proclaim that temporary urban design projects can stimulate property markets and commercial enterprise, rebuild the negative image of derelict neighbourhoods, and reactivate abandoned sites. These outcomes dovetail neatly with the interests of real estate developers, who stand to benefit 'as interim uses add value, prevent squatting and pave the way for permanent projects' (Dovey, 2014: 261–2; see also Dotson, 2016).

Framed through the lens of civic engagement, celebration of DIY culture's spontaneity and creativity has become a touchstone for a particular vision of hipster urbanism, reflective of a fascination with the perceived impulsive, quirky, whimsical side of DIY urbanism. By contrast, for residents excluded from mainstream urban life, improvisational DIY urbanism does not fall under the rubric of spontaneous leisure and frivolity, but rather represents a precarious means of survival and self-help in the absence of public assistance or resources (see Kinder, 2014, 2016). Here, 'going-it-alone' is less a choice than a necessity for urban residents confronting 'greater urgency', fewer options and 'higher stakes' (Kinder, 2017).

These grassroots efforts directed at remaking places display wide variation in their degree of radicalism, their commitment to addressing social inequalities and redressing grievances, and the extent to which they are sanctioned by those in power. Sometimes, bottom-up strategies are more 'guerrilla-like' when they involve transgressive activities that deliberately take place outside the law, without official approval. By contrast, other activities operate with the tacit sanction or even enthusiastic endorsement of municipal authorities. Ultimately, DIY urbanism and similar terms are capricious, free-floating concepts, lacking any precise definition and conveying multiple meanings (Finn, 2014a: 382).

It is not immediately obvious that gathering these various self-initiated actions under the 'umbrella concept' of DIY urbanism is a necessary or helpful move, given that it risks 'conflating disparate processes and their distinct antecedents and consequences'.[2] More fundamentally, it is inevitable that in encompassing as much as can be covered under the concept of makeshift urbanism, scholars from wildly diverse theoretical perspectives and points-of-view will be attracted. As a result, it is not difficult to see how unconvinced sceptics may consider the DIY concept as too elastic a term – an idea that means too many things to too many different people.

It is important to acknowledge how concepts like DIY urbanism are 'never purely empirical categories or analytical tools, but are also discursive formations, loose in the world, producing effects, and possessing social, cultural, and political lives of their own … Their sphere of influence extends far beyond' their use in scholarly discourse (Zeiderman, 2008: 33). 'As such, the socially-constructed category' of DIY urbanism 'should be seen to enframe a field of thought and action [and] consolidate networks of actors, thus enabling abstract policies and programmes to be implemented concretely in particular locations' (Zeiderman, 2008: 33).

When applied as a universalizing conceptual framework relevant to any situation involving grassroots initiatives in urban settings, DIY urbanism inevitably loses its critical edge. As such, it is best used as a contextually specified concept that can assist in understanding how ordinary people negotiate everyday life in struggling cities. Despite the fact that various unauthorized activities – ranging from illegal squatting in abandoned buildings to unsanctioned informal trading – are a permanent (and sometimes invisible) feature of struggling cities (Anjaria, 2016), grassroots efforts aimed at 'getting by' and 'making do' are poorly accounted for in mainstream urban studies.

Fundamental ambiguity

In seeking to get to grips with the diversity of grassroots initiatives and unauthorized practices taking place in urban settings, scholars, policy-makers and local activists have sometimes grouped these bottom-up activities under such broad banners as (in addition to 'DIY' urbanism) 'insurgent' urbanism, 'guerrilla' urbanism, 'everyday' urbanism, 'participatory' urbanism, and 'grassroots' urbanism (Iyeson, 2013). Some, such as Mike Lyon and Anthony Garcia (2015), appear less concerned with distinguishing the various terminologies, and in doing so have attached themselves to the catchall phrase 'tactical urbanism'. This indiscriminate blending of disparate activities – which have subtle differences in terms of their implied political and aesthetic sensibilities – ignores whatever nuanced dissimilarities exist. Perhaps more than other terms with similar connotations, the phrase 'tactical urbanism' has gained a degree of popularity in official urban policy circles as a politically mobile ideology that 'adheres to the agile, precarious and "creative" characteristics of contemporary neoliberal urban development' (Mould, 2014: 532). Yet, at the same time, advocates of tactical urbanism often support interventionist, disruptive and even subversive activities that appear directly opposed to this prevailing neoliberal discourse of urban governance (Daskalaki and Mould, 2013). Put broadly, many of the activities that tactical urbanism advocates endorse depend on urban residents 'effectively taking matters into their own hands and reconfiguring their local environment' without official sanction or legal approval (Mould, 2014: 532). However, while at first glance these activities may seem opposed to existing regulatory frameworks and to subvert the laws governing private property, in reality such 'edgy' interventions are frequently subsumed under the logic of consumer capitalism, becoming part of a creative or 'cool' urban aesthetic (Frank, 1998). Indeed, as Luc Boltanski and Eve Chiapello have suggested, the malleability inherent in the logic of the capitalist marketplace enables 'the pursuit of profit at any price' to 'recuperate' the autonomy that it intermittently extends, in large measure by implementing new flexible modes of governance (2005: 425). In a similar vein, Herbert Marcuse (1965) long ago called this malleability of the logic of capital a kind of 'repressive tolerance'.

The re-packaging of various activities (ranging from so-called 'guerrilla gardening' to 'pop-up' restaurants and retail outlets; temporary parks to impromptu music concerts) into celebratory narratives used in mainstream urban policy programmes effectively neutralizes the oppositional, potentially subversive character of these interventions (Day, 2017). By taming what initially appears to be a creative re-using of the built environment, municipal authorities are able to both deflect 'resistance' and maintain the illusion that they are responsive to the interests and needs of ordinary urban residents (Daskalaki and Mould, 2013; see also Adams and Hardman, 2013; Adams, Hardman and Scott, 2013).

DIY urbanism conjures up a new urban imaginary in which ordinary residents take matters into their own hands, engaging in all sorts of self-help activities outside existing regulatory frameworks and without official authorization (Vasudevan, 2015a). Many scholars hail these efforts as expressions of popular resistance, celebrating them as exemplars of 'bottom-up' initiative in the face of unresponsive governance regimes and repressive state authorities. However, a more sanguine assessment suggests that DIY urbanism pulls in two directions. On the one hand, it opens up the possibility of an embryonic grassroots communitarianism, grounded in local participation, mutual aid and decommodified exchange. On the other hand, DIY urbanism can easily fall prey to neoliberalism by stealth. By taking a 'hands-off' (*laissez-faire*) approach, municipal authorities relieve themselves of responsibility for overseeing the necessities of everyday urban life: access to decent housing, stable and functional infrastructure, and reliable public services. If ordinary residents take the lead in self-help innovation, then public authorities can justify their withdrawal from delivering services by putting the onus on self-mobilized, localized, grassroots efforts, ultimately leading to residents providing for themselves without public involvement (see Spataro, 2016).

Rescuing the critical edge

The current discourse of DIY urbanism places particular emphasis on identifying practices whereby ordinary people carve out spaces for themselves in the 'makeshift city' (Ferreri, 2015). While this idea of 'do-it-yourself' self-help is 'often understood as encompassing a highly heterogeneous variety of practices' (Ferreri, 2015: 181) and interventions that defy strict definitions, the proliferating use of such terms as tactical urbanism, temporary urbanism and guerrilla urbanism 'bears witness to the existence of a shared imaginary of marginal and alternative temporary practice' (Ferreri, 2015: 181; see also DeSilvey and Edensor, 2013; and Bishop and Williams, 2012; Hou, 2010).

Though supplementing ideas related to urban informality, concepts such as DIY urbanism can capture the widespread realities of the improvisational (and largely spontaneous) activities undertaken by ordinary residents in distressed urban settings where state regulatory regimes are stretched too thin or virtually non-existent, and where formal housing and stable income-generating options are highly circumscribed (Martinez, Short and Estrada, 2017). The way in which ordinary people in struggling cities insert themselves into the mainstream of urban life is under-theorized and largely misunderstood – inventive strategies remain shrouded in mystery, in part because they often take place in the shadows of legality and outside official sanction.

In struggling cities, the practice of DIY urbanism takes place in circumstances where existing formal regulatory frameworks have proven incapable of accommodating ordinary people's needs, including access to affordable housing, opportunities for wage-paid work, and social protection against everyday adversity (Jabareen, 2014: 425). The introduction of such concepts as 'invisibility' (Simone, 2003), 'suturing' (De Boeck, 2016), 'pirate modernity' (Sundaram, 2010), 'spectrality' (Appadurai, 2000), 'quiet politics' (Bayat, 1977), and 'insurgent citizenship' (Holston, 2008) all point to a path forward when it comes to uncovering ordinary people's modes of collective action in struggling cities (see also Rao, De Boeck and Simone, 2007).

In his study of post-2000 Zimbabwe, Jeremy Jones (2010: 285, 286) coined the term '*kukiya-kiya*' economy to describe a new logic of economic action that originated on the urban margins but eventually came to mark a 'sweeping spatio-temporal shift' in the country's economic life. In local parlance, '*kukiya-kiya*' refers to multiple forms of 'making do' and 'getting by'. For Jones, straightforward, above-board transactions carried out in accordance with enduring, jointly held conventions and shared rules have given way to 'zigzag deals' and impromptu bargaining that are limited to particular times and places, and directed at individual 'survival'. Under circumstances where expectations governing formal transactions under the rule of law are suspended, the dictates of 'survival' and temporary 'necessity' drive economic activity and become justification for transactions of dubious transparency (Jones, 2010: 285, 287–9). In a similar vein, as Tatiana Adeline Thieme (2018) argues, the 'hustle economy' is a localized yet 'globally resonant condition' embedded in the operative logic of precarious labour markets, where regular wage-paid work is the exception rather than the norm. Hustling brings together the 'generative possibilities' arising from the 'everyday experiences of uncertainty and management of insecurities' associated with precarious urban environments that fall outside the boundaries of formal rules and 'normative social institutions' (Thieme, 2018).

It is useful to recast the concept of DIY urbanism as an umbrella term in order to highlight the family resemblance that exists between 'do-it-yourself' practices and similar ideas such as tactical urbanism, guerrilla urbanism and rogue urbanism. Approaching DIY urbanism from this angle allows for the connections and commonalities between the related concepts and 'doing-it-yourself' within scholarly research to be exposed. In this way, it can be said that DIY urbanism is a useful concept that fits many circumstances reasonably well, though not always perfectly. As such, the concept of DIY urbanism offers a useful entry-point for making sense of how ordinary residents in struggling cities are able to adopt 'copying strategies' under precarious circumstances, with the caveat that the concept should be employed with restraint and not applied indiscriminately (Finn, 2014a; Talen, 2015).

Notes

1   Talen (2015: 135–48) (ideas taken almost verbatim from p. 136).
2   For the source of this quotation (which is taken out of context), see Adler and Kwon (2002: 18).

Chapter 3

REFLECTIONS ON THE DIY PARADIGM AND URBAN LIVING IN NIGERIA

Mohammed-Bello Yunusa

Introduction

Urbanization and urbanism are concepts that have long been present in development literature (Aluko, 2011; Jelili, 2012). While *urbanization* represents a continuous process of people and activities agglomerating within particular areas, and is often expressed as the proportion of the national or regional population living in such areas (Levy, 2009: 9), *urbanism* has both spatial and social components (Pacione, 2009: 376). Urbanism finds expression in towns and cities, and, socially, is composed of the lived realities of urban spaces. Thus, urbanism is associated with the behaviours, relationships, styles and practices of those who are considered to have been 'urbanized'. As a result, the discourse here is less about urbanization as a demographic and spatial process and more about *how* people live in cities.

However, urbanism cannot be understood without understanding urbanization, the latter of which can be regarded as 'the concentration of communities into cities' (Macionis and Plumber, 2014: 841). Contained within this are the processes of population distribution, value formation and ways of living that occur as people seek to take advantage of this concentration. An urban area can be succinctly defined as 'a relatively large, dense and permanent settlement of socially heterogeneous individuals' (Wirth, 1938: 8), with such heterogeneity representing a diversity of cultures, interests and needs, some of which will inevitably manifest in new and perhaps unexpected ways. Durkheim and Tornnis – both cited in Macionis and Plumber (2014: 8, 19) – present a continuum of societal transformation that involves progressive disintegration of community bonds and values, and increased individualism fostered by capitalism and industrialization. Despite such disintegration, the predisposition of simple and organic societies tends to endure.

Based on a paper presented to a workshop co-organized by the Nordic Africa Institute on the 'Practice and Politics of DIY Urbanism in African Cities', held at University of Abuja, 4–7 December 2017.

According to this continuum, the extent of urbanism depends on levels of transformation. Here, it should be noted that the emergence of a new society does not necessarily entail the complete eradication of the old order. Instead, the old order co-exists with the new at varying scales, even amid the new order circumstances of capitalism, industrialization, and information and communication technology. Given this, it is useful to determine the extent to which the old order (i.e. 'rural' values, behaviours and practices) influences how the new, 'urban' order is navigated, thereby helping us to define 'new urbanism' in the sense of friendly neighbourhoods characterized by walkways and life opportunities.

High population densities, heterogeneity and a multiplicity of activities combine to form complex living circumstances in urban areas. Here, a variety of actors – ranging from individual to institutions – respond to common interests and needs, all the while influenced by values, beliefs and modes of living that are in the process of disintegration. Given this, how do people live and survive in cities where transformations are ongoing, and in what ways do the characteristics and values of simple societies persist? Such a question presupposes that the city – rather than the slum, as argued by Roy (2011: 228) – is the entity through which the transition from village or rural (simple) society to large, heterogeneous, complex capitalist communities is processed. According to this perspective, residual rural values and emerging individualistic and capitalist values combine to give identity to African towns and cities, with both 'ruralism' and 'urbanism' providing various means of responding to the needs and aspirations of city dwellers. However, the extent to which these links between 'simple' community values and new urbanism constitute a frame for urban living remains a nagging question. The 'do-it-yourself' (DIY) perspective offers a means of addressing this.

This chapter highlights the urban space 'hacking' currently taking place in Nigerian cities, looking at how it occurs and what facilitating factors are relevant. In doing so, the chapter delves into issues surrounding who engages in urban space 'appropriation', why such places are 'captured' with or without authorization, and the implications for urban living and form. Through such efforts, the aim is to show how DIY systematically contributes to urban functionality through the (re-) making of physical urban structures.

Do-it-yourself and urban living

Durkheimian society is characterized by considerable communal provision, alongside individuals and groups being more or less independent. Here, the only way for individuals and groups to mobilize resources to meet their specific needs and interests is through the spirit of DIY. Such an approach tallies with how life is lived in rural communities – in other words, DIY as a mode of living corresponds with ruralism. Ruralism can therefore be regarded as a process of resource mobilization in circumstances where individualism and capitalism have yet to take root.

Thus, in relation to new urbanism, the DIY paradigm is essentially a carry-over of survival techniques used by simple society dwellers following their move to the city. As such, it provides concrete ways of understanding how resource provisioning operates in both rural and urban environments. According to this way of thinking, DIY is not merely an urban living strategy, or a means for all the urban classes to meet their own needs, but a process by which rural-to-urban migrants deliver programmes and projects to communities in their places of origin. Sometimes, this can undermine urban development, as it has been observed that urban residents' rural commitments may discourage investment in the urban areas where they now live (Andreasen, 1990: 168).

Technology, capitalism and industrialization – along with the individualism that goes hand-in-hand with them – have not entirely erased community ties or ruralism (Augustine, 2010: 2205). The DIY paradigm therefore provides a means of understanding enduring phenomena that have endured in the face of contemporary development. As such, it is a useful frame for analysing new urbanism in Africa, which can be seen as a mixture of integrated and disintegrated – Durkheim's organic and inorganic – modes of survival and city living. It is this concoction that provides a 'shock absorber' to urban residents, and thus renders Africa's cities more governable and sustainable. Through the notion of DIY, we can examine the prevailing interfaces between the state, private capital and civil society in terms of urban construction, development and governance.

The socio-spatial processes of urban formation are intricate and complex. Even so, a number of efforts have been made at understanding how such processes operate in cities (Kent, 1964; Spreiregen, 1965; Keeble, 1969; Pacione, 2009). Furthermore, the socio-economic and spatial processes that shape cityscapes can be seen in early discourses regarding urban life in Africa (Mabogunje, 1968; Hanna and Hanna, 1971; Little, 1974; Gugler and Falanagan, 1978). Building on this, and as outlined above, there is a need to analyse and understand how age-old DIY practices operate within urban spaces. In terms of the preliminary discussion offered by this chapter, the focus is on the use of space in an urban context, and how this operates in relation to informality, and to processes of urbanization and urbanism. Specifically, the chapter offers insight into DIY modes of urban living in Nigeria, as manifested in space hacking or appropriation.

Urbanization in Africa

According to McGee (1975: 18), urbanization is a pervasive phenomenon irreversibly affecting all aspects of life at a vast scale. The way in which populations use urban space is significant when it comes to making cities liveable and sustainable (or otherwise). Residents want sufficient space, necessary infrastructure and functioning services, and the capacity of the cities to meet these needs is what makes them sites of economic power, investment, capital accumulation and consumption (Macionis and Plumber, 2014) – all of which provokes competition for urban space. An inability to meet such needs, as was the case in the Soviet Union, can result in urban growth and liveability becoming unsustainable (Kaplinsky, 2013).

Urbanization in the previously mentioned sense of 'concentration of communities into cities' (Macionis and Plumber, 2014: 841) represents a process of population redistribution, as well as inducing changes in people's lifestyles. Through this ongoing concentration of people – mainly youth – and activities into urban spaces, the city becomes 'a synergy of people in space, ecology and infrastructure' (Jain, 2015: 3). This synergy manifests through individuals making contacts as a means of meeting their needs, with the networks thus established being the essence of functional urban life. In other words, urbanism is 'perceived from the angle of "function" (or) the particular purpose' the city serves (Little, 1974: 100). Basic wants for the urban mode of life consist of:

1) Places to live (housing and circulation, such as roads or walkways).
2) Places to earn a living (fulfilling livelihoods at given places without hindrances).
3) Places for recreation or development of sporting skills.

In order to meet these wants, certain 'patterns of private conduct and decision making that by and large make successful (or unsuccessful) governance' (Rae, 2003: xiii) emerge as constituents of urbanism. Thus, urbanism consists of the various ways social categories in cities live, meet their wants and survive.

The cogent issues here are space, policy and support infrastructure, such as water and energy (Vanderschueren, Weglin and Wekwete, 1996). Faced with an ever-growing city population, the private and public sectors are often unable to meet all these wants, which then manifests as exclusion in the form of, for example, pavement dwellers (Vanderschueren, Weglin and Wekwete, 1999), street families and outright squatting as an 'illicit consequence of the struggle for urban space' (Caminos and Geothart, 1978: 197). Thus, with individuals and groups engaged in constant negotiation as they attempt to meet their needs and wants within the city system, rapid urbanization creates focal points at different scales for growth or decay, opportunities or deprivation. The extent of opportunity or deprivation translates into how exclusive or inclusive a city is, which in turn shapes DIY behaviour or urbanism when it comes to altering land use, street appearance or urban forms/shapes (Simpson, 2015: 3). As such, DIY urbanism can be seen to impact the construction of urban morphology, policies, governance and the wellbeing of city dwellers.

How people, individuals and groups relate to and organize the use of urban spaces to meet their needs indicates a 'complexity of traits (and interfaces between agencies) which make up the characteristic mode of life in cities' (Wirth, 1938: 7). Despite the individualism that marks urban life – often characterized by competitive externalization and survival strategies – a pattern of community-life-sharing opportunities persists or emerges. When it comes to constructing this community sharing, the city's physical structure plays a key role in shaping the capacity and defining the opportunities open to individuals and groups.

While on the one hand the city shapes the lives and behaviours of its residents, on the other, residents can be seen to influence the cityscape through constructing and altering urban space to meet their daily needs. This dialectical relationship must be appreciated if the governance of urban processes, politics and construction is to be understood. Here, city living can be viewed as akin to a complex web of distinct or related formal/informal activities constantly being spun together amid the available urban space. Extrapolating from this, the essence of urban planning is the mediation of formal and informal relationships in the city space.

DIY urbanism – A new debate?

The notion of DIY denotes individuals or communities initiating, executing and utilizing certain facilities, resources or infrastructure to meet their own or others' needs. In order for DIY urbanism to occur, there must exist a gap or constraint that prevents individuals or communities from realizing some or all of their needs in the city. Through the appropriation of resources – mainly in the form of urban space – DIY creates space for activities and induces changes in land use and the city's spatio-temporal character (Pagano, 2013: 338). Such DIY may proceed with or without the permission of land owners, and may or may not involve collaboration with public or private agencies (Pagano, 2013: 338).

In particular, where the public and private sectors are unable to meet the land, space or service needs of individuals and communities, openings emerge within which DIY tendencies can bloom. Such deficits in meeting residents' wants and needs increase in line with a city's population and the multiplicity of activities requiring space. Thus, DIY as both a practice and process has implications for a city's inclusiveness. Indeed, given that a process of DIY is often needed to address these increasing deficits (Farah, Cabrera and Teller, undated: 1), the absence of such practices can potentially result in rising urban exclusion. By appropriating space or resources in order to ensure delivery of services, individuals and communities can meet their needs and in doing so become part of urban system. In this context, it can be said that the spread of DIY urbanism is occurring in tandem with the struggle for social, economic and physical space occasioned by 'economic crises and the rolling back of public responsibility for funding, (delivering) and managing infrastructure' (Bradley, 2015: 91), which limits the capacity of private and public agencies to meet the daily wants of citizens.

As has been asserted, the fact that individuals and groups in integrated (rural) or disintegrated (urban) communities may have 'access to the same form of (city facilities) … education and radio communication does not automatically mean that this will lead to lessening of the differences in rural–urban attitudes' (McGee, 1975: 57). DIY urbanism, though it may only operate in the marginal areas of private capital and state responsibilities, is an expression of people's values and attitudes. Thus, DIY practices can be regarded as a critique of government-and-private-capital-led urban development, which is often unable to meet the wants of citizens. As claimed by Wendler (2014), DIY urbanism potentially offers new urban configuration and practices that lie outside government and private capital.

The DIY paradigm, ruralism and informality

The notion of DIY is inseparable from the various processes of informality that are a part of urban living. Such informality involves individuals and communities attempting to meet daily wants outside the realm of private capital and public programmes. Thus, DIY urbanism can be seen to operate outside or at the margins of city rules and regulations. As has been asserted, 'the informal nature of urban development is an age-long issue and is expressed by the tension arising from what a state organ controls and what is beyond its control' (Abdoul, 2005: 237). Here it should be noted that most African cities have, from their foundation onwards, lacked the spatial development controls and governance characteristic of the Euro-American model. Instead, they have often been constructed according to the rural spatial cosmology held by incoming migrants. As a result, African urbanism is a manifestation of the values and practices of both Euro-American urbanism and African ruralism (in the sense of individuals and groups providing for themselves and others in a more or less unregulated manner). African urbanism therefore falls between what is regulated and what is not, and as such links together formal and informal urban processes.

Ruralism can be seen as a mode of living in which needs and aspirations are pursued not within written regulations and controls, as is the case for industrial and capitalist societies, but within commonly understood norms and values. Here, though the pursuit of needs is not guided by specific rules, it should not offend the community's common sensibilities. The habits, values and practices of simple societies, which migrants to the city bring with them, do not really disappear. Thus, the assertion of 'territorial claims' (Roy, 2011: 228) in the city may be viewed as not only confined to the dispossessed, but something reflected in all social groups, arising from rural traits that have refused to die when confronted by capitalist and industrial-driven individualism.

Ruralism manifests in processes of space appropriation that fall outside established rules of urban land acquisition, development and use. This can be seen in space being utilized for what some may view as peripheral or marginal activities, but are in fact activities that meet people's needs, despite being absent from any official urban development plan. Often, it is these official development plans that establish controls on the use of urban land. When controls were introduced in the colonial period, they were more firmly implemented in some city areas (where the Europeans and elites resided), than others (those hosting the indigenous population). This is exemplified by the classification of Lagos' residential sectors by Mabogunje (1968), who primarily relied on the Euro-American model of spatial forms.

DIY urbanism has been adopted by urban researchers as a frame of analysis for economic, social and political processes within spatial formation and functioning. Here, the concept of informality can be adopted for similar purposes, as, like DIY, it is:

> a permanent instrument for observing changes in urban development. It takes into account the complex nature of the process of evolution within a given space, a series of interactions not only between the stake holders, the nature

and objectives of their actions, but equally between the stakes and strategies the stakeholders map out for the development of a type of urban area.

(Abdoul, 2005: 237)

Informality becomes noticeable when unwritten mores and values can be seen to guide how urban affairs are conducted. Informality enables certain decisions, activities and behaviours to occur outside a city's control system. Such activities are more prone to be guided by rural values and practices, which may either compliment or contradict urban values and controls, but ultimately enhance urban living. It this way, informality and ruralism blend together in cities. The persistence of simple society traits in complex urban life renders Euro-American modes of urbanization and urbanism somewhat utopian in Africa, something that will remain the case for as long as the traits of both simple and complex communities continue to co-exist. This observation informs the assertion that:

> In taking the virtual symbols of urbanisation (particularly in Africa) to be marks of the important qualities of urban society; we have compared these symbols with other ideological precepts of order and found that they do not conform; and so we have mistaken for 'urban chaos' what is more likely to be a newly emerging order whose signal qualities are complexity and diversity.

(Weber, 1969: 25)

However, notions of DIY urbanism and informality as being driven by unwritten mores and values, as opposed to formal urban controls, allow us to gain insight into the interwoven connectivity between urban stakeholders, processes of space capturing or appropriation (both of which make up hacking), and how this produces a particular type of cityscape. Similarly, DIY and informality offer useful lenses through which to understand urban space construction and usage, as well as socio-economic processes and dynamics.

At this point, it should be noted that – regardless of government controls – in most African cities (Nigeria's included) it is individuals and group initiatives that drive space construction and use, along with urban socio-economic processes. Thus, due to pervasive individual and community initiatives, along with some instances of private capital and public programmes, urban development can be seen to go far beyond 'self initiated urban improvements' (Bradley, 2015: 91). This is very much verifiable with respect to the presence across residential sectors of such facilities, services and utilities as housing, access ways, shops and, more recently, water (growing borehole culture) and electricity (massive installation of electricity generators and solar facilities). This is evident in the analysis of housing shortage and supply in Marrakesh (Gheris, 2005), as well as the profile of Angwar Mai Gwado in Zaria in northern Nigeria, which represents a response to 'urban expansion and need of low income earners for housing' (Yunusa, 2005: 182).

Some DIY practices may be illicit, particularly among the urban poor, who are often engaged in a constant struggle to access basic urban services. One study has noted that in Kaduna urban area in north-western Nigeria, 'the poor are seeking illegitimate access through illegal (in the sense of unauthorized) connection of service lines of various services, utilities and facilities' (Yunusa, 2004: 153). The means by which such activities are pursued offers a window onto how the excluded contest and defend their rights to the city, as well as navigate access to city infrastructure. Suffice it to note here that both the DIY and informality paradigms, and the overlap between them, can assist in understanding how individuals and communities influence cityscapes, as well as meet their daily wants outside the assistance of private capital and state programmes.

Again, it is important to emphasize that cities – as spatial points where people and activities are concentrated – incorporate a variety of social-economic categories, each of which exhibit or encounter varying lifestyles, opportunities and challenges (Macionis and Plumber, 2014: 845). These groups have differing relationships with respect to the types of activities engaged in, and the modes of space acquisition or appropriation employed. Hence, urbanization processes create cities that 'are spatial manifestations of human activities (land values) and exhibit a dynamic relationship between various elements (space and socio-economic segments and activities)' (Jain, 2015: 3).

The manifestation of DIY is more noticeable in demands for and consumption of city space required for various human activities. Such demands may be met through official channels, which can be influenced by informal negotiations, or be realized through entirely unofficial processes. These unofficial processes require navigation across various dimensions in order to access and appropriate city facilities and opportunities.

Urban planning, development and urbanism

From the early nineteenth century onwards, the intensity of physical planning increased as a response to the Industrial Revolution, which was causing increased population concentration, environmental degradation and health hazards. As a reactive measure, land use planning was, and still is, directed at safeguarding the public interest – that is, protecting individuals and groups from the dangers of city expansion, as well as meeting the needs and aspirations of existing and prospective city inhabitants (Duruzoechi and Duru, 2015: 57). Physical planning addresses the provision of space and the delivery of support infrastructure to various socio-economic activities within a city on a permanent basis. It is common knowledge that 'the provision of public facilities is also a traditional (physical) planning emphasis' (Gan, 1968: 235). The socio-economic and spatial fabric of a city incorporates a synergy of people in its physical space and web of infrastructure. However, within the city space allocation plan that arises from this synergy, some people and/or activities tend to be left out. These unprovided-for people must then, of necessity, contest their existence in the city, creating space for their activities as a means of gaining access to infrastructure and recognition. The marginality of such individuals or groups may in some cases relate to their status in terms of poverty, power and influence.

Physical planning is the conscious effort to organize people and activities within a defined space, thereby providing the city with a spatial form and mode of life that can accommodate everyone. Land use planning provides a framework for safeguarding individuals and groups from potential dangers, while at the same time meeting their space needs. In this way, physical planning mediates relationships between land, activities and the urban population. Thus, physical planning is – or should be – the provider 'of satisfaction for every day wants' (Binns, 1977: 11). However, such planning involves predetermined, coded land use provisions, which does not provide for daily, often unforeseen, ephemeral space needs.

These ephemeral space needs arise from activities that, rather than having a permanent presence, only occupy urban spaces for a limited amount of time – whether just a few hours or for a day or two. Coded land uses, by implication, cannot accommodate the diverse land use needs of every urban social category, a situation exacerbated by the in-built tendency for physical planning to be rigid and controlling (Simpson, 2015: 6). This rigidity manifests in the application of zoning by-laws, which define the uses to which urban spaces can be put. As a result, the need for land of various sizes at various locations, for common or even individual activities, is not comprehensively met. Hence, though urban planning plays a key role in guiding the construction of cities, it often fails to meet the fluctuating exigencies experienced by many city dwellers.

Given this context, city residents will inevitably start doing things in 'their own ways', which, regardless of cultural multiplicity, will often be reflective of past experiences of rural living. The need to accommodate the myriad space needs that go unforeseen in urban land use plans forms the basis for a range of individual and group interventions that shape urban spaces for the common good (Pagano, 2013: 337–8). This is illustrated by the increasing tendency for city dwellers and communities to barricade neighbourhoods and hire their own security guards (Silver, 2008: 10), while appropriating public spaces and alleyways for a variety of activities, including economic. Such processes have led to individuals and/or groups appropriating urban spaces that in some cases have been designated for other uses. It is this appropriation of city land outside physical planning controls that offers a platform for space hacking and alternative utilization tendencies.

While space stealing can be seen as an indictment of urban planning and management provisions, and as innovative as DIY may seem as a frame for analysing the processes through which these spaces are taken, adopted, reorganized and utilized by individuals or groups, it should be noted that the motives, manifestations and purposes of DIY are not necessarily the same across different cities – or even within a particular city. Even so, the DIY frame offers a plausible means of unveiling the extent to which ruralism pervades contemporary urbanism in Africa, and for establishing commonalities or generalizations that can be applied to city modes of life. Extrapolating from this, the differences in how DIY manifests across and within cities in various regions – such as sub-Saharan Africa, Asia and Europe – can be established.

Space capturing and use in Nigerian cities

As of 2015, over 87 million Nigerians lived in urban areas, a figure that continues to increase by the day, while as of 2017, Nigeria had 7 cities with a population of over one million people; 79 with 100,000–1,000,000 people; and 249 towns/cities with 10,000–100,000 people.[1] Urban formation is an age-old process in Nigeria, predating colonial administration. As such, Nigerian urbanization is characterized by traditional or indigenous cities, colonial cities and post-independence cities. All these types of city have been created, driven and sustained by different modes and scales of social, political and economic development. This section presents a brief overview of the DIY use of urban space taking place in Nigeria – specifically, the variety of activities observable in the cities of Zaria, Minna Lokoja and Abuja. It should be noted that the intention here is simply to present a selection of the DIY urbanism activities that are observable in these cities – analysis of, for example, how modes of communication and networks are constructed is left for further studies.

Space use in Zaria

Over the course of its existence, Zaria has served as the headquarters of the Zazzau dynasty's kingdom, of Zaria Province during the colonial period, and since then Zaria Local Government Area of Kaduna state. Outside the traditional walled town area, Zaria is highly cosmopolitan and contains a variety of educational institutions, including a university, a polytechnic, a collage of education and a collage of aviation technology. Within Zaria – which has a population of about 975,153 – a variety of space capturing and usage activities can be seen.

The herbal market that appeared in Durumi offers an illustrative case of gradual space occupation without authorization. The market was started by a herb retailer who took over a portion of roadside land next to the perimeter wall of a local government department in the walled town. The retailer's success attracted other herbalists and traders, leading to the strip of land becoming a huge Monday market that prevented the road being used by motorists. In response, local authorities developed a market in Magajiya, relocating the herbal traders there in order to restore traffic flow.

In Zaria, space is also hacked for recreation, particularly football, with vacant plots appropriated to create playing surfaces. In an attempt to ward off players and spectators, property owners put up notices prohibiting such usage. Such notices are placed on walls. In some situations space hackers put up notices to indicate that the appropriation is without government authorization. Space capturing is also common on circulation routes, particularly along major roads, with newspaper and book vendors targeting the moving population on road shoulders reserved for pedestrians.

Urban space hacking also manifests in public space being annexed for private use. For example, a mosque in Sabon-Gari put up 'No Parking' signs on the stretch of service road alongside it, thereby contesting its status as a public space. The road is a busy one, only metres from an open concourse market. Ordinarily, shoppers will park on the street and proceed to the market. Thus, how the public negotiates this annexation of land with the mosque's management has potentially significant implications for urban governance and security, as religion remains a sensitive part of Nigerian public life.

Space use in Minna

Minna – with a population of around 291,905 – first emerged as a train station and is therefore a colonial creation. Having previously served as the district headquarters for Bida province and the local government headquarters for Sokoto state, it is currently the capital of Niger state. The city is also the seat of Bahago traditional authority. Like Zaria, Minna hosts of number of educational establishments, including two universities, a collage of education and the Niger State School of Nursing and Midwifery. All these institutions attract a diverse population with correspondingly diverse interests, activities and land needs. This has capacity to heighten space hacking.

Physical space appropriation in Minna is predominantly for the purposes of recreation or livelihood activities. In terms of livelihoods, an example can be seen in physically challenged individuals collectively occupying roadside pedestrian walkways to solicit alms, thereby forcing pedestrians to share the carriageway with vehicular traffic. In doing so, the physically challenged have managed to capture a fixed space within which to negotiate their livelihoods. In terms of recreation, children and youth frequently convert undeveloped plot of land into playgrounds, from which it may be inferred that their needs are not being fully met in the urban development process.

Space use in Lokoja

Lokoja – with a population of around 60,579 – is located at the confluence of the Niger and Benue rivers, in the central area of Nigeria. It was the headquarters of the Royal Niger Company and capital of colonial Nigeria. As a river port, it handled both internal and external trade. After serving as the headquarters of Kwara Native Authority in Kabba province, it became the headquarters of Kogi local government area in Kwara state, and later of Lokoja local government in Kogi state. It is currently the capital of Kogi state and serves as a gateway between the north of Nigeria and the country's south-western and south-eastern regions.

Space capturing for sporting or recreation activities can be observed in Lokoja, with local teams competing for various prizes on apparently unmarked football pitches, regardless of the fact that the owners of the plots may at any time employ the land for other uses. In addition, rollers share roads with vehicular traffic in order to practise or display their skills, which has implications for road safety.

Space use in Abuja

Abuja, currently the headquarters of the Federal Government of Nigeria, is estimated to have a population of 590,400 and was created, planned and developed as a new town from the 1980s onwards. The city thus represents a test ground for the extent to which physical planning meets the wants of citizens, as, given this development plan, it should in theory be the case that all land use needs across social categories and demographic cohorts are provided for. In practice, however, it appears that the city is not meeting these needs, prompting residents – such as joggers, rollers and car drivers – to capture space without authorization.

Drivers engaging in racing and stunts present problems to urban managers and security agencies due to the inherent dangers of such activities. The racing/stunts take place in the city's Central Area (near NICON Insurance Building and Karimu) in the evenings or dead of night. Despite the efforts of the police and security agencies, drivers are often able to outsmart their pursuers and escape capture. Even when arrests are made, drivers are often released before they have made it to the police station. This is because such activities are usually engaged in by those from rich and influential families, meaning parents can negotiate settlements in order to keep their children out of jail.

Rollers represent another category of space invader, and are mainly to be found in Jabi Lake area, with some spotted at the CBN Senior Staff Quarters at Karu. Moreover, at weekends, various public areas are taken over for the purposes of aerobic exercise and jogging. The four-lane road that passes in front of Primus Hospital in Karu is one such area given over to such activities – here, in addition to the exercise itself, sportswear sellers carry out their trade on the kerb, road shoulder and setbacks. Besides sporting activities, opportunities are provided for socializing and networking with other cultural groups and nationalities.

One particular DIY activity of note in Abuja concerns youth contributing to infrastructure maintenance in the absence of a public agency taking responsibility – specifically, youth assumed responsibility for repairing damaged portions of an access way in Gwarimpa. In the same area, vendors can be observed selling goods and services while they sat on road shoulders or drainage covers.

Concluding remarks

Urbanism as a way of life relates to urbanization, ruralism and informality. The notion of DIY can be seen as the string binding ruralism to urbanism, as development does not inevitably cause established habits, ideas and practices to disappear. Ruralism is not necessarily a critique of urbanization or meant to contradict it, as indicated by Ferguson (1992), nor is it the exclusive preserve of the excluded, as posited by Bayat (2000) – rather, it is an inherent part of city dwellers' lives, aiding their navigation of urban opportunities and livelihoods. Thus, the role of ruralism and the practice of DIY urbanism provide a unique frame for understanding African cities.

The glimpses of space occupation and usage in Nigerian cities outlined above make clear that land use planning has not provided space for all the activities that residents wish to participate in. In the four cities examined, a variety of public and private spaces are being captured – sometimes in direct confrontation with the public interest, as in the case of the herbal market in Zaria or the 'No Parking' signs planted outside the mosque. Meanwhile, the car racing and stunts in Abuja only highlight the inadequacies of planning when it comes to envisaging and providing for 'new' modes of recreation.

If cities are to continue to be perceived as places of opportunity and innovation when it comes to economic and social development (Cohen, 2006: 63), urbanization and urban living should not simply be taken for granted (Nordhag, 2012). Instead, we must constantly seek new understandings of the roles played the state, private sector capital and communities in urban construction, space usage and sustainability. This point is underlined by the fact that 'what the state has done or has not done has been of great importance in the social and economic development of modern societies' (Dowd, 1977: 267) – it is precisely what the state provides (or not) that forms the basis for how DIY urbanism manifests itself in cities.

A major but unresolved issue arising from the discussion of space capture in the four cities is the extent to which 'DIY' coincides or conflicts with informality, as both notions tend to involve citizens providing for themselves or their communities in areas where the government or private capital have been deficient. When it comes to space appropriation in African cities, while the 'national and local government have (partial) influence over layout of urban space' (Therborn, 2017: 70), it may be that capital has lost the ability to control access to urban space (Therborn, 2017) due to a combination of DIY urbanism, ruralism and informality. The contention that urbanism in African cities is essentially an extension of ruralism is reinforced by the observation that Yoruba cities have village-like (rural) houses, with many primary producers (Gugler and Falangan, 1978: 19).

With this in mind, subsequent studies should explore in greater detail which of the various forms and processes seen in DIY African urbanism constitute an extension of ruralism and informality. Such investigations should be conducted in relation to city type and size, as well as the types of space hacking in evidence, thereby establishing what links and interfaces exist between urbanism, ruralism and informality, and how African urbanization and urbanisms fit into contemporary global processes.

Note

1   These population figures, together with those for Abuja, Minna, Lokoja and Zaria, were found at http://worldpopulationreview.com/countries/nigeria-population/cities.

Chapter 4

DIY URBANISM IN AN AFRICAN CONTEXT AND ITS POTENTIAL AS A COLLABORATIVE PLACEMAKING TOOL FOR BRIDGING AFRICA'S URBAN INFRASTRUCTURE DEFICIT

Mathias Agbo Jr.

Introduction

In 1950s Paris, the Situationists International – a group of artists, filmmakers and poets – created a distinct brand of urban exploration that was, in essence, a form of street ethnography. The group was highly critical of the models of urban renovation and planning prevalent in Paris at the time, which involved slums being cleared to make way for middle-class residents (McDonough, 2010). According to Shepard, the Situationists viewed urban life as a contested terrain, malleable to the needs of various users, each with different visions of what a city space could or should be (Shepard, 2014).

Over the years, urban activism has taken a number of forms around the world, all of them connected in some way to the Situationists' legacy. According to Hern, while these urban interventions typically vary in terms of aims, forms, legality and communal participation, they share a key component: community engagement at the grassroots through a bottom-up approach, thereby ensuring all-round citizen participation (Hern, 2010).

Long before the Situationists, however, there were urban activists such as English planner Ebenezer Howard, who rather than pursue an incremental DIY (do-it-yourself) urbanism proposed a radical, large-scale, citizen-led urbanism aimed at building idiosyncratic cities (what he termed 'Garden Cities') from scratch. In his 1898 book, *To-morrow: A Peaceful Path to Real Reform* (which was later significantly revised and reissued in 1902 as *Garden Cities of To-morrow*), Howard proffered practical solutions to the overcrowding and industrial pollution afflicting growing Victorian cities. He wanted to build self-sufficient, egalitarian suburban cities that were of limited size, planned in advance and surrounded by agricultural land. Overall, he had a utopian vision of cities without slums, wholly owned and financed by residents who would live harmoniously as equals (Howard, 1902). Although Howard's urban dream did not exactly become reality, it did influence the planning of a number of cities, and even now continues to shape urban discourses around the world (New Garden City Movement, 2013).

Today, the concept of DIY urbanism has evolved significantly. Whereas once upon a time it was only members of avant-garde activist groups who were involved in citizen-led urban interventions, now every citizen has the opportunity to have their say about how cities are shaped. As Duncombe observes: 'The idea of just going out and doing it – or as it is popularly expressed in the underground, the do-it-yourself ethic … is not just complaining about what is, but actually doing something different' (Duncombe, 1997).

Pagano describes DIY urbanism as urban interventions that occur with the permission of the private or public entities that control the spaces used, and that are built/designed by urban planning professionals, often in close cooperation with city officials and a cross-section of community members. On the other hand, he employs the term 'guerrilla' urbanism to distinguish a subcategory of DIY interventions that break laws, ignore regulations and/or circumvent democratic processes (Pagano, 2013).

Although not every contemporary DIY urban activist will share the radical political ideologies of their forebears in the Situationist International, the Lettrists, or any of the other movements that shaped the urban politics of post-war Europe and the United States, it is clear that they are driven by the same motive of 'asserting their right to the city' (Lefebvre, 1996), and that the urban interventions they are involved in are largely premised on building egalitarian urban spaces where all citizens have equal rights. A good example of this can be seen in the cycling activism that – at various periods – has swept across cities in Europe and the United States. For these groups:

> the bicycle became an apt metaphor for independence and an iconic signifier of freedom itself. European Socialists viewed it as a symbol of freedom and a means for articulating the cultural politics of the left. Feminists embraced it as a source of empowerment, as a way to escape coerced domesticity.
>
> (Furness, 2010)

The rest of this chapter will provide an overview of the current state of DIY urbanism in Africa, before proceeding to discuss in detail the socio-political and socio-cultural factors that have motivated citizen-led urban interventions across the continent, and in particular, Nigeria. Specifically, the following questions will be explored: What are the social narratives that have created and sustained the deplorable spatial circumstances found in African cities? How have socio-cultural and socio-political realities on the continent shaped citizen-led approach to DIY urbanism? What are the political implications of these responses? Moreover, the chapter will interrogate the potential for harmonizing citizen-led placemaking into mainstream urbanism across Africa.

The state of contemporary urbanism in Africa

A visit to Africa's first-tier cities – such as Lagos, Nairobi and Luanda – reveals landscapes replete with construction projects, ranging from upscale apartment blocks to luxurious retail developments. In some places, there are even purpose-built 'smart' cities being built entirely from scratch. Behind this facade of utopian urban development, however, lies a spatially fragmented society – one in which wealthy neighbourhoods receive high-grade infrastructure, while their less affluent counterparts are left entirely to their own devices. Such spatial dysfunction, previously confined to slums and low-income communities, is now spreading throughout cities, including to middle-class neighbourhoods (Agbo, 2017a).

Residents of neglected neighbourhoods are burdened with the responsibility of building their own public infrastructure – such as access roads, potable water sources and street lights – despite the huge ground rents and multiple taxes they already pay to municipal authorities. Such discriminatory patterns of urban infrastructure distribution have led to citizens embarking on everyday, self-led interventions aimed at building infrastructure and amenities in their neighbourhoods (Kimmelman, 2013).

Participatory, citizen-led DIY interventions are typically initiated and executed outside the 'legitimate' channels of conventional urban planning and city building. Instead, they are built around 'everyday people' playing active 'hands-on' roles in redefining their urbanscape, filling palpable infrastructural gaps within their communities. These prosaic but essential interventions are a response to the shortcomings of traditional urban development in Africa, which has resulted in a colossal infrastructural deficit of at least $108 billion (AFDB, 2018).

Case study: Lokogoma community, Abuja

On 24 August 2017, residents of Lokogoma – a growing middle-class neighbourhood of around 400,000 people in Dakwo district of Abuja – marched in protest to the offices of the Federal Capital Development Authority (FCDA) over the death of one of their members, Mr. Kenneth Nwoga, and his two children. The three had been killed the previous week when their SUV was swept by flood waters off a makeshift bridge into the surrounding gorge. The FCDA became the target of blame for the infrastructure deficit present in the district, which – it was felt – had led to the needless suffering of residents and the eventual deaths of the Nwogas.

Residents complained that they had written on several occasions to the FCDA regarding the decrepit state of infrastructure in their neighbourhood, yet nothing had been done to address their plight. As a result, they had often elected to build their own makeshift public infrastructures (Premium Times, 2017). The improvised bridge built by the local community was the only access point in and out of the neighbourhood, meaning that residents were often cut off from the rest of the city during periods of heavy rain. Regardless of such dangers,

Mr. Nwoga had decided to brave the crossing in order to get his children to summer school on time.

The tragic incident in Lokogoma highlights the dire conditions under which residents of Abuja's low-income and middle-class neighbourhoods live. Like Lokogoma, most of Abuja's new districts have little public infrastructure – acting at the behest of wealthy speculators and influential land grabbers, city authorities have opened up these districts without providing basic amenities (Agbo, 2017a). As such, DIY urbanism has become an essential element of the urban culture of these communities, with many residents initially unaware of the infrastructural obligations city authorities had towards them. For residents of Lokogoma and other districts faced with similar spatial challenges, embarking on self-help urban interventions has become a survival strategy without which life would be intolerable. Across Africa, similar stories can be seen, with most neighbourhoods outside the traditional upscale districts left to fend for themselves. These neighbourhoods typically have to build their own public infrastructure or face being cut off from the rest of the city's population.

Below, I outline the peculiarities of citizen-led urbanism in Africa and how the continent's eccentric socio-political milieu has created and sustained the need for these interventions. Moreover, I highlight how the pre-existing sociocultural makeup has shaped responses to these peculiar spatial circumstances.

DIY urbanism in Africa: The socio-political context

Africa's recent history has been marked by some dramatic and significant developments on the continent's political terrain. These developments have been as varied as they have been contradictory. They have also constituted a major source of challenge to political theory, as different schools of thought grapple with them in terms of their weight and meaning.

(Olukoshi, 2004)

Africa has come a long way since the great wave of national independence swept across the continent six decades ago. Today, the political systems that succeeded colonialism have evolved from widespread absolute dictatorship to a potpourri of democracies, quasi-democracies, autocracies and systems too complex to append any known nomenclature to (Lynch and Crawford, 2011). It is ultimately these political developments that shape everything else, with urban development patterns – as with almost all social issues in contemporary Africa – built mostly along socio-political contours. Hence, the distribution of public infrastructure and amenities has long been a challenge for most African cities due to the underlying politics that characterize these urban developments (Bamidele et al., 2017).

A near consensus of opinion points to poor political leadership as chiefly responsible for the infrastructural dysfunction most African cities are currently faced with, holding that if the political class had been more prudent with available resources, the spatial situation would have been much different (Nworgu and Ijirshar, 2016). This urban dysfunction is exacerbated by the short-sighted machinations of the political class, most of whom have turned urbanism into a currency of partisan political patronage, designed to 'colour' socio-political engagement and drive a discriminatory brand of identity politics (Bamidele et al., 2017).

Today, Africa's ruling political class often prioritize urban infrastructure provision in communities where they have broad political support, or where they socially identify with residents. Given this, it is not uncommon to hear such comments as 'we won't build roads here because you didn't vote for us'. For those seeking or in power, public infrastructure such as roads has become bargaining chips to be used in political horse-trading, with supporters rewarded and the 'other side' punished (Ibelema, 2000). Some elected officials in Nigeria have even devised ways of evading their infrastructural obligations altogether, commoditizing public infrastructure or instead providing 'stomach infrastructures' – a euphemism in Nigeria's urban lexicon for food hand-outs and meagre stipends in lieu of tangible urban infrastructure and amenities (Gabriel, 2015).

In light of these harsh but sobering realities, and as a means of ameliorating the difficult spatial circumstances brought about by such crude political scheming, residents of neglected neighbourhoods have resorted to DIY urbanism. For them, DIY interventions are not part of a calculated strategy aimed at furthering a particular political ideology – rather, they are survival strategies driven by acute indigence and the need to access basic urban amenities, such as adequate roads, electricity or potable water.

Despite Africa's urbanism having largely been shaped by its politics, citizen-led urban interventions are often devoid of any underlying political motivation. Though for some it may be comforting to ascribe a significant political undertone to citizen-led urbanism across Africa – hailing it as an example of political resistance waged by the masses against the ruling class's age-old hegemony – it would in reality be misleading to do so. Contrary to many other geographical contexts, where DIY urbanism has become an agitprop and tool for political resistance, in Africa it constitutes a desperate act of survival. Sadly, most Africans do not yet have the luxury of appending lofty political ideologies to their urban interventions.

DIY urbanism in Africa: The socio-cultural context

Nearly every indigenous ethnic group in Africa is bound by a set of values, which is often dictated by local culture and traditions (Gyekye, 2011). Although these cultures are in no way homogenous, it can nevertheless be observed that each one is influenced by a set of overriding common beliefs. One such manifestation of this system of beliefs can be seen in *Ubuntu*, a traditional African philosophy that emphasizes communal living and so acts as a means of binding members of a community together. As van Nierk explains: 'Though the word *Ubuntu* is derived from Nguni languages of Xhosa and Zulu, the philosophy is not exclusive to these cultures. Instead, it encapsulates numerous sets of values that have their roots in various African cultures' (van Nierk, 2013).

Ubuntu is built around African humanism and provides an indigenous socialist system that advocates communal well-being and the collective responsibility of community members. It dictates that individuals must be subservient to the sovereignty of the community, as well as responsive to its needs, and that in turn the community is obligated to look after each individual (Tschaepe, 2013). From this profound philosophy arise a plethora of other values inextricably linked to how each community member engages with wider society.

Ubuntu represents the unwritten constitution of traditional African societies, and dates from long before cities evolved into the formal social structures they have now become. This communal statute is so entrenched in African societies that it is often seen as the primary symbol of authority within communities, one so potent that every member of a community is by default bounded by the 'invisible' bonds of communalism (van Nierk, 2013). It is cultural ideologies such as *Ubuntu* that motivate citizens to execute their own urban interventions, rather than wait endlessly for city authorities to act. Thus, long before societies from other parts of the world understood the concept of people-led urbanism, local communities in Africa believed it their natural duty to shape their urban space. Hence, whenever residents needed a road, the community simply mobilizes its local population and goes about building it. These interventions are usually quick builds that do not in any way measure up to conventional public infrastructures built by municipal authorities. Nevertheless, they are labours of love and stem from a desire to make life easier for members of the local community (Pieterse, 2011).

Urban communities in Africa have so perfected the art of citizen-led intervention that – despite the huge taxes city dwellers are paying – they were they have become almost oblivious of the existence and/or obligations of city authorities. In Nigeria, for instance, almost every low- and medium-income neighbourhood has a neighbourhood residents' association. These self-governing associations are primarily set up by local residents to midwife DIY interventions within their communities, and periodically raise funds by levying their members a service charge. These funds are directed towards public interest interventions – such as fixing roads, borehole construction and waste management – in fulfilment of the socio-cultural obligation (*Ubuntu*) mandating each citizen to improve the condition of their community (Neighbourhood Review, 2017). Even those who have a tendency to evade communal obligations are often wary of communal retribution if they fail to conform, and so will join in (even if against their will).

An interesting attribute of DIY interventions in African cities is that, for some communities, such interventions have evolved to become multi-faceted. For instance, while the larger district residents' associations take on broader urban challenges – such as building access roads and stormwater drainages – subsets of these associations, representing a particular street or neighbourhood, will focus on local provision of street lights, communal waste disposal systems and other everyday needs. These subsets can be further divided up into local units of, for example, people living in the same apartment block, who can then focus on immediate issues such as sanitation and provision of clean water sources (Echessa, 2010). Finally, wealthy individuals within a community may, of their own volition, elect to single-handedly provide basic amenities for those living within their immediate neighbourhood.

DIY urbanism as a collaborative placemaking tool

Although local governments are well developed in North Africa, in SSA (with the exception of South Africa), municipalities are marginalized and lack the required capacities and resources to plan and manage the more and more complex situations. The role of African local governments in urban development is indeed highly constrained. Many countries have sought to decentralize service delivery to local governments, but without a commensurate transfer/increase in revenue sources/financing. Moreover, most towns and cities in Africa have limited professional capacity for managing urban development. Municipalities lack legal and administrative frameworks for efficient service delivery and management of urban planning, land tenure and finance.

(ECOSOC, 2014)

Municipal authorities in Africa face a number of significant challenges (some of them self-inflicted) as they daily confront spiralling expenditures – such as pensions, salaries and other statutory obligations – amidst dwindling government revenues. The situation is even more acute in a commodity-dependent economy, as can be seen in Nigeria, where public infrastructure funding for local municipal authorities is largely tied to monthly subventions received from the federal account, which in turn is largely funded by oil revenues (over which the country has little control) (Budgit, 2017). While not discounting the effects of corruption and poor political leadership, it is nevertheless clear that city authorities are faced with a genuine fiscal handicap, which hinders them from meeting their local infrastructural obligations.

In Nigeria's 2017 national budget, for instance, the proposed allocation for capital projects was pegged at about 6.9 billion dollars (31.7 per cent of the overall national budget) – barely enough to bridge the infrastructure gap in the city of Abuja, let alone the entire country. Moreover, as of October 2017, a mere 15 per cent of this allocation had been released to fund the capital projects budget, a situation the Minister of Budget and National Planning ascribed to the National Assembly's failure to approve the proposed borrowing plan, as well as the country's inability to meet estimated revenue targets, which are largely dependent on crude oil revenues (Punch Editorial, 2017). Given that almost all of Nigeria's thirty-six constituent states are wholly depend on monthly subventions from Abuja to fund their local budgets, this depressing picture is replicated across the country's major cities, with the exception of Lagos (which now has a substantial locally generated revenue base) (Olowolaju et al., 2014). Despite the dire financial situation currently facing municipal authorities, however, the legacy of their profligate forerunners means that most citizens are unwilling to extend them any sympathy.

Consequently, most local governments in Nigeria – and indeed Africa – have unwittingly relinquished their traditional role in building public infrastructure to the residents of local communities (Odalonu, 2015). Even so, municipal authorities often feign ignorance of, or simply refuse to acknowledge, the fundamental role local communities play in shaping city urbanscapes through DIY urbanism. Exacerbating this situation, instances abound of city authorities carrying out urban development without input from local communities, meaning the latter often end up with infrastructures that are of little if any relevance to their most pressing needs (or are built in ways that prevent them being easily used). As a result, these urban infrastructures go underused or, in some cases, are never used at all.

An example of this can be seen in Nigeria's $470 million National Public Security Communication System (NPSCS), which aimed to install CCTV cameras and related security infrastructure across Lagos and Abuja. Despite being initiated by the Nigerian government in 2010, city residents are yet to feel the project's impact – at present, very little of the equipment is functional, with much of it either stolen or vandalized (*Sunday Guardian*, 2016). While, if probably executed, the project may have proven an asset in keeping the city safe, its objectives are at the very bottom of local communities' hierarchy of needs. Instead, the considerable sums of money involved could have been used to provide good roads and/or other public infrastructure for neglected urban communities, ultimately preventing the needless hardship and even deaths that have resulted from the absence of such infrastructure.

Case study: Makoko Floating School

In 2013, a new school building was completed in the coastal slum of Makoko, in Lagos. The project – known today as Makoko Floating School – was designed and built by Kunle Akinyemi-led NLE Architects, with sponsorship from the United Nations Development Programme (UNDP) and the Boell Foundation. The designers worked with the local community to draw up plans for the school, and residents also formed the corps for the project's building workforce.

The Makoko floating school was situated at the centre of the squalid waters of the Lagos Lagoon canals, amidst aging wooden homes on stilts in the watery slums of Makoko. The building typology is a re-adaptation of the existing Architecture of the Makoko people, making use of existing local materials. The school which is on three floors has a playground on the ground floor and the first and second floors are classrooms. The main construction material is wood which was used for the structural supports, roof members and floors, which float on a raft of 256 plastic drums. Labour was provided by the local community with local artisans and labourers forming the corps of the building workforce (Okeke and Chukwuali, 2019).

Makoko, home to at least 100,000 inhabitants – mostly fishermen, fishmongers (sellers) and their families – is situated just a few nautical miles from Eko Atlantic City, an under-construction Manhattan-styled neighbourhood expected to become the heart of Lagos' new business district. Makoko Floating School, constructed at the heart of Lagos Lagoon amidst ageing wooden homes on stilts, was built to take the pressure off Whaniyinna School, which had been the only primary school available to the community for many years, and had become overcrowded and dilapidated. Though Makoko Floating School collapsed in June 2016, after torrential rainfall and violent storms which caused its stilts to give way, while it lasted, it offered many of Makoko's children an opportunity to gain an education they would otherwise have been denied (van Zeijl, 2016).

Sadly, despite the far-reaching influence of community-led urbanism, municipal authorities in Africa remain indifferent to the significant role it plays in shaping local urbanscapes, with enterprising communities neither compensated nor encouraged to do more. While DIY urban interventions may not be able to instantly correct the immense spatial dysfunction faced by communities, they do have the potential to significantly cushion its effects. Makoko Floating School, like most pragmatic DIY urban interventions, not only highlighted the challenges faced by communities, but also demonstrated to city authorities how they could be resolved. As such, the project – and others like it – demonstrates how city authorities and local communities can harmonize their urban visions, synergize their efforts and pool resources in order to create better urban spaces. It also shows how DIY urbanism can, when it comes to reconfiguring urban spaces in a manner that ensures all-around inclusiveness, present city authorities with a rare opportunity to tap into local knowledge and goodwill. Moreover, it demonstrates that by engaging in dialogue with communities prior to building public infrastructures, city authorities can be directed towards allocating resources to the types of project that benefit the local population.

Many urban interventions in the United States and Europe represent deliberate acts of defiance, which overlap with political protest movements built around citizens staking their claim to the cities in which they live. Such claims are premised on building egalitarian urban spaces, with all citizens having an equal right to shape these spaces (Hou, 2010). For the most part, these interventions fit Pagano's characterization of guerrilla urbanism (Pagano, 2013). The problem with employing guerrilla urbanism in Africa is that its modus operandi is confrontational and accusative, and therefore likely to provoke city authorities into a combative response, rather than to be receptive of the ideals championed by such campaigns. Democratic institutions in Africa are still in their infancy, meaning political establishments are likely to exhibit different (that is, lower) levels of tolerance to guerrilla urbanism's harsh non-verbal criticisms (Joseph, 2016).

The peculiarity of Africa's socio-cultural and socio-political reality has often made DIY urbanism the de facto urbanism for most of the continent's communities. Due to the infrastructural emergency Africa's urban populations are currently faced with, nothing is beyond the remit of DIY urbanism (Agbo, 2017). Despite this, city authorities remain suspicious of the quality of work conducted through DIY efforts, and would rather communities waited until such time as the government has sufficient resources to build the required infrastructure (Olowoopejo, 2013). Such fears are not entirely unfounded as, given the meagre resources available to communities, it is probable that any infrastructure built will fall short of acceptable safety standards. A case in point is the Makoko Floating School, which collapsed barely three years after it was constructed (Gaestel, 2018). Yet, for communities the construction of such infrastructure may be a matter of life and death, meaning they are reluctant to wait – perhaps indefinitely – for city authorities to act.

Conclusion

Rather than the mutual contempt and finger-pointing that generally ensues between residents and municipal authorities, DIY interventions should offer a means of bringing together actors from both sides of the divide. With Africa's growing infrastructural challenges set to worsen over the coming years, this has become ever more imperative, particularly in light of the continent's exploding population and the inability of city authorities to fund new public infrastructural developments (AFDB, 2017). Thus, rather than getting defensive about or resisting DIY interventions, city authorities across the continent should seek to accept the 'new spirit of the times'.

As such, I propose that we – as researchers, theorists and built-environment practitioners – commit to developing a trans-disciplinary blueprint that will lay the groundwork for incorporating citizen-led urbanism into mainstream placemaking across urban centres in Africa, ultimately becoming the operational framework for initiating, executing and funding citizen-led urban interventions across the continent. With this in mind, I also propose further research on the subject, with the aim of producing a malleable DIY urbanism toolkit that citizens and local municipal authorities can use to drive citizen-led urban interventions in their local communities. This will offer all parties a platform for forming alliances and becoming development partners, allowing them to bring their insights, resources and expertise to the table for the common good of local communities.

A citizen-led, state-backed DIY urbanism platform offers a number of advantages, including offering third-party supporters and development partners – such as the World Bank, African Development Bank and even local citizens – the opportunity to manifest their support for such interventions. As a corollary of this communal urbanism, citizens will come to view public infrastructures in their neighbourhoods as common patrimonies, and so will do all they can to protect them from abuse, thereby ensuring their longevity.

Chapter 5

POLITICAL ECONOMY OF COMMUNITY-LED SECURITY PROVISIONING IN URBAN AFRICA

Victor Adetula

Introduction

Self-help strategies in social services are spreading fast across urban Africa, such that the provision of security that was hitherto the exclusive preserve of government is now shared between state and non-state actors. A number of non-state groups and informal structures dot the urban African landscape – while most are on a self-assigned mission to provide security at the local level, some are working in partnership with state security agencies. Urban residents across Africa have become increasingly frustrated by the state's weak response to insecurity and crime, with the consequence that they have taken to engaging alternative security provisioning strategies, which can take the form of either individual or collective action. These informal arrangements include neighbourhood watches and self-organized policing groups, religious police, ethnic/clan militias, political party militia groups, vigilantes and ethnic militia. The structure and form of these alternative security systems vary from one place and period to another, and exist at a variety of levels. Regardless of form, however, law and order is maintained through plural and multi-choice policing (Baker, 2010). Although the visibility of non-state actors in security provisioning has increased across Africa, their role is more pronounced in conflict and post-conflict countries. Here, insecurity is widespread, and state security forces usually suffer from indiscipline, underfunding and lack of enforcement capacity.

It could be argued that the proliferation of communal security arrangements has its historical, social and cultural roots in pre-colonial forms of African security practice, which were often designed primarily with the 'collective security' of the community in mind. Security is 'a unilateral action from the communities' in most parts of Africa where 'community self-rule is ubiquitous' and 'informal policing a net contributor to local safety enjoying popularity, while it is the state that appears distant to local residents, and sometimes inhospitable' (Wisler and Onwudiwe, 2007: 4). However, it is the objective economic, political and security conditions in African countries – influenced and constrained in turn by global forces and processes – that shape their security governance, and thus the alternative security provisioning arrangements arising in urban centres. While the privatization of security in Africa and the interactions of security companies with the state have received considerable scholarly attention (Berg, 2007; Mkutu and Sabala, 2007), there remain a number of concerns about self-help defence and community-led security provisioning. Moreover, there is a need to examine these self-provisioning arrangements as they relate to the role and character of African states. How are such relationships influenced by the status of African states in the international division of labour, particularly their capacity to mediate the effects of globalizing forces such as capital? In what ways does security emerge at the interface of state and non-statutory agencies? What are the dominant modes of engagement between state and non-state security providers in Africa's urban centres? In cases where statutory bodies have the power to recognize, proscribe and dismantle community-led self-help security groups, how do government agencies carry out their regulatory functions without political interference?

It is crucial to understand how the multiplicity of security actors and practices in urban Africa shape security governance. What are the operational dynamics of these self-help security groups and associations? What resources and means do they apply? In pursuing their agendas, urban self-help associations are competing with the police and other security agencies, what are the opportunities for cooperation between the actors? Are non-state security actors accountable to the community? What are the potential hazards of working with non-state actors involved in security provisioning?

Using anecdotal data from across Africa to complement existing literature on the subject, this chapter attempts to go some way to answering the above questions. In doing so, it explores the social-cultural background, motivations and dynamics underlying 'alternative' security systems in urban Africa, including the sustainability of the self-help measures adopted by residents to secure their lives and property in a context where the state has failed. Furthermore, the chapter examines how self-help measures have become increasingly interlaced with the security architecture of the urban areas in which they operate, and the implications this has for urban governance and politics.

Analytic framework

The Hobbesian notion of the state puts it at the centre of governance functions. This includes the maintenance of order within a defined territory through, among other things, a monopoly on the use of coercive force. However, the interplay of social processes at various levels (global, regional and national), particularly since the end of the Cold War, has redefined the status, role and power of the state vis-à-vis other social forces. The adoption of market-driven economic policies has resulted in many countries signing away the power of the state to regulate the power and influence of capital. Moreover, the capacity of the state to effectively mediate in social struggles and conflicts has been significantly eroded.

The discourse on civil society usually conceives it as existing outside the state, independent from higher authority. In addition, civil society is generally regarded as being a collective of individuals involved in asserting their rights to satisfy their specific needs and interests. Civil society, therefore, exists in the form of mainly private voluntary groups and associations that are autonomous of the state. However, conceptualizing civil society is no easy task (Mamdani, 1995: 3). Mark Robinson and Gordon White warn against the tendency to invoke the 'virtuous stereotype' of civil society, as 'any attempt to compress the ideas of civil society into a homogenous and virtuous stereotype is doomed to fail' (1997: 3). Mamdani, meanwhile, questions the universalist pretensions of civil society-governed perspectives, in doing so rejecting both the conventional state–civil society dichotomy and the prescriptive modernization view that denies the existence of civil society in Africa (1995). Mamdani is not alone. According to Peter Ekeh, limiting civil society to civic organizations 'points up the danger of transposing the raw notion in the West in its entirety to African circumstances and it raises the important question of what types of associations qualify for inclusion in the conception of civil society in Africa' (1992: 194). Claude Ake's submission is that 'the elements of civil society are a mixture of secondary and primary groups' (1997: 6).

The relationship between the state and civil society in Africa is further complicated by unnecessary binarism. The debate on the state–civil society dichotomy is not a new one and so will not be dwelt on here. However, it should be highlighted that the idea of civil society being entirely separate from the state is at the root of the assumption that the state's abdication of its responsibility to provide security has created a vacuum that non-state actors are now filling in response to rising urban insecurity. These non-state actors consist of both organized private structures such as security companies, and ethnic or cultural associations that are part of urban civil society.

The erosion of state capacity in Africa can be seen in the growing number of governments failing to fulfil the responsibilities of a sovereign government, resulting in, among other effects, a rising tide of conflict and violence. The logic of 'rolling back the state' that was part of 'adjustment culture' triggered unprecedented budgetary crises at all levels of government, with especially troubling implications for social service delivery. Government agencies, departments and parastatals subsequently cut budgets for social spending, public works and public safety, thereby hastening the disintegration of public goods provisioning systems. For example, as the state security sector in many African countries fell victim to inadequate funding, urban centres across the continent recorded an unprecedented rise in crime and insecurity.

Governance in a weak and failing state is associated with a political 'culture of informality', which also relates to the 're-traditionalization of society' and the 'instrumentalization of disorder' (Chabal and Daloz, 1999). Here, formal security institutions are generally weak or absent, and even where they are available, are informalized to the extent that they are almost indistinguishable from militias, gangs and other non-state armed actors (Menkhaus, 2007; Raeymaekers, Menkhaus and Vlassenroot, 2008; Trefon, 2009). This is the context in which 'the state in sub-Sahara Africa is nothing other than a relatively empty shell', and 'the real business of politics is conducted informally and, more stealthily, outside the official political realm' (Chabal and Daloz, 1999: 95). Governments incapable of performing essential state functions litter 'the countries in the bottom billion' (Collier, 2007), characterized by low GDP, widespread unemployment, a thriving dark economy, poor public health, a high level of inequality and insecurity. Unlike in most Western countries, where the state is still regarded as having Westphalian attributes, including the absolute power to maintain order, in these countries 'hybrid political orders' are discernible (Boege et al., 2008).

The nodal governance framework is useful for understanding how 'a variety of actors operating within social systems interact along networks to govern the systems they inhabit' (Burris, Drahos and Shearing, 2005; 5), and is adopted here to help explain the multiplicity of non-state security actors evident within many of Africa's urban centres today. Nodal governance acknowledges the proliferation of 'public', 'private' and 'mixed' providers of social services, and rests on the theoretical and normative assumption that the state is 'but one among many' governing nodes. The theory of nodal governance depicts state and non-state actors as sharing the responsibility of governance. Peter Ekeh provides useful insight into the public realm in Africa, which he maintains is not a single consolidated public realm, 'which effectively offers common platforms for the activities of the state and the public behaviours of individuals' (1992, 200). Rather, the public realm in Africa is segmented into 'civic public realms' over which the state presides, and 'primordial public realms', which offer a platform for individuals' public behaviours (Ekeh, 1992: 200). The trend in urban Africa, where 'more influential and stronger informal governance' exists alongside statutory agencies and performs governance functions, presents a hybrid governance model.

The application of the nodal governance framework presents urban security governance as the product of polycentric nodes that mobilize actors' knowledge and capacity to operate within the broader system and produce security outcomes (Burris, Drahos and Shearing, 2005; Boutellier and Van Steden, 2011). Within this framework, the activities of various informal networks – including community-based security and self-defence groups, and vigilante groups – can be seen to reflect the multicentred power figurations, legal pluralism and multiple modes of political action that emerge from below in African societies. The *Zwelethemba* model in South Africa, which entails a set of arrangements for governing security in impoverished townships, presents one example of such a nodal governance system (Shearing and Froestad, 2010). These governing nodes can promote democracy and self-efficacy within collectives, and have the potential for far-reaching impacts depending on where they are constituted. For example, in a situation where the state is unable to deliver public goods to the population or even exercise control over much of its territory, nodal governance can fill in the gaps.

Background, motivations and dynamics of self-provisioning security arrangements

Community-led security predated the modern state system in Africa, with the 'police idea' in its rudimentary form already known in the pre-colonial African societies, where systems of security were organized based on social values (Tamuno, 1970).

At the centre of this security governance was a mandate to provide safety, security and defence against threats. However, colonial authorities instead introduced alien security systems aimed primarily at serving their interests, which ignored the social and cultural values of African people. In Africa, 'individuals are not perceived as being meaningfully and instrumentally separate from the (various) communities to which they belong', and are instead 'placed within the family, kin and community networks from which (s)he is issued' (Chabal and Daloz, 1999: 52). Thus, confronted with the challenges of urban life, 'the ordinary individual' has always 'sought to attain his security and welfare needs' from an organizational setting that is closer to his/her ascribed identity (Ekeh, 1992: 191). Associational life is dominated by identity solidarities, which operate within the confines of their particular concerns and ethnic/clannish orientations. According to Claude Ake, associations based on primary identities 'especially, ethnicities, nationalities, kinship groups, communal groups, language groups, and religious sects tend to be very influential in such societies' (Ake, 1997: 6). Developing societal 'pressures and anxieties', which are mostly the consequence of 'state building and the push of development', create a strong tendency among people to focus on holistic identities, which provide 'the requisite solidarity for dealing with threats that are cultural, ubiquitous, and multifaceted' (Ake, 1997: 6). Many of urban Africa's self-help security provisioning arrangements are built around – among other primordial identities – ethnic, cultural and religious solidarity, through which they are connected to customary societal structures and traditional authorities. As Tunde Adeniran explains:

> before the present experiments there had been some vigilantism ... brought about by internal wars among and between various ethnic and sub-ethnic nationalities as well as between communities over different issues ... Agile men and, in some cases, cunning women were mobilised and deployed for surveillance to serve as gatekeepers either to alert their people about any imminent invasion or provide information on ways of securing the communities against external enemies.
>
> (2002: 3)

Many of the vigilante systems that have emerged in Africa's urban centres are, arguably, a response to security threats associated with systemic collapse (Adeniran, 2002: 3). The failure of the social contract framework – whereby the state is obliged to protect its citizens – in most African countries has disrupted state–society relations, generated inequality and engendering a widespread lack of trust in state institutions. The latter has responded with a significant shift towards self-help social services and security provisioning. The current realities of most African states' political economy, including the poor state of the formal security apparatus, have contributed to the increased visibility and prevalence of self-help, community-led, networked security governance structures in urban Africa. As crime rates have surged, overwhelming state-led security systems, urban residents have – particularly since the late 1980s – sought alternative means of addressing their safety concerns. The result has been 'the simultaneous communalization of private security and privatization of community policing' (Diphoorn and Kyed, 2016).

There is, undeniably, an economic dimension to how urban residents have responded to rising security challenges. The rich, dissatisfied with state-led security provisioning, have increasingly withdrawn into 'gated communities', residing in housing estates with high walls and fences that convey an 'architecture of fear', buttressed by security surveillance systems mostly operated by private security companies. Conversely, those in low-income brackets have had to rely on self-help measures to construct community-led security systems. In South Africa, for example, there has been a surge in the number of private security companies as the rich demand safety for their lives and property. Alongside this, the previously mentioned *Zwelethemba* model has flourished for the benefit of the poor in urban communities (Shearing and Froestad, 2010). There is a similar trend in Ghana, particularly in the capital, Accra. Residents in high-income areas use their 'connections' to government to obtain security and protection, or in some cases contract private security companies. In low-income neighbourhoods, such services are provided by community policing groups called 'the Watch Dogs'.

Building on the above, the background, motivations and dynamics of a number of illustrative informal security structures across sub-Saharan Africa are examined below.

Ten-cell units (Tanzania) and Nyumba Kumi (Tanzania, Kenya, Uganda)

In Tanzania, under President Julius Nyerere, the ruling Tanganyika African National Union (TANU) party set up the 'ten-cell unit' system, which while deeply rooted in the community system fitted into a 'communist-style party'. This structure aimed to facilitate political mobilization and security provisioning in communities but had a strong link to the ruling party (Proctor, 1971; Bjerk, 2015; Lal, 2015). The ten-cell unit system operated as a grassroots institution by assigning locally elected party representatives 'the task of monitoring all activities and providing a channel of communication between the party and the people' (Bjerk, 2015: 124). Although the system was intended to ensure political mobilization at the grassroots level, it also served as a platform for intelligence gathering and an early warning system for communities and villages. Moreover, it was involved in mediating conflicts between households in various communities. The ten-cells unit system was eventually renamed 'Chama Cha Mapinduzi' in 1977. While the system was community driven and communally oriented, its fortunes were shaped mainly by TANU party politics. Thus, when the multiparty system was introduced in Tanzania in 1992, the system underwent significant restructuring.

The government-initiated community security initiative called *Nyumba Kumi* which in Swahili means 'ten-households arrangement', is very popular in East Africa. The model involves informal community policing at various levels, beginning at the household level, and borrows a number of elements of Tanzania's ten-cell unit system. The *Nyumba Kumi* model is used in Kenya, Tanzania and Uganda, where it assists in identifying threats, complementing state security agencies in combating crime, and providing local intelligence to prevent the expansion of terrorist group activities (Ndono, Nzioka and Kariuki, 2019). While this security initiative has been effective in strengthening trust between locals and law enforcement officers (Ndono, Nzioka and Kariuki, 2019), and the relevant governments seem happy with its performance, there have been concerns in some quarters that the model is eroding civil liberties and the right to privacy.

Kinyinya Irondo (Rwanda)

Elsewhere, Rwanda has a strong community-led security provisioning mechanism that differs in a number of respects from those of the other countries in the region. Unlike its immediate neighbours, who mostly rely on government-driven models, the dominant model in Rwanda reflects its recent history as a nation divided along ethnic and religious lines, resulting in genocidal violence. The absence of proper governance structures following the genocide in 1994 created gaps in public service delivery, including security provisioning. A shortage of security personnel and other related challenges further complicated the security situation. It was within this context that citizens came up with self-help initiatives, such as routine night patrols by volunteers to keep the community safe. This community-led security provisioning arrangement was later christened *Kinyinya* night patrol, otherwise known as 'Irondo'.

Social awareness at both the national and individual levels, proper organization, and cooperation among state security services contributed immensely to the development of *Kinyinya Irondo* as a community-led model. Moreover, the model benefits from the adoption of technology and the availability of resources in the community, as well as financial contributions and technical support from the government. *Kinyinya Irondo* has professional government-recognized night patrol teams that collaborate closely with public security agencies such as the Rwanda National Police, thereby ensuring the capacity building of patrollers (Barihuta, 2017). Despite these attributes, however, the model lacks adequate financial capacity, while access to technologies and resources is uneven across communities.

Association des Jeunes (DRC)

In the Democratic Republic of Congo (DRC), the 'Association des Jeunes' (youth association) has strong links with key elements of Congolese civil society. Areas of active engagement include information gathering and keeping track of insecurity in local neighbourhoods (Hendriks and Buscher, 2019). The Association des Jeunes has proven to be very effective at the community level, where it enjoys a 'high level of legitimacy' partly made possible through its 'horizontal and gender-based' structure, as well as its commitment to creating 'a shared engagement on the challenges of everyday urban insecurity', as observed in the city of Goma (Hendriks and Buscher, 2019: 49).

Aside from the Association des Jeunes, there are other 'policing groups' and platforms that draw on 'members of different ethnic communities who live together in their respective urban neighbourhoods'. Although not formally organized, they are spurred by 'a shared sense of abandonment by the government', and are engaged with the 'auto-defence' model of security provision. This is a community-based self-defence system aimed at reducing the threat of criminal gangs, organized by neighbourhood youth working as volunteers. The effectiveness of these self-defence groups is, however, dependent on the level of support they receive from state authorities, as well as the level of risk they are exposed to (Hendriks and Buscher, 2019: 53).

Yan Banga and Amotekun (Nigeria)

'Yan Banga' or 'Yan Sintiri' in Hausa simply means 'vanguards'. The origins of the Yan Banga date back to 1973, when a group of hunters in Kano city joined forces with the police to check the menace of armed robbery. These hunters deployed their knowledge of the city and affinity with Kano residents to uncover the hideouts of the armed robbers and other criminals. Initially, the Yan Banga had no legal recognition, though members of the group 'enjoyed the goodwill of the authorities and the general public as a result of their useful activities' (Dawha, 1996: 15). Throughout the 1970s and even beyond, 'the Yan Banga not only gave vital information on robbery and theft-related cases, they engaged hoodlums in battle and if apprehended, they handed them over to the police' (Dawha, 1996: 15). Since then, the Yan Banga has evolved from 'a group of rugged hunters' into 'a para-law enforcement group' with reach across northern Nigeria and parts of Niger.

The role of primordial identities – notably ethnicity, culture and religion – in the emergence and development of community-led self-help security provisioning is quite pronounced. Most informal security structures in African cities are run by youths drawn from the urban population, who are nevertheless bound together by common cultural, ethnic, language and/or religious identities, which they often emphasize and exaggerate. For example, in Nigeria, the activities of the Odua People's Congress (OPC), a community-led security outfit, are largely concentrated in Yoruba-speaking areas in the southwest of the country. Similarly, 'Agbekoya', an association of indigenous farmers and hunters in Yorubaland, until recently dominated the community security landscape across southwest Nigeria, carrying out private security functions at the grassroots and providing neighbourhood watch services.

In January 2020, a new security outfit codenamed 'Amotekun' ('tiger' in the Yoruba language) was created by the governments of the six southwestern states (Ekiti, Ondo, Osun, Ogun, Oyo and Lagos states) where the Yoruba language is widely spoken. It is a plausible argument that the homogeneity of the Yoruba, as expressed in their shared history, culture and social values, has helped Amotekun gain traction across Yorubaland. The collective action taken by the sub-national governments was a response to growing insecurity and rural violence in the region, particularly banditry, highway robbery and kidnapping. Amotekun builds on existing local security structures and socio-cultural groups, notably Agbekoya and the OPC, and taps into their experience. Initially, the federal government was opposed to the idea of regional police. Moreover, the creation of Amotekun provoked fear and suspicion among other ethnic groups residents in the Yoruba-speaking states, who imagined they may become targets for ethnic cleansing, particularly the Hausa and Fulani, who were alleged to be involved in widespread violent attacks on farmers across the country. To address such concerns, efforts were made at the launch of Amotekun to present the outfit as a modernized version of the traditional hunters who had previously had neighbourhood watch responsibilities in Yorubaland.

Koglweogo (Burkina Faso)

In Burkina Faso, militias – popularly known in the Mossi language as *Koglweogo* ('to protect') (Hagberg, 2010) – made up primarily of young volunteers have mobilized to combat robbery and armed assault. Amid a context of limited or non-existent security, corrupt law enforcement officials and unbridled lawlessness in the judicial system, these armed self-defence groups have emerged to occupy the space previously dominated by the police and other law enforcement agencies. The members of *Koglweogo* dress mostly in ways that reflect their grassroot origins, and use archaic tools and hunting equipment for weapons. Though there was initially severe tension between *Koglweogo* members and the police, through dialogue the two sides have been able to build trust and work together to improve security.

Youth militias

The rise of political vigilantism in Africa is bound up with the political context and its related dynamics. For example, as electoral competition has become more intense, so the incidence of election-related violence has increased, with youths paid by unscrupulous politicians to intimidate and victimize political opponents.

In Ghana, the role of political vigilantes in the country's electoral process is not new, with the list of vigilante groups including the 'Macho Men', 'Verandah Boys', 'Girls Club', 'Kandahar Boys' and 'Delta Force'. In the 2012 elections, the concept of 'Macho Men for Peace' was floated following the formation of the 'Macho Men for Good and Justice Association', a group of bodybuilders in the Ashanti Region supposedly committed to maintaining peace during elections. In that instance, the group's attempt to partner with police to ensure peaceful polls was rejected. A similarly feared group was the Azorka Boys. During the 2016 election, leading Ghanaian politicians regularly threatened to deploy well-built macho men and other unofficial armed men to protect their interests, with some parts of the country witnessing clashes between youth groups associated with the ruling party and others associated with the main opposition parties. In the run-up to the 2020 elections, concerns were expressed that the activities of the vigilante groups expanded to include women. Moreover, rumours abounded that the two major parties – the National Patriotic Party (NPP) and National Democratic Congress (NDC) – were deploying vigilante groups to perpetrate violence, with efforts to persuade them to check the activities of their youth wings proving unsuccessful.

In Nigeria, meanwhile, youth militia involvement in electoral politics can be dated back to the latter days of the colonial period, particularly as public agitation for self-government became increasingly intense. The struggle for power between the Northern Peoples' Congress (NPC) and the Northern Elements Progressive Union (NEPU) was the context for the cultivation of 'a core of political thugs' that would later spread across northern Nigeria (Ya'u, 2000: 170). The use of youth militias by power-hungry politicians 'to maintain themselves in power' continues to this day, with militias employed 'to cow the populace and make it difficult for the latter to organize for their removal from office' (Okonta, 2012: 11). Until recently, when it sued for peace, the 'Sara-Suka' gang operated in Bauchi almost without constraints, due in part to its powerful connections to notable members of northern Nigeria's political elite. The same is true for the 'Kauraye' gang in Katsina and the 'Jangaliya' and 'Kalare' gangs that operated in Kano and Gombe states, respectively.

A similar situation prevails in most other African countries, as evidenced by the following illustrative cases of youth militia complicity in election-related violence. In the DRC, during the President Mobutu Sese Seko era (1965–97), the youth wing of the Mouvement Populaire de la Revolution (MPR) maintained a militia gang called the 'Disciplinary Brigade'. The group's responsibilities not only included conducting night-time patrols but also carried out arbitrary arrests and extorting innocent citizens. In Cote d'Ivoire, the armed youths that fought in support of the incumbent president Laurent Gbagbo and his challenger Alassane Ouattara were drawn from the Patriotic Galaxy (for Gbagbo) and Ressemblenment des Houphouetistes pour la Democraticet la Paix (RHDP) and Forces Nouvelles (FN) (for Ouattara). In Kenya, youth groups – including 'Mungiki youths', 'the Taliban' and the 'Baghdad Boys' – were reportedly involved in 2006–07 post-election violence. In Malawi, between 1963 and 1967, President Kamuzu Banda commanded a paramilitary group formed from among the members of his political party's youth wing. The group was called the Malawi Young Pioneers (MYP), and President Banda freely used it to intimidate activists opposed to his rule. In Cameroon, Paul Biya's government co-opted President Biya's Youth (PRESBY militia) which was founded in 1996 into the state's machinery for dealing with agitation for self-determination in Southern Cameroon.

The 'Kiboko Squad' in Uganda, which allegedly worked for senior members of President Yoweri Museveni's government, was visibly on the ground in the capital, Kampala. The group first emerged in 2007 to beat up citizens demonstrating against the proposed Mabira forest giveaway. Many Kiboko Squad operations since then have targeted opposition members and innocent civilians. In the run-up to the 2011 elections, for example, a group of political parties came together under the Inter-Party Cooperation (IPC) and organized demonstrations calling for electoral reform, only for demonstrators to reportedly be assaulted by members of the Kiboko Squad. Moreover, the activities of the Kiboko Squad have provoked violent reactions from rival groups, such as the 'Kifesi' gang.

The impacts, evolution and drawbacks of self-provisioning security arrangements

The deployment of self-provisioning security arrangements is fast becoming a common feature of African urbanism, with instances abounding of vigilante and neighbourhood watch groups conducting quasi-security activities aimed at ensuring the safety of residents. These activities sometimes involve working in partnership with state security agencies. In fact, self-provisioning security arrangements can complement state security structures, particularly in circumstances where state agencies are unable to deliver security services to the population, such as when conflicts or wars mean the state's control over its territory is contested. In this context, a well-coordinated partnership between state and non-state actors can produce effective security governance. Here, the activities of the Civilian Joint Task Force (Civilian-JTF), which has been assisting the Nigerian military in the fight against armed insurgency and banditry in north-eastern Nigeria, are illustrative of the values and benefits of nodal security governance.

Recent community-level security structures in Nigeria, such as the 'Lagos' Area Boys', emerged in the early 1990s as a neighbourhood watch. The same applies to the 'Bakassi Boys' in Southeastern Nigeria and the 'Egbesu Boys' of the Niger Delta region. The Area Boys, though operating mostly in Lagos, are present in all the nearby Yoruba-speaking towns of southwestern Nigeria. A similar story applies to the Bakassi Boys and Egbesu Boys in terms of identifying with a particular ethnocultural group, and comparisons can be made with the OPC's claim that it traces its lineage to Oduduwa, the legendary father of the Yoruba nation, and therefore the group is commissioned to defend those of the Yoruba race wherever they may be. Lagos Neighbourhood Watch and the previously mentioned Amotekun operating in southwestern Nigeria typify hybrid security provisioning systems within the nodal governance framework. These community-led security structures were established through the enhancement of state laws, with their operations providing synergy with the formal state security apparatus. Similarly, the Yan Banga quasi-security outfits operating across northern Nigeria and the *Kinyinya Irondo* in Rwanda are recognized by their respective governments and are integrated into the formal state security apparatus, essentially providing useful intelligence to the police.

In Tanzania, the ten-cells unit model – before its reorganization in 1992 – operated mostly at the grassroots and was an essential part of the national security and justice system, contributing to intelligence gathering and the monitoring of security threats. As mentioned, the system was well connected to the structures of the ruling party, TANU, which was then the only political party in Tanzania, and so served as a veritable platform for political mobilization at the community level. Since the sidelining of the 'ten-cell unit' system, however, community influence has declined, robbing the country of a security system linked to the people at a grassroots level. As a result, Tanzanian society has become more susceptible to violent conflict and crime, exemplified by the infiltration of villages by extremist groups spreading growing radicalization across the country. In Tanzania and some parts of Kenya, *Nyumba Kumi* has, in addition to helping reduce the influence of terrorist groups, contributed to maintaining peace through dispute settlement at the community level, promoting inter-religious and communal trust among various groups, and maintaining an early warning system (Andhoga and Johnson, 2017; Sambaiga, 2018: 50).

In Kenya, members of the Mungiki gang generally claim to be offshoots of the Mau Mau movement, providing them with a strong link to the Kikuyu ethnocultural identity group. Members of the gang not only see themselves as security actors – curbing crime and maintaining order in urban slums through mob justice – but also flaunt their engagement in public service provision (Ruteere, 2009; Landinfo Country of Origin Information Centre, 2010; Sana and Okombo, 2012). Mungiki, to its credit, was reported to have asserted a form of 'law and order' in the Mlango Kubwa, with its activities driving large numbers of criminals out of the area (Ayiera, 2017). However, this was not without cost, with the gang charging fees for the system of protection it unilaterally and violently imposed on residents:

> They conducted public trials for crime suspects, gave summary judgements and meted out corporal punishment or even killings. This protection system also brought the Mungiki gang into conflict with local property owners and business people who bore the greater weight of the extortionist practices. Due to their pattern of abductions, macabre killings, terrorising public transport operators and fomenting conflict between communities beyond Mlango Kubwa, the groups quickly came into conflict with the police.
>
> (Ayiera, 2017: 40)

The Mungiki gang's self-defined 'law and order' mandate has generated contradictions as well as challenges for urban governance and national politics in Kenya. For instance, while on the one hand, the gang is providing a system of protection for residents (albeit contested), on the other hand its complicity in electoral violence poses a threat to security. Furthermore, despite the gang's claims that it is providing security for local people (Servant, 2007), members are associated with activities that range from forcefully extracting fees to dispossessing residents of their personal belongings. In terms of pursuing these activities, the Mungiki gang was until recently so established that it could afford to operate freely on certain routes in Nairobi, referred to as 'Mungiki routes' (Ayiera, 2017).

Elsewhere, the role of the Macho Men in Ghana's electoral politics has not been well received in many circles, as, despite members of the group claiming they are for 'good and justice', they are perceived to be a threat to peace. Meanwhile, in Burkina Faso, the unorthodox methods of the *Koglweogo* groups often border on human rights abuses, with, for example, suspects tied to tree trunks and whipped with pepper-soaked whips until they confess. Nevertheless, the effectiveness of their activities – for example, in terms of ensuring that stolen goods are returned to their owners – means that group members tend to be well respected by the community.

Cases of vigilante justice and inhuman treatment of suspects (and sometimes ordinary citizens) are not limited to the *Koglweogo* and *Mungiki*, with a high percentage of informal security outfits in Africa engaged in illegal forms of popular justice. For example, alleged thieves in some parts of the DRC, such as Goma, are 'either stoned to death or burned alive by a crowd of people' (Hendriks and Buscher, 2019: 16). In Benin, it is with impunity that self-defence organizations impose 'extralegal justice, using self-made small arms in action against criminals passing judgements on them' (Gratz, 2010: 84).

There have been numerous other cases of quasi-security groups – mostly the vigilante groups – being complicit in criminal activities and threats to security in the areas where they operate. In Nigeria, the Bakassi Boys, OPC and Area Boys have degenerated into groups of aggressive youths on the streets, extorting money from members of the public and becoming involved in criminal activities that threaten public order. Moreover, there are allegations of their complicity in political thuggery and other forms of election-related violence. Similarly, in post-conflict Liberia, many of the non-state actors that initially provided local security at the community level – particularly neighbourhood watches and vigilante groups – later became security threats, particularly in the face of the state policing system's ineffectual response to the breakdown of law and order.

The use of ethnic-based vigilante groups to victimize other groups has been widely noted. Here, the overbearing influence of ethnicity and religion on community self-defence groups is problematic, especially for countries that are already polarized along ethnic or religious lines, such as Nigeria and Kenya. Moreover, the politicization of any form of identity – whether based on ethnicity, language, religion or other primordial characteristics – hinders security governance in situations where ethnic nationalism and religious politics have supplanted the original purpose of community-led security strategies. The activities of the Mungiki in Kenya and the OPC in Nigeria are often viewed with suspicion by members of other ethnic groups. Similarly, the creation of the Amotekun security outfit in Nigeria's so-called Yoruba-speaking states provoked fear in other ethnic and cultural groups resident in these areas. In northern Nigeria, where the Sharia Islamic legal code is in operation, there are allegations of victimization of non-Muslims by overzealous members of the vigilante religious police group, the 'Hisba'.

The relationship between the state and community-led security provisioning platforms varies from place to place, as well as over time, with instances of both cooperation and conflict between the two. Amid the plethora of community-led initiatives aimed at ensuring security in urban areas, the state–civil society dichotomy is not as clear-cut as often assumed. On the one hand, there are 'top-down' initiatives launched and largely controlled by the state. These include vigilante and neighbourhood watch groups that have legal status, and whose activities are regulated by state laws. On the other hand, there are 'bottom-up' security provisioning strategies linked to civil society. This reality, which has far-reaching implications for security governance, must be taken into consideration when examining the relationship between quasi-security outfits and the state.

Cooperation and contestation between state agencies and community-led security arrangements

Factors such as public perceptions, mutual trust and level of mutual dependence mediate the relationship between state agencies and informal security providers. While collaboration between state and non-state is desirable, there are significant challenges that must be overcome, such as the disparity between the capacities – whether in terms of human or material resources – of state and non-state actors. Regardless of this disparity in resource endowment, however, formal and informal security platforms can work in tandem. For instance, while state agencies have funding, competencies and organizational capacity, non-state actors have the benefit of social capital. In East Africa, particularly Tanzania and Kenya, the *Nyumba Kumi* model has helped bridge the gap between locals and state security agencies, providing 'ears to the ground and eyes on the street, which enhanced effective intelligence gathering and threat assessment' (Maza, Koldas and Aksit, 2020: 16).

Where non-state actors limit themselves to quasi-security functions that complement the activities of state security agencies, the prospects for collaboration are strong. On the other hand, in most cases where the state has collapsed, social services end up being provided by non-state actors, which in turn influences the direction of urban politics and governance, including changes in power relations. For example, in South Africa, the emergence of 'Amadlozi', a vigilante group operating in the townships of Port Elizabeth, was justified on the grounds of the state's failure to provide adequate security. Here, the group's activities implied a desire for a new legal-political order that was at odds with existing state structures (Buur, 2006). Moreover, the proliferation of informal security outfits in South Africa must be understood within the context of post-Apartheid security dynamics, which are rooted in the legacies of the Apartheid system's repressive and authoritarian policing. This has resulted in a sustained lack of trust in the state security system, particularly among black South Africans, who seem more inclined towards re-ordering society through vigilantism. Where the security provisioning strategies of quasi-security groups seek to radically alter the existing social order, they usually face strong resistance from the state. In Kenya, for instance, the government declared 'total war' on the Mungiki (Servant, 2007: 521), while in Burkina Faso, the *Koglweogo's* efforts to promulgate a new legal-political order came close to running 'a parallel government', which the country's government vigorously opposed.

Elsewhere in Africa, illustrative cases of cooperation between state security agencies and community-led self-defence groups can be pointed to. In South Sudan, the community policing system relies greatly on grassroots structures, which received substantial assistance from state security agencies. In Liberia, meanwhile, state security agencies enjoy the support of Police Community Forums, which have responsibility for policing activities in communities. In Mozambique, too, state security agencies collaborated well with the local policing structures (Kyed, 2009). Such models provide a positive indication of the prospects for collaboration between state and non-state security providers in post-conflict societies.

Non-state actors usually have strong links to the grassroots, which state security services can leverage to the benefit of urban security governance. In most of Africa's urban areas, state security agencies are regarded as corrupt and are treated with far less respect than traditional and religious leaders within communities. For example, in Changanyikeni and Kigezi Chini sub-wards in the Dar es Salaam region, Tanzania, the *ulinzi shirikishi* participatory security system operates to keep residents safe – a function that has traditionally been assigned to the state. Some have attributed the decline in the number of insecurity incidents to the operations of *ulinzi shirikishi* (Godfrey and Dixon, 2017), with residents apparently more comfortable with these community-led security mechanisms than with the state police, who are generally perceived as inefficient.

Conclusions

As this chapter has made clear, the hierarchical state-led provision of security and policing is fast eroding in Africa, supplanted by a nodal network of state and non-state actors. These hybrid public–private security provision arrangements involve both conflict and cooperation, and in a sense may be viewed as ironic, given the private elements are generally perceived as 'a psychological source of security as well as a palpable threat to it' (Adeniran, 2002: 1). While community-led security provisioning is not new in Africa, its prevalence has been accelerated by neoliberalism, as manifested in the enthronement of the market, the decline of state capacity and the consequences of intense electoral competition on urban security. As has also been pointed out in this chapter, the quasi-security activities of self-help groups and community security outfits, as well as their relationships with state security agencies, are shaped by wider political, social and security dynamics. These in turn are mediated by the political economy of the relevant African state, and the pressures brought to bear by global forces.

Where state services are absent, inaccessible or inadequate, self-help security provisioning is welcomed by the majority of citizens as an effective model. Such arrangements do not enjoy similar popularity among state officials and policymakers, however, who are generally unwilling to concede their benefits. Moreover, substituting state policing systems with self-help arrangements may have negative consequences for at least some citizens, with certain self-help security groups operating with little regard for human rights or the law. This has prompted concerns in some circles that the dominance of self-help security provisioning in urban governance contributes to a state of nature where life is 'nasty, brutish and short'.

Despite the proliferation of 'public', 'private' and 'mixed' providers of security, the state remains the dominant actor in the security sector, belying the claim that the state is 'but one among many' governing nodes. There can be no doubt that the police and other state security services have a leading role to play in the urban security space, with no informal self-defence group seriously able to compete with these state agencies in terms of exercising (symbolic) authority or accessing human and material resources.

Even so, the security sector in Africa is constituted by a complex mixture of state and non-state actors and institutions. One policy implication arising is the need to strengthen non-state security provisioning systems and mainstream them into national governments' security sector reform (SSR) and good governance initiatives. The focus of most SSR programmes is on strengthening the state's capacity to provide comprehensive security, thereby facilitating a more reliable social contract. However, this does not necessarily fit with the reality of many African countries, where state agencies share the urban security landscape with a number of non-state actors. Thus, without dismissing the state's long-term role in security provisioning, the benefits of non-state informal security systems must be acknowledged and incorporated into security reform programmes.

Further research is required to help African states and other stakeholders identify the possibilities and challenges of nodal urban security governance. There is some concern about the ambiguity of the term 'community policing' in self-help narratives employed by community organizations and groups. Associated with this is the application of the Western notion of policing to the African context (see Berg et al., 2013: 169). If the concept of community policing as developed in the West is to be transplanted to Africa, it must be reconfigured to reflect the local context and history. Also, some narratives have included vigilante and neighbourhood watch groups dominated by misguided youths exploiting citizens under the umbrella of self-help security systems, thereby unwittingly elevating their predatory activities to the level of security provisioning.

On the other hand, an increase in youth rebellion indicates that youth groups and their modes of engagement within wider society need to be re-conceptualized. This includes examining the opportunities that exist for youths' social and economic empowerment, as well as the constraints that limit their self-actualization. Moreover, it is important to understand the class interests and logic underlying their behaviour, including their role in quasi-security activities in urban areas. Such knowledge would prove invaluable in, for instance, unpicking the complicity of youth groups in violent conflicts in Africa.

Studies on the political economy of alternative security provisioning in urban Africa should be encouraged, with questions to be explored including: What is the relationship between local vigilantes and private security companies? And what is the link between the latter and the formal state security apparatus? Answering such questions would help explain why some community-based groups do not enjoy stable support in countries where the activities and operations of private security companies are well-pronounced. Moreover, it would assist in addressing concerns that the growing private security culture in Africa may prove to be another risk factor for conflict.

Finally, research initiatives should consider the importance of gender in security self-provisioning. To touch on the subject briefly, there are several instances of women becoming members of quasi-security groups. In north-eastern Nigeria, for example, there are female members of the Civilian-JTF, while in Ghana, female members of political vigilante groups have been reported. Generally, though, women's participation in the activities and operations of vigilante groups and neighbourhood security watches has not been pronounced. It would be interesting, therefore, to learn of the status and role of femininity in community-led security provisioning. What position(s) do women occupy in quasi-security organizations? Are women banished to the periphery of organizations, or do they form part of their leadership and decision-making structures? How is the abuse and undignified treatment of women by some vigilante groups perceived by the public? These and other questions beg further investigation.

Chapter 6

THE POLITICS OF URBAN INSECURITY: HYBRID RELATIONS AND PARTY DOMINANCE IN LAGOS, NIGERIA

Henrik Angerbrandt

Introduction

As the largest city in both Nigeria and Africa, Lagos is often depicted as a place for the ambitious and resolute, where everybody is looking for opportunities to get to the top (e.g. Packer, 2006; Howden, 2010). Each week, the city welcomes some 10,000 new residents. This in turn contributes to every aspect of the city being claimed – and/or contested – by someone. Whether it concerns clean water sources controlled by local strongmen (Gandy, 2006), or sleeping spots under highway bridges – as illustrated in Chibundu Onuzo's novel *Welcome to Lagos* (2017) – someone is always attempting to protect their carved-out space within the city, often on behalf of someone else. Militia groups, youth gangs, thugs and an often brutal police force contribute to making security a daily challenge for much of the population, in a context where threats of violence are typically presented as offers of protection. Self-regulation seems to form the basis for urban relations in a city that is 'not for the lazy and ... not for the old' (Howden, 2010).

However distant the state might seem, a technocratic approach to governance has provided the city with a reputation for innovation and entrepreneurship in line with prevailing neoliberal urbanism (Peck, Theodore and Brenner, 2009). State reforms are, however, historically specific processes that are contextually embedded and politically mediated. Urban renewal plans tend towards planning for the rich, illustrated in the fact that 'actually existing neoliberalism' usually amplifies inequalities (Peck, Theodore and Brenner, 2009), which in turn provokes instability (Ferguson, 2006, in Marr, 2016). This contributes to making life unpredictable and insecure for the poor. As a result, citizens in the urban margins often have little trust in the state's ability or willingness to provide security, prompting do-it-yourself (DIY) citizen-led security arrangements that make use of extra-legal and informal means (Kyed, 2018). Adverse state attitudes towards marginal populations have generated competitive authorities that thrive on the ever-present threat of violence. However, though DIY initiatives are largely a reaction to a non-responsive state, little focus has been placed on how they can become enmeshed in competitive or cooperative relations with state actors, shaping a hybrid security governance that imposes its own hierarchies (Bagayoko, Hutchful and Luckham, 2016).

Nigerian politics is infused by prebendalism, with the resources of a political or administrative office commonly appropriated by the officeholder and distributed with the aim of retaining office (Joseph, 1987; Adebanwi and Obadare, 2013). For citizens, their defining links to state resources come through connections and political affiliations. This tends to disfavour those living in poor areas on the city's fringes, who are largely unconnected. It is also in these areas that instability is most pronounced. So-called 'area boys' extort illicit tolls and instigate violence; militia groups claim entitlements with violence, while other actors attempt to build alternative structures – such as vigilante and community policing groups – to prevent crime and violence. In Lagos, these groups co-exist with a police force notorious for utilizing excessive force and corrupt practices (Hills, 2008). The informalization and/or privatization of security structures seldom, however, results in citizens being granted more control. Instead, authority is negotiated and disputed among powerful groups within and outside the state (Baker, 2009; Hagmann and Péclard, 2010; Bagayoko, Hutchful and Luckham, 2016). We should therefore be wary of viewing DIY initiatives as free of hierarchies and discrimination, and instead – to understand their potential for reshaping the state – analyse their linkages to state and non-state actors and processes. This chapter examines how urban instability and local security initiatives in Lagos are intertwined with the wider political context. This context is informed by a federal system characterized by politicized security institutions and prebendal politics, within which the city has long served as an opposition stronghold.

Cityness and hybrid security institutions

Perhaps more than any other African city, Lagos has since the early 2000s been subject to neoliberal urban restructuring with an emphasis on technocratic governance. In line with Peck, Theodore and Brenner's (2009) concept of 'actually existing neoliberalism', urban restructuring processes should be regarded as contextually embedded and politically mediated, rendering diverse socio-political effects and contradictions. In practice, however, much of what has been written on Lagos has been preoccupied with what has made the regeneration possible, and see its effects primarily in terms of output, such as increased taxing capacity (e.g. Cheeseman and de Gramont, 2017). The assumption underlying such an approach is that Lagos is now on its way to becoming a world-leading 'mega-city', reinforced by the official slogan 'Lagos is working' (cf. *Financial Times*, 2018).

Urban scholars are increasingly exploring 'cityness' in ways that focus attention on how – especially non-Western – cities work, rather than what they lack (Pieterse, 2010). The Western city has long been held up as the model of how a city should work, with non-Western cities analysed primarily in terms of the extent to which they comply with this ideal. Such lines have, though, become increasingly blurred, as it is not only African and other non-Western cities that fall short of this ideal, but also – in the wake of de-industrialization and declining production – many cities in the West (Marr, 2016). Where the state has little motivation or ability to formulate inclusive strategies aimed at counteracting widespread poverty and vulnerability, the urban poor must find their own survival strategies. For male youths, this often entails violence. In fact, a defining feature of city life in postcolonial states is the decisive effect violence embedded in enduring inequalities has. According to Pieterse (2010: 213), 'the focus on cityness, on the inventiveness of survivalist practices and the worldliness of African cities, is first and foremost a story about terror'. It is not by coincidence that Lagos is one of the prime examples given in Pieterse's article: the city is infused with 'specialists in violence' who routinely employ terror and violence as a means of control and regulation (cf. Tilly, 2003). This includes not only non-state actors such as area boys, militias and vigilante groups, but also state authorities such as the police.

The police mandate in Nigeria is primarily connected to regime interests and has little to do with serving the public. The reputation of the police force – notorious for its violence and corrupt practices – is abysmal. As one newspaper column observes: 'If there is one institution with a near total disconnect with the Nigerian people, it is the police. Half the police force is devoted to supplying VIP security cover and the other half to extorting Nigerians' (Ibrahim, 2017). Thus, residents expect little from state authorities, with the police regarded, if anything, as a threat (Hills, 2008: 219). This does not imply, however, that citizens are passively awaiting state reform – experiences elsewhere show that when the state fails to provide basic functions, communities make their own arrangements (Menkhaus, 2007). Similarly, residents of Lagos have set up alternative security measures. Whereas upmarket areas rely on private security companies, low-income neighbourhoods tend to depend on community-based vigilante groups with a preference for 'jungle justice', including lynching offenders (c.f. Owumi and Ayadi, 2013). The latter's violent mode of operation further contributes to instability, as these groups spread fear and are frequently involved in inter-ethnic clashes.

The violence in Lagos has generated a thriving 'securo-commerce' (Ismail, 2009), in which both formal and informal actors take part. In other words, security institutions are not limited to neither necessarily controlled by state authorities. Within a context of unconsolidated formal state institutions, however, DIY solutions cannot easily be separated from state authority interests. Studies analysing linkages between politicians and violent non-state actors emphasize that non-state security providers are enmeshed in a variety of interactions, including with formal state institutions. This results in a form of institutional multiplicity, which in turn causes parallel lines of influence to proliferate (Bagayoko, Hutchful and Luckham, 2016). These informal connections to the state indicate that vigilantism is interwoven with a struggle for political control and, as such, are part of state formation processes (Anderson, 2002; Reno, 2005; Fourchard, 2008; Pratten, 2008). This is in line with the observation that in states characterized by weak or contested formal institutions with patronage systems, power is often vested – through networks 'closer' to the grassroots than formal state institutions – in informal modes of governance (Helmke and Levitsky, 2004). Contrary to the tendency to depoliticize local relations in the city (Bekker and Fourchard, 2013), local and informal institutions involve contestations, have their own power hierarchies, and 'do not work equally well for everyone, least of all for the weak, vulnerable and excluded' (Bagayoko, Hutchful and Luckham, 2016: 1).

Prebendalism and urban (in)security in Lagos

A defining feature of the prebendal Nigerian political system is 'the competition for, and appropriation of, offices of the state' (Joseph, 1987: 63). Offices are administered for the benefit of officeholders and their supporters. To be able to compete successfully for office, whether by vote or appointment, a contestant is dependent on both vertical and horizontal networks. In Nigeria, political networks centre around 'godfathers' who can – through access to state resources – support politicians and others in instrumental positions (Sklar, Onwudiwe and Kew, 2006). Electoral politics has tended to reinforce prebendal politics, as opportunities to access state resources proliferate when politicians canvass for votes. The character of Nigeria's political parties has changed from being regionally based in the 1960s to today becoming what can best be described as coalitions of elite factions from different parts of the country (Obi, 2011). It is common for politicians to shift from one party to another in their attempts to gain office.[1] Despite Joseph emphasizing the 'fundamental instability' of the prebendal order as being 'in part attributable to the absence of a continuous authoritative force and a legitimizing ideology' (Joseph, 1987: 65), Lagos has been remarkably stable in terms of the political control exerted by a single godfather, Bola Tinubu, the first governor of Lagos in 1999–2007. After party politics were reintroduced in 1999, Lagos became a stronghold for the political opposition against the federal government. As one of the few states in Nigeria with substantial internally generated revenues, Lagos State continuously challenged the federal government, for example when the state government attempted to create thirty-seven additional Local Government Areas (LGAs) in 2003.[2] The federal government, for its part, deemed the reform illicit and responded by withholding federally allocated revenues, prompting a stalemate that lasted six years. More recently, the 2015 shift in federal power has meant that the ruling party at the national level – the All Progressives Congress (APC) – is now the same as the ruling party in Lagos.

Support for the ruling party in Lagos is not, though, primarily based on any appeal to public sentiment, with patronage tendencies limiting the scope and representativeness of policymaking. The result has been a vast expansion of informal social and economic networks, which serve to sustain everyday life. However, neither the local nor the federal state is sufficiently challenged by Lagosians to prompt any reshaping of the politics of entitlements and citizenship. A lack of programmatic politics has bred a passive citizenship, many of whom are quite willing to sell their vote for 3–4 US dollars in lieu of any alternative political vision.[3] Lagos also had the lowest voter turnout – a mere 18 per cent – in the 2019 national elections. According to Gandy (2006: 253, 257), '[p]ervasive problems of corruption in combination with widespread indifference have produced a scenario that is particularly antithetical to more socially responsive forms of urban policymaking' in Lagos. This has opened the door to a technocratic turn in policymaking, which has bestowed on Lagos a reputation as a city going through a 'historic reconstruction'.

The 'regeneration' of Lagos, for which Tinubu is regarded as being the architect, has contributed to increased service provision in large parts of the city. At the same time, however, inequalities have widened due to a business-led model that has failed to renew the dynamics between the state and its citizens. While service delivery and tax collection are carried out by state agencies in prosperous neighbourhoods, in less affluent areas and informal settlements, governance is delegated to civil society (in the form of, for example, traditional institutions and NGOs). Service provision, such as access to clean water, relies on community-based markets, which puts traditional authorities in charge of collecting fees. The system is thus beneficial to those in control of provision, meaning that reforms are contested and often subverted by violent means (Gandy, 2006). As a result, people access the city on unequal terms.

Despite the state governor's dubious claim that 'Lagos right now is the safest city across Africa' (*Vanguard*, 2018), insecurity and the risk of violence are part of everyday life.[4] This is especially so in low-income, densely populated areas of the city. The phenomenon of 'area boys' (a term that includes girls) refers to youths engaged in criminal activities and violence, who often rely on menial jobs and extorting illicit tolls. A typical illustration of their activities can be seen in the instance when area boys took a generator delivered to a civil society organization 'hostage', demanding money from the owners in order to allow access. The way in which the situation was resolved is likewise illustrative of the dynamics involved. The organization contacted an influential man in the area, who suggested that the organization 'bring them some soft drinks and snacks'. The man then contacted the area boys, who proceeded to withdraw.[5] Although rooted in a longer-term history, the area boys' phenomenon in its contemporary form stems from the rising levels of urban poverty seen during the structural adjustment programme of the 1980s. Area boys are entrenched in Lagos city life and are often central to mass political action, though their activities are primarily motivated by material gain rather than ideological commitment (Momoh, 2000, 2003). As such, they are susceptible to use by political actors for rallies, as well as for intimidating the opposition. Politicians allegedly arm the area boys to the degree that 'what the boys have, the police do not have'.[6] In the months leading up to elections, there is a perceived reduction in petty crime, which local actors explain as due to politicians recruiting area boys and giving them handouts.[7]

Another critical actor in Lagos' security landscape is the ethnically based Oodua People's Congress (OPC). A violent wing became more active ahead of the transition from military rule in 1998, campaigning for a federal restructure granting increased regional autonomy to be put in place prior to the elections.

While violence initially targeted the police, from 1999 the OPC increasing took the form of an ethnic vigilante group involved in both crime control and inter-ethnic clashes (Akinyele, 2001; Fourchard, 2008). Today, the OPC is a major actor in Lagos' private security market, though the group's brutal approach and inclination towards jungle justice causes some to avoid using them in favour of training their own guards.[8]

Militia organizations have been a contentious issue between the federal government and the state government in Lagos, due to state politicians engaging them to enforce sub-national political control. State governments are prevented from establishing their own police forces and so have, whether officially or unofficially, supported vigilante groups. The violence associated with the OPC prompted the federal government to ban all ethnic militias in the early 2000s, and there was even a threat of a state of emergency being declared in Lagos State. Even so, Lagos state government refrained from pursuing any repressive strategy aimed at preventing the groups (LeBas, 2013), though the police force – which is a federal institution – raided suspected OPC sites in Lagos' suburbs (Akinyele, 2001: 630). The reluctance of the state government to suppress the OPC is likely due, at least in part, to the role played by the militias in controlling the city, as well as their political instrumentality, not least in times of elections. Fourchard (2008: 34) argues that 'vigilante practices are part of the historical and ongoing formation of the state', emphasizing that militias are not outside social control. The sub-national dimension of this is highlighted in Lagos, where state government has had fluid relationships with both organized and less organized vigilante groups and militias, and politicians use local groups as political enforcers during election campaigns (LeBas, 2013; de Gramont, 2015: 23).

In Nigeria in general, the political predisposition of violent actors can be negotiated. In 1999, the OPC supported the regional Alliance for Democracy (AD) party, which was associated with Yoruba politics. However, the efforts of the Nigerian president, Obasanjo, to speak to the southwest was largely successful, with the result that the PDP gained a stronger position across the region in the following elections. Ahead of the 2003 election, the OPC sided with the PDP in many Yoruba towns, with the AD regarded as representing the old regional elite, who were effectively shutting the younger generation out (Nolte, 2007: 227). In many southwestern states, this contributed to a weakened position for the AD. In Lagos, though, such actors have more established connections with the state's ruling party, with the city's politics expressed as being 'more or less one-way traffic – Tinubu calls the shots'.[9] Tinubu's influence was illustrated ahead of the APC's primary elections in Lagos State in 2018, when Tinubu fell out with incumbent governor Ambode, and decided instead to support another candidate, Babajide Sanwo-Olu. To Tinubu's irritation, Ambode decided to contest the primaries regardless. Ultimately, though, Ambode received less than 7 per cent of the vote (*Guardian*, 2018), with not even the deputy governor voting for him. The general mood was captured as 'Ambode tried to challenge Tinubu, but we all knew it wouldn't work. There is party discipline here in Lagos'.[10]

Contrary to other parts of Nigeria, party structures in Lagos are ingrained in the city. Tinubu has been able both to control the party in Lagos and to link it to informal associations, making Lagos State a virtual one-party state. There are regular local party meetings and every street has a Community Development Association (CDA), which together function as another arm of the party, imposing party consistency. Following the primary elections, people referred to Sanwo-Olu as the 'incoming governor', indicating that the forthcoming election was a mere formality. Moreover, there is a general perception that Tinubu controls the area boys, with, for example, leaders going to him when someone is arrested in order to secure their release. There are, though, limits to this relative impunity. When the activities of area boys have impacted on land-related matters, and thus economic growth, the state has responded harshly. Or, as one local politician puts it, 'anywhere in Lagos, when they [area boys] hear certain names they know it is a no-go area for any miscreant'.[11]

There are, accordingly, fine-grained relations based on reciprocity, and though the area boys may appear to be an anarchical force in society, an underlying hierarchical structure exists connected to a leadership with political connections. The control of area boys is instrumental to regulating the use of violence, and in turn political control, in the state. The police force is a federal institution and has been used by the federal government to interfere in election processes (Omotola, 2010). In response, the state government has established an alternative security structure it can control and deploy as a counterforce to the federal government's politicization of the police.

Community policing and hybridity

Lagos' high level of insecurity, exacerbated by a defective police force, has triggered demands for protection among citizens. A diverse group of people – youths, elders, men, women, Christians, Muslims, politicians, community leaders – awaited me in a meeting I attended with those involved in community policing in some of the city's more insecure areas. Their initiative began in 2004 with the objective of 'implementing the concept of community policing', and was supported by the Nigerian police, the UK Department for International Development (DFID) and the NGO, CLEEN Foundation. Though the concept of community policing was new to Lagos, the practice of communities establishing their own security arrangements was not. Indigenous vigilante practices have a long history in southwestern Nigeria, taking various forms according to the political context (Fourchard, 2008). The community policing approach was not, however, initiated by the communities themselves, but rather by international actors in an attempt to foster community–police relations, following models developed in the United States and the UK in the 1980s and 1990s (Brogden, 2004).

Before community policing was introduced, neighbourhoods organized vigilante groups that were 'more or less community policing without state actors', having been in place since, so it is claimed, the 1830s.[12] In effect, community policing is an attempt not only to make the police more responsive but also to discipline the vigilante groups. Community policing groups differ in their operational mode, with the group mentioned above describing their primary objective as conveying information to the police regarding criminal activity. Other groups – who refer to their activities as 'voluntary policing' – take an operative stance, patrolling the streets and making arrests. Typically, these groups had engaged in a more ruthless form of vigilantism prior to embarking on the community policing approach: 'if we saw you during the odd hours, we would not ask you "where are you coming from" [as we do now]. The first thing that we did was that we slap you or we give you the cutlass'.[13] This type of group exerts a kind of 'street authority' with the capacity to intervene directly and often violently, ascending from informal DIY organizing to become important actors in society. Though the groups embody a critique of the political system, their focus on instant action makes them susceptible to political co-optation (cf. Kyed, 2018). Despite the ambition among community policing groups to cooperate with the police, the latter are also seen as undermining security efforts, for example by leaking information to criminals.[14] The effectiveness of community policing initiatives seems to rely on the local police being responsive. It is not only a lack of capacity on the part of the police that matters, however – they are seen as constituting a threat to residents through their actions. This reinforces the population's perception of the police as non-reliable, further spurring citizen-led alternatives.

That the police give primacy to regime protection is particularly evident at election times. Area boys are recruited as thugs by politicians, with, for example, violence and intimidation preventing voters in some areas from casting their ballots in the 2017 Lagos State local government election. Elsewhere, ballot boxes were snatched and electoral officers attacked by thugs (i.e. area boys) (*Premium Times*, 2017). Police are often present at polling booths, but adopt different approaches to the various parties' thugs, tending to be more indulgent to intimidation that favours the ruling party. The general assessment following the 2017 local government election was that there had been no real election. Local government elections are administered by the State Independent Electoral Commission, which is more or less controlled by the state government. In the election, the APC won all the chairmanship positions in the 20 LGAs and the 37 Local Council Development Areas, as well as 369 of the 376 council seats (*Punch*, 2017).

The tangled relations between politics, violence, the police and communities are further illustrated when examining area boys' connections. Communities know who the area boys are, with one community leader who is also a community policing chair stating that: 'The area boys from time to time interfere. But they know I know their heads, their elders. If anyone misbehave, I will just tell who is leading them and they will deal will them.'[15] While there are leadership and administrative structures that the area boys follow (Ismail, 2009; Howden, 2010), respect for community authority is not definitive:

> Sometimes we cannot control them [the area boys]. When they come with guns, we move away. We do not want to risk our lives. But when they hear siren [of

the police] they will run. The funny thing is that when police come they will ask us 'Where are they? Who was it?' They [the police] say we know them [the area boys]. True, true we know them. But we are not so bold [as to tell them who it was]. We are afraid that they will come later and beat us or even kill us.[16]

There is a fluid relationship between the area boys and the rest of the community, with youths involved in community policing attempting to convince area boys to choose a different path in life: 'They are the people within us. We talk to them and tell them that it determines their future.'[17] Elsewhere, more operative community policing groups try to co-opt and monitor the area boys by encouraging them to join the community policing groups.[18] On the other hand, the community leader involved in community policing quoted above is also a politician, and during campaigns the services of the area boys come in useful: 'There is no politician that do not have security. We have some strong boys that come to help.'[19] Consequently, community leaders attempt to restrict the activities of area boys while simultaneously utilizing their capacity for violence, thereby contributing to terror becoming a routinized method of control (cf. Pieterse, 2010: 215).[20] Furthermore, interweaving several roles – politician, community leader, community policing chair – for political purposes muddies the lines between political interests, the community policing group and actors of insecurity:

> I belong to so many groups. Wherever I am, I campaign. I let them know that I am running. As I am here [with community policing]. I was the secretary for another association; I am chairman of the CDA for my area. I use all this as avenues [for my political campaign].[21]

There is, accordingly, a significant risk of community policing being politicized. This risk is reinforced by the prebendal nature of Nigerian politics, which both makes leadership of community policing groups – that is, acting as an intermediary between the community and government officials – an attractive position, and raises expectations that leaders should contribute to the community. For the latter, it is necessary to connect with the political sphere in order to access resources, even if people within that sphere are identified as 'looters'. In this regard, one community leader who is also community policing coordinator claims that: 'I just have to belong to their party [i.e. the party in power]. I have to manage the political space. If I do not manage the political space, they will not support my programme. Then you are seen as an opponent.'[22] The state government in Lagos, by linking these structures to the ruling party, reinforces its control at the grassroots.[23]

In parallel to the politicization of security structures, interviews indicate that the area boys are likewise highly organized. Specifically, the ruling party has 'mapped *every* area in Lagos' and this has stopped other violent actors, such as Boko Haram, from entering the city and potentially undermining the state government.[24] Indeed, Tinubu has declared himself 'the leader of the structure in Lagos' (*Daily Post*, 2018). In this context, the 'structure' should be understood as including not only the formal party organization but, equally critical, some level of control over the specialists in violence, such as the area boys, the National Union for Road Transport Workers (NURTW) and the OPC. Moreover, it includes linking community leaders to the party, such as ensuring party stalwarts are chairs of the CDAs. As such, there is little space for sustained independent organizing along DIY lines, despite the state government being largely non-responsive to the marginal population. Patronage channels mean that DIY initiatives in Lagos that potentially constitute a societal force typically become enmeshed in prebendal politics.

While, at a national level, Nigeria's political parties are unstable and weakly institutionalized, local security arrangements have played a crucial role in a single party institutionalizing itself as the dominant political force in Lagos. The use of community policing and other security actors to expand the ruling party's reach into the urban population does not, however, mean that these actors are effective and coherent in their approach to the politicization of local arrangements – an observation also illustrated in Di Nunzio's (2014) study of Addis Ababa. The linkages between community policing groups and state politics do not mean that control is effectively enforced from above. In line with how neoliberal restructuring projects are contextually embedded (Peck, Theodore and Brenner, 2009: 49), the multiplicity of security actors in Lagos demonstrates how emerging networked governance systems hinge on pre-existing institutions. It also points to the continued negotiation of urban authority within a national political context.

Conclusion

This chapter has examined how having unresponsive state institutions has led Lagos residents to initiate local DIY initiatives in the field of security. Given the inherently political character of security, these local arrangements have become entangled in relations that encompass both state and national politics. In other Nigerian cities, community policing and vigilante practices have become part of the political struggles taking place between the central state and local communities (e.g. Kyed, 2018; Jackson, Kassaye and Shearon, 2019). In Lagos, however, Nigeria's federal system and prebendal politics have contributed to non-state actors becoming embroiled in the field of violence and security, provoking political contestations between the central and regional state.

Political parties in Nigeria are generally weakly institutionalized. In Lagos, by contrast, the ruling party has built party networks that extend down to the street level, with alternative security structures helping to secure sub-national political space. Citizen initiatives in response to the absence of state provision of security are thus politicized by the dominant party in an attempt to enforce control. Urban security is accordingly a critical sphere for negotiating authority and statehood (Lund, 2006; Hagmann and Péclard, 2010), with non-state actors as an integral part of Lagos' security structure. These actors do not, however, challenge the prevailing order or present an alternative urban future – instead, they are instrumentalized by the elite through patronage relations. In other words, given the instrumentality of violent actors in keeping the political elite in office, they are left to carve out their own space (within limits). As such, non-state violent actors do not represent a challenge to the technocratic urban renewal project that speaks to Lagos' 'helicopter class' (Howden, 2010), and which includes projects such as the futuristic Eko Atlantic City – expected to host 250,000 of the city's richest citizens in environmentally-friendly buildings on an artificial island. Meanwhile, 70 per cent of Lagos' estimated 20 million inhabitants will continue to live in unsafe and informal settlements.

In the absence of political challenges that support active citizenship, community groups with links to state authorities and institutions help enforce political control. Actors in the field of security operate according to their own moral systems but these are at the same time negotiated in relation to political actors. While the traditional vigilantes of the colonial era could be characterized in terms of institutional multiplicity, the merging of state authority with alternative institutions of crime control and justice has now resulted in institutional hybridity. As a consequence, rather than demands that challenge the state with alternative systems of organization, we instead see demands for *more* – not less – state involvement, in a context where state capacity is distrusted but still requested. This approach does not entail active citizenship – all that is required is an understanding of politics as transfer of resources from politicians to individuals.

The alternative model of governance purportedly being pursued in Lagos relies heavily on access to, and distribution of, resources, in a manner that promotes prebendalism. That Lagos is effectively a one-party state ensures citizen-led initiatives are enmeshed in political relations. This one-party domination is, however, not conclusive, but rather illustrates the unsettled character of state domination (Hagmann and Péclard, 2010). Actors such as the OPC have a relatively autonomous agenda, and are more consistent in their approach than, for example, area boys (Reno, 2005). The capacity of non-state actors to undermine or sustain security is an expression of a mediated form of statehood, with authority exercised through a variety of institutions in which local practices and institutions become entangled in wider forces (Lund, 2006; Raeymakers, Menkhaus and Vlassenroot, 2008). This underlines how both state reform and citizen-led initiatives are contextually embedded and politically mediated. Relations between formal and informal institutions are shaped not only by the form and extent of people's organizing, but also by the means and opportunities open to the political elite in reaching the city's margins.

Notes

1   One example is Aminu Tambuwal, who was first elected to the House of Representatives in 2003 on the All Nigeria Peoples Party (ANPP) platform. In early 2007, he switched to the Democratic People's Party (DPP), before switching back to the ANPP a few months later when the DPP denied return tickets to former ANPP legislators in the 2007 election. He then switched to the Peoples' Democratic Party (PDP), following the example of the ANPP governorship candidate. In October 2014,

he abandoned the PDP for the All Progressives Congress (APC) and became governor of Sokoto State following the 2015 election. In August 2018, he re-joined the PDP.

2   While the stated aim of the reform was to bring development, the number of LGAs is also a factor in the distribution of resources (i.e. oil revenues) from the centre. There were claims that the existing structure favoured the northern part of the country, and a frequent comparison made being that Kano State had forty-four LGAs compared to Lagos State's twenty. When Lagos attempted to create new local governments, other states also followed suit.

3   Interviews in Lagos, October 2018.

4   In the Economist Intelligence Unit's Safe City Index, Lagos is placed bottom both in terms of overall security and personal security (https://safecities.economist.com/safe-cities-index-2019).

5   Interview with deputy director of civil society organization, Lagos, 15 February 2017.

6   Interview with secretary of community policing group, Lagos, 16 October 2018.

7   Interviews with civil society organizations and community leaders, Lagos, October 2018.

8   Interview with chairman of residential association, Lagos, 26 October 2018.

9   Interview with a journalist, Lagos, 7 February 2017.

10   Interview with women's rights activist, Lagos, 24 October 2018.

11   Interview with local politicians, Lagos, 16 October 2018.

12   Interview with community policing chair, Lagos, 16 October 2018.

13   Interview with voluntary policing leader, Lagos, 14 February 2017.

14   Interviews, Lagos, October 2018.

15   Interview with community policing chair, Lagos, 16 October 2018.

16   Interview with community policing chair, Lagos, 16 October 2018.

17   Interview with community policing youth leader, Lagos, 16 October 2018.

18   Interview with volunteer police service leader, Lagos, 14 February 2017.

19   Interview with community policing chair, Lagos, 16 October 2018.

20   Those (few) politicians who do not use private security tend instead to rely on *juju* (Yoruba magic also used by the OPC): 'There are things you can swallow so that machine gun is not going to have effect on you' (Interview with politician, Lagos, 26 October 2018).

21   Interview with community policing chair, Lagos, 16 October 2018.

22   Interview with community policing coordinator, Lagos, 11 February 2017.

23   While there are some community leaders who prefer to keep a distance from politicians, this comes at the price of not being able to rely on their support when times are tough. One community leader who provides electricity for the streetlights in his neighbourhood from his generator illustrates the dilemma: 'I was scared when I was taking up the responsibility. It has been rough, but I thank God. There have been challenges. Sometimes you don't get diesel, sometimes it's expensive. I am facilitating it from my own business. Sometimes you have made sells so you can afford it, but sometimes you have not made sells but you know you have a commitment that you need to fulfil towards your community.' Accordingly, it is primarily more affluent community leaders who can afford such a strategy. Even so, it was a local politician who provided for the lampposts.

24   Interview with director of civil society organization, Lagos, 23 October 2018.

Chapter 7

'ACCRA WE DEY': PRECARIOUS HISTORIES, CREATIVE PLACE-MAKING AND REIMAGINED FUTURES IN URBAN GHANA

Jennifer Hart

A new Accra for a better Ghana

Driving down Accra's High Street from the old commercial district and the historically Ga districts of Jamestown and Usshertown towards the modern centre of cosmopolitanism on Oxford Street, you encounter a roundabout. Rising from this roundabout can be seen Independence Arch – a symbol of independent Ghana's promise atop which Kwame Nkrumah stood on 6 March 1957 to declare, 'Ghana, your beloved country is free forever!' Travel just a little further and you reach a branch in the road, which leads to Christiansborg Castle, the seat of both colonial and postcolonial government. Between Independence Arch and the castle, the Accra Metropolitan Assembly (AMA) has erected a sign proclaiming, 'A New Accra for a Better Ghana'.

This 'new Accra' signals a renewed political commitment to urban planning and development, articulated in the AMA's 2009 vision for the city and embodied in the 2012 National Urban Policy (Government of Ghana, 2012). As Accra's mayor Alfred Vanderpuije declared at the laying of the cornerstone for the new sign in January 2010, 'The AMA is resolved to play its role effectively to ensure the future as a sustainable urban landmark' (GhanaWeb, 2010). Despite budgetary and other practical challenges, Vanderpuije promised that this would not be an empty declaration, and that the AMA would immediately get to work improving 'public infrastructure, health, water and sanitation, education, transport, housing, waste management, energy and economic opportunities' (GhanaWeb, 2010). While these changes would have varied effects on urban residents, they were – according to government officials – necessary in order to achieve a sustainable future.

Over the subsequent ten years, Accra has indeed changed. While the AMA's promises arose out of the Millennium Development Goals (MDGs) and the more recent Sustainable Development Goals (SDGs), the changes witnessed by urban residents have more complicated roots. Particularly in the city's most elite districts, old buildings are being torn down and long-vacant properties cleared to make way for glass and concrete high-rise structures, funded by the expanded investment of real-estate developers. Within the existing city, new districts such as Airport City have grown rapidly, distinguished by award-winning architecture, international hotel chains, and upscale restaurants and shops. In 2017, the city began work on plans for a massive urban extension into the Ningo-Prampram District east of Accra. The construction boom coincides with what some have labelled a 'cultural renaissance' – art galleries, street art festivals, fashion boutiques, cafes, bistros, cocktail bars and music venues that cater to a tight-knit community of artists, architects, intellectuals and designers (Gittlen, 2016).

In both symbolic and substantive ways, these new developments appear to exacerbate the social and economic inequalities that have long defined city life in Accra. Today, an estimated 43 per cent of Accra metropolitan residents live in 'slums' (Benzoni, n.d.), and an estimated 80 per cent of the country's workforce finds employment in 'informal' sectors like market trading and transport (Osei-Boateng and Ampratwum, 2011). Accra's urban poor operate side businesses out of their homes, purchase food in open-air markets, cook over coal fires, use underfunded public transportation, live without water or electricity, and either send their children to apprenticeships with family members or keep them at home because they cannot afford school fees. Elite residents, by contrast, have access to a much wider range of resources and infrastructures at the local, national and global level. They access the internet on smart phones, own their own cars, purchase imported food from grocery stores, work in air-conditioned offices, buy water to fill giant tanks, run generators, and send their children to elite private schools in Ghana and abroad. As elite residents travel between work, home, shopping malls, bistros, cafes and clubs in air-conditioned comfort, largely insulated from the lived realities of the street outside, they reproduce socio-spatial inequalities that have their roots in colonial residential and social segregation policies.

While this vision of an increasingly segregated Accra – an Accra marked by what AbdouMaliq Simone calls 'the conceit of enclosure' (2019: 127) – may be driving the actions of developers and government officials who embrace new urbanist theories and so fuel property speculation, it is far from the only vision of the city's future. In Jamestown – the heart of old Accra – artists have created their own statement about the city, using graffiti and street art to proudly declare 'Accra we dey'. A popular phrase that draws on a cosmopolitan form of 'pidgin' spoken throughout Accra, 'Accra we dey' stands as a challenge to governmental and development visions of 'A New Accra for a Better Ghana'. Multilayered interpretations of the statement itself evoke claims of belonging, engagement and ownership ('we are *in* Accra'); the politics of survival and thriving ('we are *living* in Accra'); and the pride of urban residents ('we are in *Accra*').

Mobilization of the term likewise highlights the complicated nature of contemporary urban politics in the city. Though 'Accra we dey' is a product of the working-class population's language, it has been championed by upwardly mobile, digitally savvy millennials, who are effectively creating/promoting a new 'branding' for the city rooted in the rich histories, cultures and practices of urban residents. Located in Jamestown, next to the legendary Brazil House, painted on a wall that leads to a colonial-era pier where Ga fishermen repair nets, dry fish and send their canoes out into the sea, 'Accra we dey' brings the complicated spatial histories of the city's oldest district into (sometimes uncomfortable) conversation with more recent place-making efforts. Brazil House, located right beside the port where goods once moved in and out of the colonial capital, is the symbolic home of the city's Tabon community – descendants of manumitted Afro-Brazilians who 'returned' to the Gold Coast in the nineteenth century (Quayson, 2014: 43–52). More broadly, Jamestown was both the centre of a precolonial Ga settlement and the site of intensive efforts at urban reform and spatial colonialism under British rule. Currently, however, these spaces are part of an artistic and cultural reimagining of the city, arguably best represented by the activities of the Chale Wote Festival and its organizers (Accra [dot] Alt), who operate out of Brazil House, as well as the independently operated 'Accra we dey' podcast, which highlights the city's cultural happenings.[1] The phrase 'Accra we dey', then, is more than a simple statement of identity or a declaration of resistance. This complicated history forces us to engage with the layers of economic and cultural creativity, social connectivity and political action that shape urban politics and place-making in Accra.

These seemingly contradictory visions for Accra – one focused on the possibilities of the new and the other anchored, at least discursively and symbolically, in the layered histories of the city's past – suggest that plans for the city's future are both complicated and contested. The inequalities of the contemporary city are indeed real, with the income gap in cities such as Accra appearing to have grown at an accelerated pace over the past ten years, reinforced and reproduced through infrastructure and urban spatial forms, and exacerbated by neoliberal economic policies, weak commodity markets and currency redenomination (UNDP, 2014). In response to this politics of extraversion, 'southern urbanism' – urban theory from the Global South – has set its sights on the practices of the local, which are cast as forms of resilience and resistance in the face of global hegemonies that marginalize local residents and knowledge. In particular, academics, policymakers, journalists and planners often categorize the adaptations of poor urban residents as manifestations of 'informality', and so target urban planning analysis and intervention on lower-class neighbourhoods, markets, transport systems and other infrastructure. In interrogating the 'informal city', theorists such as Simone, Pieterse and Enwezor rightly emphasize the experiences of the 'urban majority', who are largely left out of (or explicitly criminalized by) planning and policy processes. However, in embracing this 'informal economy' framework, these scholars reify the artificial categories that have come to shape development practice, often at the cost of obscuring the more complex socio-spatial histories of African cities.

Keith Hart's original formulation of the 'informal economy' in Ghana was defined primarily by self-employment. In response to a lagging wage labour sector, Hart argued, many Ghanaians pursued more precarious economic opportunities not easily accounted for in economic surveys. While some of this work was, indeed, low-wage, Hart acknowledged that 'informal activities encompass a wide-ranging scale, from marginal operations to large-scale enterprises' (1973: 68).

Despite the broader economic conditions shaping the labour market and economic opportunities of 1970s Accra having not improved significantly over the last forty years, the term 'informal economy' – and the broader category of 'informality' – is today exclusively associated with the urban poor. Market traders, trotro drivers, cooked food sellers and beer brewers are all 'underemployed' members of an 'informal economy' – in Ga, '*kobolo*', a good-for-nothing street lounger who embodies the precarity of 'urban crisis' (Quayson, 2014: 199). Independent social media managers, café owners, fashion designers and Uber drivers are more often 'entrepreneurs', even if their work carries the same risk.

In Accra, as elsewhere, this politics of categorization has meaningful consequences for urban residents. As Hart notes:

> Most enterprises run with some measure of bureaucracy are amenable to enumeration by surveys, and – as such – constitute the 'modern sector' of the urban economy. The remainder – that is, those who escape enumeration – are variously classified as 'the *low productivity* urban sector', 'the reserve army of *underemployed and unemployed*', 'the urban *traditional* sector', and so on. These terms beggar analysis by assuming what has to be demonstrated.
>
> (1973: 68)

Today, 'informal economy' and 'informality' appear to have fallen into the same trap. In defaulting to these terms as a means of explaining contemporary African cities, we reify and reproduce categories that are deployed in oversimplified and highly politicized ways by government institutions and development organizations. While scholars often use these terms to identify groups that are underrepresented in development policy and yet are vital to the economic and social life of African cities, these same forms of demarcation have been deployed by politicians and others to delegitimize, even criminalize, the activities of the urban poor, transforming them into targets of government sanction, demolition and, at times, violent attack.

To understand the meaning and function of these activities, we must explore informalization as a contested historical process through which government officials and urban residents have reshaped the infrastructures and practices of urban life in cities like Accra. Much as Mayne (2017) has demonstrated for the word 'slum', in historicizing the process of informalization through the politics of planning, we illuminate the contested nature of categorization and regulation in African cities and in so doing place African experiences, practices and values at the centre of analysis. In particular, through exploring the history of urban politics and grassroots place-making, we can better understand the ways in which a wide range of Accra residents claim a 'right to the city', often bridging the gaps between the socio-spatial inequalities inscribed in urban planning policy and practice – what Simone refers to as 'leaks' in the structures of segregation (2019: 135). Accra residents describe these daily acts as 'managing' (Schauert, 2015: 8). In contrast to such phrases as 'making do' or 'getting by', which are often associated with informal practices and imply survivalism, 'managing' 'highlights the ways in which participants engage in meaningful acts, strategically harnessing the resources at hand not only to accomplish objectives but also to construct satisfying lives' (Schauert, 2015: 8). Acts of managing transcend the socioeconomic class distinctions present within the city, uniting Accra's population in a process of grassroots place-making, simultaneously reifying and resisting the city's economic inequalities.

In Accra, this grassroots place-making, or 'managing', constitutes a form of DIY urbanism that has shaped not only the culture of the city but its infrastructural, regulatory and spatial form. 'Managing' in Accra is far from new, with its roots extending back to precolonial urbanism and colonial-era urban politics. These are in many ways particular to Accra, and a historical perspective is essential to understanding the cultures and politics shaping the city's urban morphologies. Beyond this, however, 'managing' provides a helpful analytical frame through which to interrogate the broader politics of place manifest in Accra: the realities of state capacity, efficiency and resources; the politics of regulation, order and marginalization; and the contestations over belonging and autochthony that raise important questions concerning urban planning processes and practices across the continent.

'The Right to the City' in colonial Accra: Autochthony, infrastructure and order

Europeans arriving at Accra in the seventeenth century met dense concentrations of contiguous Ga settlements along the eastern portion of the Gold Coast, organized into family units or clans. Seven of those clans gathered around the English, Danish and Dutch forts at Accra, intermarrying and forming political alliances that unified them as the core of the Ga Mashie, constituting what is now central Accra. Through their interaction with traders who operated out of European forts, Ga Mashie expanded their political and economic influence, intermarrying with other African ethnic groups and European merchants. Despite this, Ga communities continued to use clan as a basis for both social and spatial organization, rooted in the seven founding families of Accra. By the early 1700s, Accra had become the capital of a broader Ga federation dispersed throughout the eastern part of the Gold Coast and organized into several towns (Pellow, 2001: 61–2).

Socio-spatial organization through kinship groups did not prevent Ga populations from interacting, engaging and incorporating outsiders into their community. Beginning in the 1670s, slaves from the coast of Benin and fishermen from Moree settled in the Alata quarter of Jamestown – both of whom were deployed as laborers by African and European leaders in and around the coastal forts and trading posts – were absorbed into the Akwamu *akutso* of Otublohum. In 1836, ex-slaves deported from Bahia in Brazil arrived in Accra and used their connections with broader returnee populations along the West African coast to establish themselves as wealthy traders (Parker, 2000: 14–15). These 'Tabon' returnees of Hausa, Fulani or Yoruba lineage were likewise incorporated into

Otoblohum in the nineteenth century (Quayson, 2014: 44–5). European and Afro-European merchants built homes and established businesses across Accra's various quarters, alongside an increasingly diverse African population of fishermen and traders. This integrative model of settlement contrasted sharply with both the 'outsider' settlement patterns of Akan populations elsewhere in the southern Gold Coast, and the increasingly widespread models of European town planning that shaped highly segregated spatial organization in cities such as Nairobi. Accra was, in other words, both a Ga town and a cosmopolitan urban settlement[2] – a social and cultural tension that raised questions about autochthony, belonging, spatial organization and political authority. Such questions grew increasingly important over the course of the nineteenth and twentieth centuries.

In establishing Accra as the new capital of a consolidated Gold Coast Colony in 1877, British colonial officials inserted themselves into the centre of these debates. Officials immediately moved to renovate Christiansborg Castle, which had fallen to ruins after an 1862 earthquake destroyed its upper floors. This renovation was one of several early building projects in the city, including a new 'government house' and hospital in the 1870s and 1880s. Colonial officials marked these moments of construction as symbols of new British political authority in the city, alongside older European structures such as the Basel Mission Society trading posts, which had been so central to the region's export-oriented trading networks. However, these early construction projects were often located significant distances from established settlements in the old Ga core. In choosing these isolated locations, British officials signalled a new vision for the city – one that broke with older traditions of incorporation and integration, and instead created space for new, segregated enclaves to be developed. Moreover, in focusing their construction efforts outside of the city, British officials highlighted the limits of their authority in navigating the complicated politics of land tenure, residency and autochthony in the old town. Despite their depictions of Accra as a jumbled mess of 'dilapidated huts' and disorganized, congested quarters, British officials were initially constrained in wading into the city's socio-spatial politics.

Disease outbreaks – attributed to residential settlement patterns in Jamestown and Usshertown by doctors and other health officials – inspired new intervention efforts, which sought to remake the city in line with prevailing theories of public health and social order. Following the recommendations of Sir W. J. R. Simpson, the colonial government established enforced quarantines in response to outbreaks of bubonic plague in 1908 and yellow fever in 1911. Africans who sought refuge from the outbreaks were settled in the new neighbourhoods of Korle Gonno and Adabraka, located outside the core of the old Ga town (Sackeyfio, 2008: 132; Quayson, 2014: 69–70).[3]

A series of natural disasters also altered the spatial dynamics of the city. A fire in April 1894 destroyed a significant portion of the city. By 1895, the Public Works Department had cleared damaged houses, laid out new streets and begun construction on a new church (Her Majesty's Stationary Office, 1887). This British eagerness to remake the city raised questions among African residents, who suggested that the fire had intentionally been set in order to secure cooperation from local political leaders and land owners. Other construction – Salaga and London Markets, the Accra Post Office, Korle Bu Hospital – cast as public welfare projects by British officials, faced less direct criticism.

Even so, complicated land tenure systems and the persistent power of local political leaders frustrated colonial officials, who struggled to secure 'public lands'. A Public Lands Ordinance passed in 1876 gave the British colonial government the legal power to compel landowners to sell land at a reasonable price 'for the services of the Colony' (His Majesty's Stationary Office, 1912: 21). Enactment of the law was, however, much more difficult. Overlapping claims of ownership were common among African landholders, resulting in drawn-out legal battles and extensive costs for the state – a situation the British government was still seeking to address through legislation as late as 1929.[4] Even in cases where officials were able to clearly identify owners and pay compensation for land seized for public projects, they frequently faced significant criticism from community members, landholders and local leaders. Early public projects usually involved little if any community consultation, despite the often significant alterations proposed to the form of urban space and practice of urban life. In this regard, colonial officials continued to underestimate both the practical and symbolic importance of indigenous spatial logics – traders protested their move to new markets and homeowners protested seizure of family lands (Parker, 2000: 22).

In passing the Town Councils Ordinance in 1894, British officials sought to diffuse criticism (and cost) by decentralizing the regulation and administration of towns such as Accra, in the process providing a means of direct representation for the city's African residents.[5] Accra Town Council, established in 1898, included four 'official' (i.e. appointed) European members and four 'unofficial' (i.e. elected) African members. Among the city's rate-paying class of property owners, Accra Town Council represented an experiment in democratic governance and a precursor to eventual independence.[6] However, among those not eligible to vote – which constituted the majority of the city's population – the elite, Western-educated African Town Council members were perceived as being just as disconnected from residents' needs and concerns as the European councillors appointed by the governor (Parker, 2000: 22).

In the context of this politics of representation, members of the Town Council set about fulfilling their mandate to provide roads, public infrastructure and services for the growing city. In doing so, they embraced the modernist logics of urban planners, who privileged the broad boulevards, open public spaces and decongested neighbourhoods of European town models over the dense settlement patterns of African residents.[7] These efforts culminated in the British response to a 1939 earthquake, which damaged homes across large parts of the city and inspired an extensive rebuilding effort. The earthquake, then, seemed like an opportunity to start afresh, buoyed by new British commitments to a 'development colonialism' that sought to modernize African colonies.

British officials used this opportunity to not only relocate African residents, but also reshape built environments and reinforce racial segregation and commercial zoning policies.[8] The reality of meagre resources, though, limited investment and inhibited the realization of these grand modernist aspirations. This reality, Bissell (2011) argues, reflected colonial attitudes towards cities like Accra – a paradoxical mixture of interventionist reform, aspirational development and strategic disinvestment.[9] However, the strength of Ga cultures of urban residence also influenced how local populations used this infrastructure. African entrepreneurs, drawing on much older cultures and practices of residence, mobility and economic exchange, translated these imported technological and spatial cultures into forms often indecipherable to colonial officials. Africans who failed to embrace European logics of industrial modernity, urban modernism and technological capitalism were labelled 'pirates' and 'profiteers', and accused of obstructing the efforts of colonial development. African commercial vehicle owners undermined colonial municipal bus systems by carrying passengers within city limits (Hart, 2020). Traders in open-air markets were criticized for taking advantage of customers in order to increase their own profits, and as a consequence shifting customers' attention away from shops and stores (Murillo, 2017). In fact, these acts of technological translation made imported technologies meaningful to local communities, enhancing existing systems of interaction and exchange while creating opportunities for accumulation and innovation.

The Gold Coast government was not exceptional in its frustration over 'the incapacity of legal and bureaucratic instruments to reorder the totality of the everyday' (Bissell, 2011: 3). However, despite colonial officials frequently pointing to the perceived messiness and disorder of the African urban milieu, their modernist plans masked a process of urban planning 'marked again and again by incoherence, incapacity, and incompleteness' (Bissell, 2011: 1). The long history of Ga urbanism, the cosmopolitanism of migrant populations and the economic autonomy of African residents further complicated these processes in Accra, as residents and officials alike argued over who should define infrastructure and order, and in whose interests. The Town Council had limited revenue available to fund the maintenance – much less the expansion – of public infrastructure. As a hub of economic, social, political and cultural activity in the colony, Accra grew significantly over the first half of the twentieth century – between 1901 and 1931, Accra's population increased from 17,892 to 61,558 (Acquah, 1958: 31; Plageman, 2013: 43). Young men and women from across the colony arrived in Accra seeking economic opportunities (McCaskie, 2001: 122–33; Plageman, 2013: 42–4; Hart, 2016: 95–120), with many settling in the oldest parts of the city, apprenticed to local craftsmen before striking out on their own as entrepreneurs or company men (Hart, 2016: 103–5). Still others arrived from the Northern territories, looking to take advantage of new trade opportunities in the aftermath of the Anglo–Asante war. Unlike earlier generations of 'strangers', these Muslim migrants formed new communities (called Zongos) outside the boundaries of the old city, marked by their own spatial logics (Pellow, 1991: 424).

Those who did embrace the plan for the city experienced first-hand the tension between aspirational plans and fiscal realities. Middle-class residents moved to neighbourhoods such as Adabraka in large numbers in the first half of the twentieth century in order to escape inner-city congestion. In embracing the 'modern' houses of the city's newest districts, middle-class Africans sought to reflect their aspirational status in built form, utilizing government-sponsored hire-purchase systems to buy land and build houses in planned communities (Quayson, 2014: 69). However, the pace of resettlement far outstripped the Town Council's ability to provide the promised infrastructure that would distinguish these communities from the old Ga quarters of the city centre. By the 1920s and 1930s, residents regularly complained to the Town Council and other government bodies about the poor condition of roads, the absence of gutters and water, and the 'unsightly' appearance of their neighbourhoods. Their complaints were born out by the Town Council's own reporting. Despite spending over £1,000 on road construction in 1934, twenty-three roads in the city were either in serious disrepair or had not been properly constructed in the first place, with the Town Council repeatedly appealing to the Colonial Governor's office for financial and technical assistance.[10] British colonial archives document extensive, persistent concerns about the condition of roads and related issues of drainage and sanitation, which not only affected the city's appearance and functionality, but also exacerbated significant public health challenges such as malaria and yellow fever.[11]

The injection of resources and energy following the 1939 earthquake ultimately proved to be a brief exception in an otherwise remarkably consistent story. Even with the significant donations and loans made available for earthquake relief, some affected residents were still living in temporary housing as late as 1945.[12] Thus, scarce resources, inadequate legislation and inept officials hampered the visions of British officials and African residents alike. Despite bringing different expectations to bear on their environment and in doing so producing dramatically different spatial forms throughout the city, the residents of Zongos, middle-class neighbourhoods and old Ga quarters were united in the work of 'managing'. While it is perhaps most intuitive to think of 'managing' in the context of want – as a metaphor for 'making do' or 'getting by' – for many Accra residents managing also required negotiating various levels of expectation. The complicated, contradictory tensions at the core of Accra's spatial politics consistently frustrated British colonial officials. As Bissell notes, in colonial Zanzibar, 'The unruliness of urban life frequently disrupted their efforts to make the city conform to a grid of abstract legal definitions and bureaucratic rules' (2011: 2). However, even if the British colonial state ultimately failed to fully plan and control space in Accra, their efforts to order the city did create a new regulatory vocabulary – laws and frameworks that constituted a new form of moral and legal distinction in the city. Zoning ordinances, town plans and resettlement programmes established new expectations surrounding the built environment and urban life practices, marginalizing indigenous practices and, through the politics of space, limiting African opportunities and access.

Colonial legacies, modernist visions, nationalist dreams

Long histories of urban residence, as well as the relative degree of African economic autonomy enjoyed in Accra and throughout the Gold Coast, ensured that African interests and voices remained at the centre of conversations about the city's future. Even in Accra, though, urban planning was marked by efforts to create and reinforce an urban form that marginalized Africans. In the years following independence, the spatial structures of racial segregation quickly adjusted to reflect new forms of postcolonial inequality and global technopolitics. In Kwame Nkrumah's vision for Accra, the city would serve as a symbol of the new nation's power and of the entire continent's promised modernization. 'Those who in the future will have in their hands the task of moulding the shape of our cities, towns and villages throughout Ghana' were tasked with both a practical and symbolic project, bringing to life the technopolitical visions of modernization, nationalism and development (Nkrumah, 1958). In 1958, just a few months after independence, the Ministry of Housing released, under Prime Minister Kwame Nkrumah's orders, a report detailing its plans for the country's capital. Despite the plan's relatively uninspiring title – 'Accra: A Plan for the Town' – the vision it conveyed was imaginative and grandiose. As indicated in Nkrumah's foreword, Accra's redevelopment was merely the first stage in a much longer-term project aimed at redeveloping all of Ghana's towns and cities and improving living standards throughout the country: 'It is fitting that we should improve our main towns alongside our rural and industrial development and that our capital city should offer improved amenities and standards of living' (Nkrumah, 1958).

Urban development, in other words, was part and parcel of a broader project of modernization, which, Holston argues, sought to force urban residents 'to adopt new forms of social experience, collective association, and personal habit' through reshaping the built environment (1989: 22). As such, the plan for Accra echoed a wider vision of economic and ideological redevelopment in Ghana. Driven by concerns about neocolonialism, the Nkrumah government sought to enhance the country's ability to resist foreign exploitation and compete on the international stage. A wide-ranging suite of policies – from ideological education to massive infrastructure projects – sought to engage citizens in a project of materialist decolonization, directed by the central government and its Convention People's Party (CPP). Inspired by Nkrumahist theories of African Socialism, the 1962 'Programme of the Convention People's Party for Work and Happiness' called for 'a rapid change in the socio-economic structure of the country' built on 'the firm foundation of mass support'.[13] In reality, however, the proposed 'two-way exchange of confidence' and populist appeals of the CPP were merely a means of securing consent for the policies of a 'strong, stable, firm, and highly centralized government'.[14] The CPP embraced socialist policies, infrastructures and models as an alternative framework capable of making Ghana globally competitive though redressing the legacy of underdevelopment wrought by colonial capitalist exploitation. Faced with the reality of dwindling resources, the CPP encouraged public participation via 'self-help' and 'community development' projects that would free up resources for large-scale industrialization, at the same time binding citizens to the nation through collective action and self-sacrifice. These policies represented 'the re-envisioning of ideals and modes of development in Ghana during the 1960s' (Skinner, 2011: 299; see also Ahlman, 2012).

As Skinner notes, community development officers often operated very differently on the ground, driven by a desire to 'work with the people on the problems as seen by them at their own level of development in terms of their values and purposes' (2011: 308). In doing so, these practitioners drew on colonial systems and theories of self-help, refashioned to the postcolonial context: 'Ghanaian academics repositioned their specialist knowledge, not as a "gold standard" inherited from the colonial era, but as a means of bringing modern social science to "African problems." The science … was international, not colonial' (Skinner, 2011: 309). Likewise, the plan for Accra laid out what Quayson identifies as 'a broadly modernist aesthetic vision' (2014: 83), reflective of colonial and postcolonial desires to transform Accra into a 'modern' city. Quayson argues and the colonial archives attest that 'the notion of Accra as a modern city comparable to others in Europe and in the wider empire had already crept into colonial government correspondence during the lengthy debates that took place around the reorganisation of the city following the earthquake in 1939' (2014: 83).

African nationalists shared this modernist vision for the city, both in terms of the built environment and in terms of the urban culture and experience it would make possible. Throughout the mid-twentieth century, newspapers advertised the latest fashions and technologies, which combined could help shape a 'modern life' – defined by mobility, cosmopolitanism and a future-oriented vision – for Accra's rapidly increasing population (133,192 in 1948 to 337,828 in 1960). Nate Plageman argues that in the years immediately preceding independence, major newspapers such as the *Daily Graphic* served as important sites for imagining what the new nation and its future might be, with newspaper staff shaping discourses about the political, social, cultural and economic possibilities of the nation-to-be (2010: 138). The pages of the *Graphic* detailed Accra's 'ever-changing face' (Plageman, 2010: 139) through descriptions of infrastructural development, urban planning and architectural design – descriptions that linked 'Accra's physical environment to the colony's growing prospects of national independence' (Plageman, 2010: 148). In the process, Plageman argues, newspaper staff projected an image of independent urban modernism that ignored the realities faced by many the country's residents – including a significant proportion of those living in Accra. Regardless, for these writers the new buildings and infrastructural development were 'markers of progress' that showed Accra had 'come of age' as a city in and of the world (Plageman, 2010: 148).

For some, built space created modern citizens, with *Graphic* writers viewing sanitation infrastructure as both the means and spark for creating a citizenry capable – through greater cleanliness – of bridging urban life's stark contrasts (Plageman, 2010: 153). Kwame Nkrumah likewise embraced this modernist rhetoric, encouraging the development of structures and institutions that would convey an innovative vision for Ghana's capital and its citizens. New department stores such as Kingsway would create 'modern consumers'. Moreover, as Bianca Murillo argues, by placing the Kingsway store in the middle of a major new thoroughfare (now known as Independence Avenue), Nkrumah sought to put 'consumerism on display' in order to help 'legitimize Ghana as a new nation and establish Accra as a desirable destination' (2012: 376–7). A new airline, steamship and other forms of transport infrastructure, as well as hydroelectric dams and industrial manufacturing plants, sought to project a dynamic vision of the nation both at home and abroad. This infrastructural modernization echoed a more experiential cultural modernism, in which highlife music and dance, as well as cinema, fashion and other expressions of urban life, projected a vision of modern Ghanaian life that was both ambitiously global and profoundly local.

The tension between colonial continuity and the rhetoric of decolonization was perhaps most clearly illustrated in the plan for Accra's redevelopment. The plan was comprehensive in its efforts to rethink and reshape the city, suggesting that the policies of postcolonial government would be guided by a coherent urban development practice and ideology. This image and ideal was appealing for both government officials and foreign observers alike – beautifully printed and bound versions of the document were sent to government offices and university libraries around the world, complete with gilded crest and full-colour illustrations. However, this coherence and comprehensiveness – and the modernizing promise of such aspirational visions – obscured the ongoing, complex contestation over the infrastructure, organization and culture of Accra as a capital city, global trade hub and Ga town. Such contestation was far from new. The plan submitted by the Town and Country Planning Division to Minister of Housing A. E. Inkumsah (and by extension Prime Minister Nkrumah) was rooted in the government's longstanding project to rationalize Accra's residential patterns and urban development in conformity with prevailing theories of public health, commerce and governance (Quayson, 2014: 82).

In 1945, the British colonial administration enacted the Gold Coast Town and Country Ordinance, which aimed to take a 'broader view of planning … orderly and progressive development of land, town and other areas, whether urban or rural to preserve and improve the amenities thereof and other matters connected therewith' (Quayson, 2014: 82). 'Accra: A Plan for the Town' was a direct product of this change in urban development and planning. Though the plan was commissioned in 1954 by the British colonial government under the direction of Kwame Nkrumah as prime minister, and assembled by a team led by B. A. W. Trevallion and Alan G. Hood, the end product was effectively a revised version of a 1944 plan submitted by city planner Maxwell Fry as part of the 1945 Town and Country Ordinance.

The Trevallion-Hood plan, then, seemed to embody both colonial-era reform and postcolonial aspirations. Minister of Housing Inkumsah (1958) encouraged Accra residents to remember:

> the moral as well as the physical importance of clean, well-designed and efficiently maintained towns, and to ask all our citizens to remember that our

daily environment means a very great deal to us. In this age of material well-being, motor-cars and advertisements we are inclined to overlook spiritual and aesthetic factors and I ask every citizen of Ghana to consider the need for beauty in his town or village and to be insistent that everything in that town from the largest building to the smallest road sign or advertisement is designed in good taste in order that the result will be towns and villages worthy of our State and one of which posterity can be proud.

In doing so, Inkumsah articulated a vision of urban planning as both infra/structure and experience. Likewise, in revising the 1944 plan the authors sought to integrate 'local knowledge acquired in the recording of day-to-day development over the last twelve years, the rise in the standard of living, the greater importance of the motor vehicle and up-to-date techniques of planning' (Inkumsah, 1958) – producing a plan that was, at least tacitly, both local and global. However, as Town Planning Adviser W. H. Barrett (1958) noted in the preface, the plan represented 'a modest design to improve present conditions and to give scope for future development to be carried out in a manner fitting to the dignity of a capital city which is also practical and economically feasible'. In other words, the plan was an effectively a continuation of/improvement on the vision already in place for the city, simultaneously capitalizing on the 'present political buoyancy and enthusiasm of the public' for urban development and modernization, while tempering expectations of a brand new capital city that would saddle the country with unrealistic financial burdens (Barratt, 1958).

As a plan rooted in colonial models of spatial control, 'Accra: A Plan for the Town' provided both a resource and a challenge for the newly independent country's leaders. It was, in many ways, a reflection of the limitations of Nkrumah's vision for the nation – limitations that chafed in the context of constant calls for 'shared sacrifice' (Hart, 2013). While some degree of debate was tolerated and even encouraged, the party increasingly policed serious opposition by arresting under the Preventive Detention Act those who did not agree with 'the political conscious leadership', as well as reinforcing ideological purity through mass education and mandatory membership in cross-cutting organizations that sought to undermine the influence of 'tribal, regional and other communal ideological influences which are penetrating the ranks of the more backward Party membership' (Skinner, 2011: 303–6). Nkrumahist decolonization was, in other words, neither a project of grassroots development nor a process of conceptual decolonization. In its materialist focus, Nkrumahism arguably (and perhaps inadvertently) reinforced the more structural, intellectual and spatial legacies of the colonial project, embracing a language of modernism and developmentalism now re-cast through modern social science.

As Quayson (2014) notes, the large financial cost of such redevelopment combined with the fiscal challenges faced by the newly independent government inhibited attempts to fundamentally redevelopment the city's downtown core, echoing the British government's financial struggles in the 1930s and 1940s. Beyond this, the discontent of Ga residents in Bukom highlighted fundamental tensions in

Nkrumahist visions of national development. Nkrumah's evocation of an 'African personality' and calls for decolonization and community self-help rang hollow for many residents, as the government invested large sums in prestige projects that privileged industrial production and provided tax breaks for foreign companies at the expense of African farmers and other entrepreneurs (see Miescher, 2012).

In the old Ga quarters of the city, these strategies were, in many ways, not new. For residents of old Accra, spatial planning was part of a century-long contestation over urban space, articulated through both indigenous and colonial politics. Colonial urban interventions intensified in the 1940s as British officials embraced a new form of 'development colonialism' designed to make their colonies more self-sufficient (Acquah, 1958: 31; Ahlman, 2012: 89). In the face of persistent urban migration, much of this development in the Gold Coast was targeted at cities such as Accra, which were experiencing an urban boom driven by more expansive educational opportunities and the return of highly trained ex-servicemen who had distinguished themselves in the Second World War (Ahlman, 2012: 88–9). By 1954, the population of Accra had more than tripled from 61,558 in 1931 to 192,047 (Acquah, 1958: 31).

For urban migrants, the city held the promise of opportunity, wealth and status (McCaskie, 2001; Hart, 2016). Films such as *The Boy Kumasenu* dramatized both the city's temptations and dangers. Colonial officials and chiefs alike sought to limit urban migration throughout the 1950s, mobilizing warnings about the dangers of city life in order to emphasize the importance of community and stability and ward off urban delinquency and criminality. While such stories did little to dissuade urban migrants from joining vehicles travelling to Accra, the young men and women arriving in the city were often disappointed, faced as they were with labour and housing markets that failed to keep up with the rapidly expanding population. This urban migration placed new pressures on land and opportunity in a place that Accra's Ga residents had long considered 'theirs'. Ga men and women competed with migrants for jobs, housing and land – a form of economic and social marginalization that undermined the power and influence of Ga people in the city, in turn raising questions about their place in the new nation. For many, Nkrumah's inability (or unwillingness) to address the challenges facing Ga communities represented a new, more enraging form of failure and government neglect, particularly given the power Ga residents had long leveraged in shaping the politics of Accra as both a town and colonial capital.

Ga members of the CPP sent a petition to Nkrumah in January 1956 protesting Akan dominance and warning of a 'feeling in the Ga-Adangme area' that 'gathers and engenders a ferment for an eruption likely to blow up any time' (Austin, 1964: 373–5). A mere five months after independence (and only a few months before the release of the new town plan for Accra), Ga people gathered in Bukom Square in Central Accra (Nkrumah's own constituency) to elect leaders for a new non-political association: the Ga-Adangbe Shifimo Kpee. The organization's aim was to restore resources, respect and opportunity to Ga people and challenge Akan ethnic dominance in the political and economic sphere, with its slogans – '*Ga shikpon gamei anoni*' ('Ga land for the Gas') and '*Gboi mli gbweo*' ('The strangers are crushing us') (Austin, 1964: 373–5) – highlighting the centrality of land and spatial politics to the broader political concerns of Accra's residents. News coverage of the association and political propaganda describing the group in the aftermath of protests and arrests in 1957 often cast its membership as 'Tokyo Joes' – unemployed or underemployed youth associated with urban criminality.[15] While a wide range of Ga society was represented among Shifimo Kpee's members, many – including founder and widely recognized leader Attoh Quarshie – worked regular government jobs. In condemning groups such as Shifimo Kpee for engaging in 'hooliganism, terrorism and subversive action', the Nkrumah government highlighted the continued importance of spatial politics in the city. This was no mere social protest – it was, in the eyes of the new government, a political threat. Localized Ga demands for greater representation, opportunity and investment seemed, in light of the government's national development priorities, to undermine the stability and order of the new nation. In November 1958, forty-three members of the political opposition – including Attoh Quarshie – were arrested for plotting a coup.[16]

The spatial violence and persistent spatial inequality against which the members of Shifimo Kpee were protesting were perhaps inadvertently written into and reinforced by the plan for the postcolonial capital. Like its colonial predecessors, 'Accra: A Plan for the Town' created new moral and legal definitions/frameworks that sought to reshape both the urban form and the everyday practices of urban life. In regulating and reforming the economic and social manifestations of spatial practice, the plan effectively politicized these practices within new postcolonial regimes of power. As the Nkrumah government cracked down on political opposition, demanding new forms of obedience and self-sacrifice in the name of national development, so the resistance urban residents had deployed in the colonial context became increasingly criminalized. Furthermore, inconsistent implementation of the plan and the ambiguities and contradictions of Nkrumah's development agenda made it increasingly difficult to navigate the terrain of postcolonial politics. The significance of regulatory frameworks, as well as the relationship between morality and legality, changed significantly both during and immediately after Nkrumah's reign. As a result, new forms of 'managing' were needed within the shifting postcolonial political and economic landscape.

The persistence of debates surrounding what it meant to create a postcolonial 'African' city highlighted the tension between the rhetoric of decolonization and the policy realities of modernization. Common narratives of postcolonial Ghana's history and politics tell a story of African elites taking up old roles in the 'gatekeeper state' established under colonial rule, embracing modernism and modernization as forms of social and economic transformation before using them to justify the marginalization of poor people and the protection of their own interests (Cooper, 2002: 156–90). It is, in other words, a narrative of corruption. Events such as the destruction of Makola Market, for example, seem to exemplify this process (Robertson, 1983). Ayi Kwei Armah's novel *The Beautyful Ones Are Not Yet Born* dramatizes the ways in which government leaders and citizens alike sought to secure and preserve their interests in Nkrumah's Ghana. Likewise, in the midst of Jerry John Rawlings's 'housecleaning exercises' and anti-corruption campaigns of the late 1970s and 1980s, stories circulated of military officers using their positions to secure special access and protection for their girlfriends and wives, who then used this political cover to sell goods outside of price control regulations. While it is easy to dismiss these acts as 'corruption', such a narrative obscures the complicated structural and systemic inequalities of the postcolony. Amidst widespread economic decline, entrepreneurial market women and drivers – who dominated the country's so-called 'informal economy' while often being criminalized as profiteers and pirates – expanded and reinforced established practices of 'managing'. They frequently did so, however, through the help of well-placed elites, who were also seeking to profit from the instability and uncertainty of the time, and so gain greater security for themselves and their families.[17]

This economic and political analysis has huge consequences for how we understand postcolonial cities like Accra. Dominant historical narratives about the history of colonialism cast cities as sites of resistance, with local residents creating or reinterpreting spatial, social, cultural and economic practices as forms of resistance to an imposed political order. In the postcolony, triumphal narratives of independence and decolonization obscure the realities of ongoing 'managing', articulated in response to persistent modernist assumptions about spatial regulation, infrastructure and urban culture. The various regimes in power during the turbulent 1960s–80s period all attempted to address issues of dependency and Western exploitation inscribed in both local- and global-level political institutions and economic networks. In doing so, however, they largely ignored the ways in which these processes were built into the very infrastructures and built forms of the city itself.

Urban models, marginalization and the politics of the present

The urban politics of the present echo these historical trends, even as they reflect the new realities of the global political economy. On 15 January 2010, development economist Jeffrey Sachs declared Accra a 'Millennium City', promising partnerships and support through Columbia University's Earth Institute aimed at helping Ghana achieve the benchmarks set out in the MDGs. Accra was, once again, at the centre of development visions. As Sachs observed, 'If Accra flourishes Ghana and West Africa would do the same' (GhanaWeb, 2010). Though the Earth Institute would partner with the Accra Metropolitan Assembly (AMA) to provide technical support, government would, he noted, have to take the lead. The Earth Institute's own reports on the Millennium Cities Initiative in Accra highlighted the need to address the 'specific challenges facing this rapidly burgeoning city', with their research addressing issues at the core of the MDGs – health, public infrastructure and environmental sustainability – alongside issues of land use policy, mapping and urban planning.

In setting out the MDGs, the United Nations called on member countries to 'meet the needs of the world's poorest'.[18] However, the commentary of local and national leaders in Accra raised questions about how these policies would manifest in the city. At the 2010 launch of the Millennium Cities Initiative, First Lady Ernestina Naadu Mills told residents that 'some actions taken by the AMA could inconvenient some of them but they should be undertaken to ensure the initiative succeeded and made the capital city a cleaner, safer, healthier and stress free' (GhanaWeb, 2010). Even as Mayor Alfred Vanderpuije promised to use this opportunity to make the city more 'people-friendly', he noted that 'the development of unplanned settlements in Old Fadama, Nima and Maamobi, the rising slums in Chorkor through James Town, development of unauthorised structures in some parts of the city and encroachment of public lands' were central challenges facing the AMA (GhanaWeb, 2010). He went on to declare, 'The new Accra is to see the end of further slum development while existing slums would be upgraded. Although it would affect some people, we call for cooperation' (GhanaWeb, 2010). The urban poor, in other words, were expected to accommodate the new changes, which would supposedly 'make Accra a modern city with the provision of utilities daily, good environment and unlettered roads, effective drainage system, healthy private and public toilets, disciplined people, effective transportation, modern hospital to meet the challenges of the time and effective housing programme to meet the accommodation needs of the people' (GhanaWeb, 2010).

In cities across the continent, urban (re)development efforts are informed by a politics of displacement that draw on visions of 'the good city' and 'the good citizen' (Byerley, 2011). In re-centring the city in development discourse, global development visions such as the aspirational MDGs and SDGs draw on much older urban spatial politics. Vanderpuije's language of discipline echoes both Nkrumahist self-sacrifice and colonial-era cultures of regulation and reform, connecting the politics of the present to a long history of contestation over urban redevelopment and reform among politicians, practitioners and urban residents. Much like these earlier models, more recent neoliberal redevelopment articulates an aspirational vision for a 'modern' city, anchoring a nation and its broader region within global economic and cultural flows. Following structural adjustment and neoliberal retrenchment, however, redevelopment is increasingly in the hands of private investors, who in attempting to reshape urban life draw on both their privileged access to government and elite strategies of 'managing'.

The vast majority of this investment in the 'new Accra' has been made manifest through the rapid increase in residential and commercial construction projects across the city, funded by international property developers and real-estate speculators. The city is inundated with construction projects, from high-rise office buildings and skyscrapers to planned 'communities' and new shopping malls. Some – 'Kente Tower', 'Gold Coast City', 'Adinkra Heights', 'Switchback Park', 'Appolonia', 'Cantonments City', 'Jamestown Boxing School' – evoke the city's rich cultural and economic history, while a select few – 'Point of No Return' in Tema and a new Ghanaian National Museum on Slavery and Freedom – engage directly with such history though creating sites for historical reflection and, undoubtedly, tourist dollars. Other projects highlight the global aspirations that informed their planning, with names such as 'Riviera Residence', 'Infinity Tower', 'Accra Twin

Towers' and 'Hope City'. Still others evoke whichever corporations – Unibank, Ecobank, MTN – the new construction will house.[19]

These sparkling new projects are designed by innovative, award-winning young architects from within and outside the continent. They are going up alongside a slightly older set of buildings – such as the World Trade Center Accra or Accra Mall – whose worn appearance belies their central role in kicking off what feels like a real-life Monopoly game (an Accra version of which is currently for sale at Accra Mall and other high-end retail shops around the city).[20] As an early investor in the city, AttAfrica partnered with Ghanaian businessman Joseph Owusu-Akyaw to build Accra Mall, the first US-style shopping mall in Ghana. Ghana, it appears, is being transformed into a regional anchor of consumer culture and economic exchange. According to the company:

> The Accra Mall is fulfilling a regional function and is strategically situated in close proximity of established residential and business areas in Accra. The Accra Mall offers high accessibility at the intersection of major roads and is located on the main Trans West Africa route that connects Ghana with Togo and the Ivory Coast.[21]

AttAfrica – a Mauritius-based company that focuses on 'investing, developing, and acquiring A-grade shopping centres in key sub-Saharan African markets excluding South Africa'[22] – has continued to expand its reach in Accra, developing the upscale West Hills Mall in the western suburb of New Weija, as well as the Achimota Shopping Centre. It is also behind a number of other new projects, all situated near the city's most affluent residential districts.

On the surface, these construction projects seem to be a realization of the promise of 'A New Accra for a Better Ghana'. Here, the 'new Accra' reflects an embracing of 'new urbanism' tenets among the city's developer class and policy elites. Glittery buildings, sleek architectural designs, upscale shops and sustainable landscaping anchor new developments that promise 'walkable blocks and streets, housing and shopping in close proximity, and accessible public spaces'.[23] While new urbanism casts itself as a rejection of modernism, these movements share a belief in the importance of the built form and its ability to reshape behaviour by creating new parameters for urban life, articulated through models and principles and enacted through urban plans (Vanderbeek and Irazabal, 2007; Hirst, 2009).

Developers are proposing not just buildings but communities. Devtraco Plus, Ltd, which is developing the East Cantonments Village property on 8.9 acres in the middle of one of the city's wealthiest and most desirable districts, says that its vision is to 'create a liveable, walkable, sustainable development with a strong identity. The development at East Cantonments is to be one of the well-planned, mixed-use developments with an international appeal mimicking the Buckhead Atlanta project, or similar, in Georgia, USA'.[24] The project includes plans for apartments, townhouses, a sports facility, a hotel, retail units and boutique offices. Such properties are not geared towards low-income residents or even, in fact, Ghanaians. As Devtraco boast, 'It is expected to attract the highest calibre of persons across the globe and retain its ambiance, relevance, and functionality over 100 years'. This is certainly a vision of design that 'transcends the ordinary' in Accra, attracting a business and young executive class who supposedly have a 'passion for beauty, serenity, and power, and place a value on convenient living' and an emergent middle class who are 'discerning in their taste and style'. Townhouses have rooftop infinity pools, residences are insulated from the noise of the street, and jogging paths cut through the development. More than a mere refiguring of space and spatial practice, however, this vision for a sustainable community of tasteful, powerful global citizens effectively represents a spatial occupation by the capitalist class. 'New Accra' is, apparently, an empty playground for cosmopolitan urban imaginaries, unmoored from the realities of the vast majority of city residents even as it claims to cultivate community.

Vanessa Watson (2013) argues that these developments represent new forms of 'African urban fantasies' driven primarily by real-estate speculation across the continent. Excitement over Africa as the 'last development frontier' arising from the continent's rapid rates of urbanization and strong economic growth numbers – in contrast to the saturation of urban land and development in Asia and the lacklustre housing markets of the West – has attracted international property developers eager to invest in cities like Accra. While these investments are most visible in the construction projects that increasingly mark the city skyline, Watson notes, 'the proposed new urban master plans for many of Africa's larger cities are now to be found on the websites of international architectural, engineering and property development companies' (2013: 215). They are, in other words, shaping both the form and substance of cities like Accra, presenting revived and reinvented visions of modernism, now touted as eco-cities or smart cities.

This 'new urbanism' seems to place African urban redevelopment in conversation with movements elsewhere in the world – for example, the rhetoric surrounding 'new Accra' sounds remarkably similar to conversations about 'new Detroit'. However, as Watson argues, in modelling the future visions of these cities on Dubai, Singapore or Shanghai, new urban master plans 'depart even further from African urban reality than did the post-colonial zoning plans' (2013: 215). While new urbanism's focus on creating walkable, sustainable development is in theory modelled on the inclusiveness of the village, in practice it has created an omnibus of planning models, some of which have become hegemonic. For example, the focus on bus rapid transit in urban plans, to the exclusion of local mobility systems/solutions and other possible technological alternatives, has been a waste of scant resources in many cities like Accra. Moreover, it has diverted attention from the central issues facing mobile urban residents. Driven by the interests of private corporations and Western urban planners, these models take on imperialistic overtones (Abourahme, 2018). To an extent mirroring critiques of gentrification, the preference for more expensive Western models marginalizes the majority of urban residents who cannot afford access to new housing developments, transit systems and other amenities.

The slick design of these new developments, the affluence of their residents, and the cosmopolitan appeal of the cupcake stores, boutiques, art galleries and coffee shops surrounding them have attracted the attention of government officials and international journalists alike. Not unlike the attention given to Accra as the capital of Britain's 'model colony' or the new capital of the 'black star of Africa', Accra has now been branded Africa's 'capital of cool' – part of a new cultural and economic resurgence on the continent, with its own global investors, stylists and tastemakers (Lobrano, 2016). However, this language of cosmopolitan 'cool-ness' and the rapid growth of a new oil economy obscures a much more complicated urban politics. These changes are unevenly distributed and embraced in the city, with official and journalistic commentary rarely reflecting on who is left out in the 'new Accra'. Such unresolved questions of inclusion and marginalization are connected to the much longer histories of precolonial urbanism, colonial planning and postcolonial modernization discussed earlier. The rapid pace of construction and the remarkable consistency of developer plans and architectural styles are driven by global tastes and investor preferences. The city has no current and coherent urban master plan.[25]

In carving out their visions for the city, these developers participate in elite variations of managing. While scholarship on African urbanism tends to focus on the actions of lower-class residents who are often excluded or marginalized in government plans, the city's affluent neighbourhoods – such as Ridge, Cantonments, Spintex, Airport Residential, Dzorwulu, East Legon – also evidence the varying ways that urban residents have shaped city life. Some of these neighbourhoods have their roots in colonial plans, drawing prestige from their historical connection to European residences in colonial segregation planning – for example, the quintessentially British colonial urban form of Cantonments, or the larger projects and grander structures of Ridge, Dzorwulu and Airport Residential are planned neighbourhoods that emerged after independence, growing up around prestige sites such as Kotoka International Airport or the University of Ghana. Others, such as Spintex, are recent additions, more directly connected to the recent spate of urban redevelopment.

Today, Spintex looks much like the rest of these neighbourhoods, with relatively well-maintained roads, expensive houses and heavy concentrations of upscale retail and services. In fact, the neighbourhood emerged in the early 2000s (notably, around the same time that the Accra Mall was under construction) when wealthy Accra residents began building large homes on vacant land alongside the Accra–Tema Motorway – an area zoned for industrial rather than residential use, for which approval had not been granted by government. Widespread condemnation did not halt construction. While more informal settlements (often labelled 'slums') are liable to be cleared by bulldozers should residents fail to heed government warnings about building in flood plains or un-zoned parts of the city, in this case the Accra government was unable to demolish the large concrete homes of some of Accra's wealthiest and most powerful residents. Instead, residents carved out their own road and later put pressure on government to pave it.

New developments sprinkled throughout the city's centre and its sprawling suburbs and hinterlands engage in a similar form of elite managing when it comes to negotiating competing claims to land, inadequate infrastructure provisions and municipal bureaucracy. Many local property owners, particularly in popular elite neighbourhoods such as Osu and Cantonments, seem eager to cash in on the new property boom. In Osu, popular spots such as Bywell Bar have been torn down to make way for new developments. Other property owners have chosen to refurbish colonial-era buildings into hotels and Airbnb rentals, drawing on colonial nostalgia to market their properties. Other expats or returnees have set up roadside cocktail bars, live music venues and private clubs that draw on the ubiquitous material culture of the city's lower classes while simultaneously remaining out of their reach. The new members-only club Front/Back, for example, asks members to enter through a shipping container identical (on the outside) to those regularly targeted by the city for removal around markets. The club is decorated with roadside mirrors, local toys and recycled materials central to the life of the street, and yet the exorbitant membership fees exclude all but Accra's most elite residents, who use the space to network and play. A recording of Ngugi reading *Things Fall Apart* plays on repeat in the bathroom, while Chimamanda Adichie novels sit on the shelves alongside books about Ghanaian art and critiques of development culture.

By marshalling the language of sustainability and casting these forms of urban development as incontestable, developers seem to circumvent public debate – consultation is rendered unnecessary and governments are pressured to accommodate the interests of the developer class (Watson, 2013: 226). The drive for sustainable cities marks the urban poor's settlements as 'uninhabitable', and so subject to demolition and displacement. Much of this land is seized and sold to property developers who promise modern, cosmopolitan communities that draw on local cultures even as they seek to transcend them (Simone, 2019: 24).

Accra residents cannot help but notice the stark differences between the privileged managing of elites and the criminalized managing of the city's lower classes, with such disjunctures spawning new forms of protest about inadequate infrastructure, government corruption and economic inequality. In 2016, frequent blackouts and load-shedding – nicknamed '*dumsor*' – provoked widespread protest in the city, as well as criticism of the former president, John Mahama. Meanwhile, the new president, Nana Akuffo Addo, has been criticized for being a member of the national elite, disconnected from the concerns of the masses and too willing to embrace neoliberalism. A 2018 military cooperation agreement with the US sparked 'Ghana First' protests in Accra (Yeboah, 2018), with citizens engaging in a vibrant debate about the city's sanitation and trash services following the claim by Dr Joseph Siaw Agyepong, CEO of Zoomlion Ghana (a private contractor hired by the government to provide trash removal services), that 'when you look on the streets now, everywhere is clean, everywhere is neat' (Larnyoh, 2018). That same week, journalists reported the popular Kaneshie market had been turned into a garbage dump due to surrounding communities having no access to refuse containers, dumping sites or trash removal services (GhanaStar, 2018). These protests mark yet another form of continuity within the longer history of urban politics. And yet, as AbdouMaliq Simone notes, the abstracted, decontextualized, transnational nature of contemporary urban development has highlighted the limits of refusal among the city's working classes (2019: 23). It is difficult to adapt and improvise in an urban landscape where you simply cannot afford to exist.

Even so, amidst these processes that seemingly exacerbate income inequalities, there appears to be an emerging creative working class capable of moving between these apparently disconnected spheres. When Accra Mall opened in 2008, it was widely regarded as a luxury space, with the high-end boutiques and global brands – such as Puma and Samsung – that filled the mall's smaller units inaccessible to all but Ghana's wealthiest. People clearly went to the mall to be seen, dressing up in their finest clothes, gathering with friends and family in the food court and hallways, proudly carrying bags that displayed their purchases. These public displays to some degree transcended class. While the electronics and jewellery stores catered to an elite class, they operated alongside Ghanaian brands such as Woodin, Kiki and Nallem, or more affordable South African stores such as Truworths or Mr Price. People from all class backgrounds picked up treats at Shoprite, checked their email at the Busy Internet kiosk, and ate meals at the fast food restaurants dominating the open-air food court. The transport options around the mall reflect this diverse clientele, from the large parking lot full of private cars to the bustling taxi rank to the busy trotro stop on Independence Avenue. When I visited Accra Mall on Valentine's Day 2009, I was struck by how quickly Ghanaians had embraced the mall as a site of celebration and socialization. Elite men and women came to watch movies in the luxury theatre or eat an expensive meal in the fancy new restaurant that served 'continental cuisine'. In doing so, they rubbed shoulders with lower-class patrons, decked out in their best suits and dresses, taking in the ambiance while sharing a plate of fried chicken and rice from Chicken Inn or a bar of local Kingsbite chocolate purchased at Shoprite.

In getting caught up in Accra Mall's slick 'newness' and seeming Westernization, I missed some fundamental historical continuities, which make the cross-class interactions seen at the mall less surprising. The act of consumption – of goods, food, drinks, culture – was certainly not new in Accra. Open-air markets, drinking spots, chop bars and highlife clubs were part of a long history of social, cultural and economic exchange both in Accra and across the country, connecting elite stores like Kingsway and Woolworths with the infamous Makola Market, and elite dance clubs with roadside bars of the late nineteenth and early twentieth century (see Plageman, 2013; Murillo, 2017). Even as Accra Mall seemed to play up its modern, cosmopolitan aesthetic, its siting suggested that its developers understood it as a space of interaction. In much the same way that people from all over the city used to flock to Oxford Street on Friday and Saturday nights to get popcorn and ice cream from Frankie's, or grab a beer or some chicken at one of the more affordable restaurants along the commercial strip, people now celebrate birthdays at KFC or Pizza Hut and take trotros to the ultra-modern West Hills Mall, where they can drink relatively affordable coffees and smoothies while walking around the upscale shops and fancy fountains in air-conditioned comfort. These spaces serve as backdrops for carefully curated selfies and social media posts, designed on computers and mobile phones charged up in generator-fuelled cafes and restaurants. Their patrons' modern style is crafted from carefully curated second-hand clothing/shoe/accessory purchases and locally produced fashion.

There are, of course, limits to this narrative of inclusiveness and interaction. Not all spaces are equally democratic, and lower-class patrons are much more likely to visit Shoprite or Woodin than a luxury jewellery store with Gwyneth Paltrow's picture prominently displayed on the wall – if nothing else because those luxury spaces seem to require modes of behaviour and dress that signal privilege, confidence, or both. In a space defined by cash and consumption, such distinctions are not just inevitable but essential. Luxury shopping malls may well be the bellwether for the 'new Accra' – the space where urban citizens envision what De Boeck calls the 'near future', a vision that 'hyphenates dream and reality; a plan predicated on incremental transformation rather than destructive, radical, exclusionary change' (2011: 76). In doing so, these citizens once again seek to reframe the processes of informalization that render them invisible and cast their homes as uninhabitable – simultaneously reshaping and reinforcing the speculative destruction and inherent volatility of urban life (Simone, 2019: 24).

African pasts and urban futures

In his introduction to *Under Siege*, Okwui Enwezor argues that African cities 'are collision points between tradition and modernity, between African development and external pressures; the new site for the reformulation of old and new influences, and the opportunity for the symbolic production of post-colonial identities'. While Enwezor acknowledges that 'as a consequence of their colonial legacy, many African cities still remain administrative systems, although disconnected from the city dynamics', he goes on to argue:

> the syntax of these cities today is not defined by the 'modern' grammar inherited from colonialism, nor by the assumption of an organic connection between individual and collective memory, of testimonies and beliefs. In these cities, where everything is interpreted and outlined by the apparent chaos of the everyday, where forms of self-organising procedures, parallel and informal economies, and the resilience and inventiveness of urban dwellers have relentlessly kept many cities still functional.
>
> (2002: 6–7)

Enwezor's assertion of the disconnection between administration and the realities of everyday life represents an attempt to grapple with the failures of urban governance and the ubiquity of alternative systems of social, political and economic order, often glossed over as the 'informal sector'. In focusing on the syntax of African cities, Enwezor seeks to understand what these cities actually *are* – not as failures or aberrations or sites of incompleteness, but on their own terms. In doing so, he is part of a much wider scholarly conversation about the parameters of 'southern urbanism' that seeks to place the 'informal city' at the centre of policy debates and scholarly analysis.

As the history of Accra's urban politics demonstrates, an exclusive focus on the urban poor and the persistent use of 'informality' as a frame of analysis obscures more fundamental questions about the systemic, structural violence of the built form and the power of spatial politics – specifically, the processes of informalization and practices through which urban residents have sought to reshape urban politics to represent their interests; 'a real, living city which exists as a heterogeneous urban conglomeration through the bodies, movements, practices and discourses of urban dwellers' (De Boeck, 2011: 81). In Accra, this politics cuts across class, with rich and poor residents alike seeking to make space and opportunities for themselves in a city that was and is increasingly not built or planned with their interests in mind. DIY urbanism and its more local articulation of 'managing' help us to understand the systemic/structural conditions shaping urban inequality and underdevelopment in cities like Accra. In doing, they direct attention towards possible alternative models and visions for the city, rooted in local understandings of space, infrastructure, technology and community. At the same time, however, they highlight a complicated contemporary politics in which 'Westernization' often stands in for 'formal', thereby privileging citizens of means, criminalizing the urban poor and perpetuating imperialistic systems of urban underdevelopment.

Notes

1   The sign in Jamestown was painted for the 'Accra we dey' organization. They have also commissioned artists to paint the sign elsewhere in the city – for example, at the Tetteh Quarshie interchange. To learn more about Accra we Dey, visit their Tumblr site (http://accrawedey.tumblr.com/) or listen to their podcast (https://soundcloud.com/accrawedey).

2   For more detailed discussions of this politics, see Parker (2000); Quayson (2014).

3   See also The National Archives (TNA): Public Record Office (PRO), ref: CO 96/769/1, 1940, 'Earthquake: Restoration of Accra' (the TNA: PRO catalogue can be found at https://discovery.nationalarchives.gov.uk/browse).

4   TNA: PRO, ref: CO 96/691/8, 1929, 'Public Lands Ordinance 1929'.

5   TNA: PRO, ref: CO 99/8, 1893–1894 'Government Gazette'.

6   TNA: PRO, ref: CO 96/740/1, 1937, 'Municipal Affairs: Petition by the ratepayers of Accra regarding the appointment of Mr D McDougall as Town Clerk'.

7   Modernist planning in the Gold Coast, influenced by architects Maxwell Fry and Jane Drew, was part of a broader modernist movement. At the centre of that movement was the Congres d'Internationaux Architecture Moderne (CIAM), which sought to bring together disparate strands of modernist practice, including colonial modernism (or what later became known as 'tropical modernism'). Fry and Drew were heavily influenced by CIAM architects, with Fry one of the founding members of the Modern Architectural Research Group (MARS), which was formed to represent Great Britain at CIAM meetings (Holston, 1989: 39; Winterhalter, 2015: 34).

8   These practices were not unique to the Gold Coast. Rather, planners, architects and administrators sought to implement models that grew out of experiences and

practices elsewhere in the empire, as well as general principles of planning, public health and architectural design (see, for example, Nightingale, 2012; Mayne, 2017).

9   Bissell argues that these contradictions were a reflection and consequence of colonial bureaucratic and administrative incompetence.

10 Public Records and Archives Administration Department: National Archives of Ghana (Accra), ref: CSO 14/1/78, 1934, 'Public Works Extraordinary Estimates 1935–1936'; PRAAD: NAG (Accra), ref: CSO 14/2/115, 1932–1935, 'Roads in Accra – Drainage and Maintenance of'; PRAAD: NAG (Accra), ref: CSO 14/2/102, 1931 'Town Roads – Payment by Town Councils toward upkeep of'. See also: Hart (2016: 58).

11 See, for example: PRAAD: NAG (Accra), ref: CSO 14/2/115, 1932–35, 'Roads in Accra – Drainage and Maintenance of'; PRAAD: NAG (Accra), ref: CSO, 14/2/205, 1943–44, 'Accra – Maintenance of town roads: Coast of maintenance of Winneba Road and Guggisberg Avenue, Accra'.

12 TNA: PRO, ref: CO 964/22, 1948, 'Correspondence with Accra Town Council'.

13 Convention People's Party, *Programme of the Convention People's Party for Work and Happiness* (Ministry of Information and Broadcasting: Accra), 1962: 4.

14 *Programme of the Convention People's Party for Work and Happiness*, 4.

15 See, for example, the following *Daily Graphic* articles: '"Our jeep was stoned" … witness tells court', 13 September 1957; 'A crowd of about 500 attacked me at Bukom Constable tells court', 17 September 1957; 'The Bukom Square incident: Police identify 10 men in court', 20 September 1957; 'I drove Fulani and others to Chorkor Beach', 3 October 1957; 'Magistrate reserves judgement', 23 October 1957; 'Twelve CPP members granted bail', 22 November 1957; 'Man said he had orders to kill us – Thompson', 17 December 1958.

16 See following *Daily Graphic* articles: 'Being arrested: PM Issues statement on "assassination" and "plot to overthrow govt"', 11 November 1958; 'Allegations against the 43', 17 November 1958; 'Zenith 7 organized Tokyo Joe group', 1959; 'Attoh Quarshie in Ussher Fort', 1959.

17 For more information on this time period and the politics of survival and accumulation, see Clark (1995); Hart (2016: 121–48).

18 'Millennium Development Goals and Beyond 2015', United Nations, www.un.org/millenniumgoals/.

19 To see images of these project plans, visit https://talkingdrumsblog.wordpress.com/2015/01/02/largest-african-ethnic-groups-or-nationalities-in-america/.

20 Playing Accra Monopoly feels like you're jumping feet first into the development game in the city. Versions of the game have apparently been developed for cities elsewhere on the continent, including Lagos and Cairo, with cooperative licensing from Monopoly's parent company, Hasbro.

21 'Accra Mall', AttAfrica, www.attafrica.com/properties/accra (accessed 2 April 2018).

22 'Company Profile', AttAfrica, www.attafrica.com/.

23 'What is New Urbanism?', Congress for the New Urbanism, www.cnu.org/resources/what-new-urbanism (accessed 2 April 2018).

24 'East Cantonments Village', Infinite Groups, Ltd., http://infinitegroupltd.com/east-cantonments-village/ (accessed 2 April 2018).

25 The last strategic plan, developed through the United Nations Development Programme (UNDP), was published in 1991. For links to that plan, see http://mci.ei.columbia.edu/millennium-cities/accra-ghana/additional-research-on-accra/.

Chapter 8

EVERYDAY SPATIAL PRACTICES AND PRODUCTION OF URBAN COMMONS IN ACCRA, GHANA

Victoria Okoye

Introduction

This chapter explores urban commoning as a process through which residents of Ga Mashie in the West African city of Accra, Ghana, self-organize (operate on their own) to meet their everyday needs. Ga Mashie is an indigenous and a densely-populated neighbourhood situated on Accra's coast between the Korle Lagoon and the city's central business district. It is one of several historic neighbourhoods in Accra, a city shaped by multiple migrations and migrant communities into an ethnically heterogenous urban area (Agyei-Mensah and Owusu, 2010). Similar to many other working-class neighbourhoods in Accra and other Ghanaian cities, its streets, buildings and open spaces are subject to a multiplicity of uses. The way in which space is used as an essential, shared resource in Ga Mashie highlights the disjuncture that can be seen in Global South cities between residents' everyday spatial practices and government visions of market-oriented, neoliberal urban modernity, as embodied in exclusive gated communities, high-income neighbourhoods, and 'world-class' commercial districts and complexes (Porter, 2011; Kuttler and Jain, 2015; Chen et al., 2018).

The concept of commoning has a long history and, until recently, was largely theorized on the basis of rural experiences of sharing natural resources. However, global and political urban crises have stimulated interest in alternative market models and state approaches to meeting human needs. In many postcolonial cities, collusion between the government and private sector has resulted in the majority of residents, particularly the urban poor, being excluded from key resources in terms of livelihood, shelter and social protections (Watson, 2009). Streets and open spaces are essential urban spaces for those who dwell in African cities, particularly the poor, who rely on these spaces for livelihood resources (Gillespie, 2015; Obeng-Odoom, 2018). Beyond this, residents demand and produce these spaces as urban commons for a vast spectrum of activities, including but not limited to recreational, social, religious and cultural practices.

The commons refer to the relationship between a defined social group and the social or physical environment on which their lives or livelihoods depend (Harvey, 2012), manifested as the interrelation between social or physical resources held in common, the social and spatial practices of commoning, and communities (Kip et al., 2015). This chapter explores urban commoning by focusing on Ga Mashie residents' self-organized spatial practices. In doing so, it utilizes historical context, examples of residents' spatial and social practices, and reflections from various urban actors. This chapter argues that urban commoning provides a means of exploring local orientations to space, as well as individual and collective transformation processes. These responses are grounded in tradition and historical influences, and therefore complicate globalization and the commodification of space as the dominant narratives governing local urban realities. This analysis draws on the concept of self-organization, described by Nonbogu and Korah in their work on everyday spatial practices in two slum communities in Accra: 'self-organising systems are not guided by external forces, but by the internal forces and interactions within the larger system (city, community) and what the system has to do in order to survive' (2016: 425). As such, this chapter is part of a growing body of research that privileges place-based narratives and urban residents' everyday social practices as a means of interpreting contemporary urbanization in African cities.

Urban and historical context

Accra, a rapidly urbanizing metropolitan area of more than two million residents, is a globalizing and regional hub of financial and economic activity. At the same time, the vast majority of its residents are the urban poor, who on a daily basis self-organize their housing, employment and social opportunities outside of government-recognized systems. This urban majority – who have limited to non-existent access to adequate and affordable housing, as well as services such as water, electricity, and sewage disposal – must make use of the available resources in their urban space to address their unmet needs. Consequently, the urban inequalities embedded within Accra's urbanization processes produce continual demands for urban commons, which poor residents appropriate to meet their individual and collective interests (Harvey, 2012; Gillespie, 2015).

Ga Mashie's history of commoning as it has traditionally been conceived provides crucial context to the contemporary practice of urban commoning. Oral history traces Ga Mashie's origins as far back as the thirteenth century, when it formed part of a series of Ga towns and village settlements situated along a 40-mile expanse of flat grassland stretching inland from the coast.[1] The Ga Mashie settlement included fishing villages and ownership of inland farming villages (Sackeyfio, 2012; Quayson, 2014), with residents engaged in mining, processing and the small-scale sale of salt, minerals and agricultural products (Mensah, 2014). While Ga Mashie people's conception of land specified family or community authority ownership, it also incorporated communal usage:

Before the advent of colonial rule in the Gold Coast, each of [Ga Mashie's] seven quarters managed the land it occupied along with property considered to be 'hunters' land', originally inhabited by hunter groups. Hunters' land, often located further inland in farming villages, constituted the property of the descendants of hunter groups and families residing in houses or *weku* in the town. Members of the different quarters could farm on any unoccupied land in their quarter of residence without specific permission. Persons who wished to farm or construct homes on specific plots of land obtained permission from the head of the family or house that owned the property. However, those who wished to farm or occupy land that belonged to a different quarter obtained permission from that quarter's chief priest, elders, and other authorities.

Outside of those who held allodial rights in land, other persons had limited rights with regard to utilitarian purposes such as hunting, fishing, cultivation, and building. Subjects or strangers recognised by a political leader could have access to 'unused' lands.

(Sackeyfio, 2012: 296–7)

In each of the seven quarters of Ga Mashie, open spaces served as geographical, social, commercial and political centres of public life. These communal spaces hosted myriad seasonal, periodic and everyday activities, including market trading, ceremonies and other celebrations, religious rituals, cultural events and public executions. The central location of these spaces, sited adjacent to the dwellings of traditional authorities, contributed to community identity while enabling protection and security during times of war.[2] Residential dwellings, internal courtyards and areas in front of dwellings were spaces for household and small-scale economic activity (Mensah, 2014). In this context, these communal sites were early examples of urban commons. Though the spaces had recognized ownership, they were made available to community members as resources for individual, familial and community livelihood, shelter and wellbeing; for public life; and for recognition of community members through the full life cycle, including celebrations of birth, various rites of passage and death.

Colonialism's implantation of western urbanization processes constrained these traditional communal conceptions of space, instead imposing private and public spaces planned and regulated by initially colonial and then postcolonial urban authorities for specified usages. Europeans first arrived in the fifteenth century, building trade linkages with the Ga people and establishing European trading posts around Ga Mashie. Colonial subjugation established the Gold Coast, from which the colonial city of Accra emerged, with a commercial core oriented around the European town and forts, and the James Town port. Key buildings (the lighthouse, multinational company offices, banks, warehouses and merchants' residences), as well as infrastructure and services (the railway terminal, docks and the main commercial High Street), were sited in proximity to the James Fort and Ussher Fort, and colonial planners employed European zoning, building codes, designs and construction materials to achieve a European sense of place (Njoh, 2009; Pierre, 2012). The British colonial government transplanted European spatial ideologies through colonial architecture and planning, and in doing so sought to re-organize spatial and social relations on the ground, thereby subjugating indigenous ways of life.[3] Colonial planners employed modernist planning and design regimes, using the rationale of epidemic and disaster management, as well as commercial, administrative and population control. This approach included residential segregation in order to separate and control populations, residences and movements in the city (Pierre, 2012; Quayson, 2014). The native residential areas inhabited by African populations were largely left to cater to their own needs, until key disasters – most notably the 1908 bubonic plague epidemic and the 1939 earthquake, which devastated key parts of Ga Mashie – enabled colonial planners to use public health as a rationale for a series of 'decongestion' practices. This included razing African dwellings, instituting new colonial infrastructures and establishing new 'planned' residential areas to extend the city (Amarteifio, 2015).

Colonial land-use zoning emphasized the strict segregation of urban space use and certain inhabitants. Outdoor recreation spaces, including the golf course, polo and cricket grounds, were open green areas that formed part of 440-meter 'building free zones' which were designed to enclose European residences from native areas in a colonial planning practice of "de jure segregration" of the races (Pierre, 2012: 27). Recreation activities were limited to parks and green areas, many of which were in European parts of the city. Moreover, many green areas were excluded from such activities and instead used to separate European and African residential areas. Small-scale commercial trading – a central part of community life and practised in communal areas – was relocated to government-planned market structures. Meanwhile, public spaces such as pavements and lorry parks were intended solely for transportation, with any confluence of activities on streets or open spaces framed as a problematic diversion from the plan.

Yet throughout the growing colonial city, Accra's African residents reclaimed urban spaces for locally-oriented commercial, residential and recreational uses that fell outside of top-down colonial and post-independent design schemes. Small-scale commercial traders sought to shift their operations from the communal areas of their dwellings to open areas in communities, such as under trees (Mensah, 2014); vehicle drivers claimed the sides of main roads to park their vehicles in the outer areas of town; young boys employed undeveloped land for 'makeshift' football pitches, while residents self-organized an 'unauthorised development' in the Nima 'slum' neighbourhood and 'slum housing' around urban commercial zones and large workshops. Self-organized commercial activities prevailed as residents set up bus repair depots and other 'non-conforming uses' around markets and lorry parks, while street vendors and hawkers made an unofficial 'overflow' from built market sites onto adjacent streets and throughout the central commercial area (Town and Country Planning Division of the Ministry of Housing, 1958: 23, 46, 58). These instances of urban commoning – again, employing urban spaces as resources to support shelter, livelihood and public life – became framed as unauthorized developments, encroachments, diversions, and misuses of space. This sentiment is captured in the city's strategic plan, published in 1958 (one year after independence) and prepared by expatriate British architects who had been working as colonial architects. Their vision, which was signed off by the country's new president, Kwame Nkrumah, proclaimed that such self-organized uses of space diminished the modern character of a postcolonial city shaped thus far by colonial planning and design:

> Open spaces, particularly in the centre of Accra, are inclined to attract a variety of unauthorised uses. This is particularly so where the open space is not maintained. As much as a site is laid out as gardens and regularly tended the trespassers generally respect it and look for an alternative pitch. In the Supreme Court area the traders have not encroached on to the gardens and the carpenters and booksellers who formerly 'squatted' on the site now occupied by the Aglionby Library and its gardens have moved elsewhere. This reclamation of open space by means of proper laying out and maintenance should however be accompanied by provision for the traders who will otherwise move to other suitable sites and create fresh problems.
> (Town and Country Planning Division of the Ministry of Housing, 1958: 26)

These practices of self-organizing to produce urban commons have intensified since independence, in part due to an absence of government planning oversight. The failure of the state-planned economy and political instability in the 1960s and 1970s led to the closure of factories and other businesses, leading to rising unemployment. Meanwhile, the demolition of the city's largest market (Makola Market) in 1972 displaced hundreds of vendors. Consequently, more and more urban residents turned to small-scale commercial trading – such as street vending and petty trading – as a means of survival, conducting their commerce in internal courtyards and open spaces, as well as alleyways and roadsides (Mensah, 2014). The introduction of market-centred planning as part of a neoliberal development regime has increased the commodification of space, resulting in reduced government provision of public goods such as affordable housing, road paving and improvements, health care, education, sanitation, and water services. Instead, such responsibilities are being delivered into the hands of private, international donor and NGO entities. Due to the increase in demand for land and the commercialization of space in Ga Mashie, many of the area's parks and open spaces have now given way to dwellings, shops, warehouses and offices, with residential houses purchased and converted into commercial shops (Osei-Tutu, 2000/2001). In addition, the departure of key administrative, commercial and trade operations following the establishment of Tema Port; the commercial rise of the central business district; an expanded ministries area in Accra; and the relocation of middle-class residents to new 'planned' neighbourhoods have all contributed to the area's economic decline (Jackson, 2019).

Urban commoning in contemporary Ga Mashie

While, in many ways, Ga Mashie's urban character has been influenced by Accra's colonial and urbanization processes, the spatial practices of its residents continue to produce spaces of commons. This section explores the everyday contemporary practices by which residents make urban commons within three material spaces in Ga Mashie: 1) two intersecting streets and their linked alleyways; 2) a dilapidated building; and 3) an open space. Through their claims, negotiation and usage of these built spaces, residents have repurposed the sites to serve their local conceptions, visions and needs.

High Street, Kwatei Kojo Street and connected alleyways

John Evans Atta Mills High Street[4] is one of the main roadways in Ga Mashie. High Street, which runs parallel to the coast, is a broad, double-lane, one-way street flanked by sidewalk pavements and lined with indigenous stool houses and colonial buildings, forts, banks, offices and commercial stores. High Street is one of only two main roads built in Ga Mashie with sidewalk pavements to facilitate pedestrian activity. These pavements are taken over for both public and private life: women wash household laundry or small children, and hang wet clothes along house walls or the sidewalk's edge to dry; vendors set up tables or kiosks, usually in front of their homes, to sell goods and services under large commercial umbrellas; young men sit on wooden benches or makeshift chairs, their cars and motorcycles parked on the sidewalk; hawkers make their way up and down the pavement, goods loaded on their heads.

High Street intersects with Kwatei Kojo Street, a paved secondary street lined by open gutters that jut against compound house walls. The lack of sidewalk pavements adds to the teeming nature of the economic, social and recreative activities that agglomerate on this road, with barely enough space remaining for vehicles to pass through. Women set up large metal bowls on charcoal fires, frying yam, donuts, fish or sausage for sale to passers-by. Outside shops, women and men place small plastic tables under enormous commercial umbrellas in order to sell foods, products and services. Men sit outside on wooden benches, debating and chatting, or gather in circles around board games such as draughts (checkers). In the afternoons and at weekends, kids compete one-on-one over table football. It is secondary streets such as this that residents close for funerals and outdoorings (naming ceremonies for newborns), blocking vehicle access with large tent canopies, under which mourners and celebrants sit in long rows of plastic chairs. Organisers may notify some members of the community through word of mouth or posters, but regardless of this the regularity with which street-based funerals take place on Fridays and weekends renders them normal, accepted and even expected. The sheer weight of activity transforms this street – once designed by government authorities for vehicular transport – into a heavily pedestrianized space often avoided by vehicles.

Kwatei Kojo Street links to numerous alleyways – intricate pedestrian paths arising from residents' construction of residential dwellings in close proximity to one another. The alleyways form an elaborate network that connect nearby main streets. These semi-public walkways and alleys, usually just wide enough for two people to stand side by side, provide passageways discernible only to residents and others who often frequent these spaces. When colonial planning left African residents to provide their own housing and improvements, residents selectively adopted aspects of European construction and design, but applied them in ways familiar to them. In addition, historical experiences, including early encounters of clan warfare and slave raiding, instilled an emphasis on neighbourhood design as being a protective measure (Amarteifio, 2015). Residents' familiarity with these internal passageways – which from a modernist standpoint appear unplanned – constitutes a spatial knowledge that has long protected residents from outsiders. The narrow widths of these alleyways and their proximity to residents' homes provide more intimate (semi-private) spaces than secondary or main streets. In this seeming extension of the home's shared living space, adult residents sit and chat with each other or run small commercial businesses; women prepare meals; young men sit and hang out; and children play games. The design produces a familiar, communal social space for residents.

In addition, the annual *Homowo* ('hooting at hunger') thanksgiving festival and cultural event make important use of the main High Street, side streets such as Kwatei Kojo Street, and alleyways. Each year, the festival commemorates a severe period of famine in Ga history and the period of plenty that followed, with most recognized parts of the festival taking place in Ga neighbourhoods over two weeks in August. The festival, which connects spiritual and historical roots and spatial practices, demonstrates how place, boundaries and space become collectively signified and recognized. One notable aspect of the festival is the *kpoikpoi* ceremony, a private ritual also replicated in the public sphere in Ga neighbourhoods, as explained by Osei-Tutu (2000/2001). Female family members prepare *kpoikpoi*, a meal of ground and slightly fermented corn dough, which is steamed and eaten with palm nut soup and fish. Once prepared, the male family heads sprinkle a portion of the dish at the main gate of the dwelling, key points of the house, and within the alleyways of Ga Mashie, followed by the pouring of libations and prayers to ancestral spirits and deities at these same spots. In offering ancestral spirits and deities food and drink before the living can partake, the ritual connects the Ga's past with its present, bringing together the worlds of the living, the deceased, and spirits. Following this ritual, large bowls of the remaining *kpoikpoi* are shared as a communal meal among family members. The ritual is then repeated by chiefs and the people along High Street and secondary neighbourhood streets. Chiefs lead the procession, followed by senior council members, then young men who fire large guns into the air, then young female virgins who carry the bowls of *kpoikpoi*. The procession, which draws large crowds of observers, follows a particular route, with *kpoikpoi* sprinkled at historically important sites within the quarter – these include historic monuments, the shrines of deities and the burial places of ancestors. The chief closes the procession by returning to the stool house, with the remaining bowls of *kpoikpoi* placed on the ground for the public to eat.

The everyday culture of Ga Mashie's alleyways, secondary streets and main streets comprises spatial practices in which residents take over and transform the street into a resource for their public and private purposes. This phenomenon is demonstrated both in everyday practices and the annual festival of *Homowo*, in which these spaces become a place to celebrate Ga's rich history, culture and traditional conceptions of spiritual life. As Ga Mashie is comprised of seven quarters, the festival is celebrated at multiple, intersecting levels – the household, the quarter and the wider neighbourhood – with residents variously spectating and participating in events. As processions, participants and observers move between alleyways, secondary streets and the main street, these sites become resources through which Ga history is remembered, recognized and practised.

Old Kingsway Building

Residents have likewise found ways to transform private but largely abandoned venues into community resources. The African and Eastern Trade Corporation[5] built the first Kingsway Department Store in Accra on High Street in 1914. The building was designed as a two-story commercial warehouse, with a rounded front to serve as a browsing emporium displaying luxury products (Murillo, 2012; Jackson, 2019). Initially, the store targeted European colonials, and was part of a chain of urban department stores and supermarkets across Britain's West African colonies, claiming to carry the 'latest and best' products from London (Murillo, 2012: 372). Over time, it expanded to cater to elite and middle-class African shoppers.

From the 1920s onwards, a general trend of commercial decline took place as both international and local businesses relocated out of Jamestown and the High Street area adjacent to Ga Mashie. Jamestown, the long-time British colonial mercantile centre, gave way to the central business district, with the latter gaining commercial strength thanks to the construction of Makola Market and an economic boom in the sale and production of cocoa, and as improved mechanical transport relieved reliance on proximity to the Jamestown port (Jackson, 2019). In 1957, a new Kingsway Department Store opened in the central business district. Ownership of the Old Kingsway Building switched hands several times, from a trading company to a shipping company, to an office company, and then to a private individual using the space for catering services. The building's open floor plan on the ground and upper floors enabled flexibility of use, but lack of maintenance and a fire destroyed the building's ceiling, leading it to fall into a state of dilapidation (Addo, 2010). City authorities, citing safety hazards, enforced the removal of the top floor and roof, with the result that the building was left as an open-air colosseum.[6] As such, interest from private companies in renting out the building declined, and the building went unused for several years.

The building's state of disuse and open-air design, however, created opportunities for residents to claim the space for their own temporal activities. Ayittey, appointed by the owner as guardian of the space, recalled playing football in the building's open space as a child. Today, for a modest price, he oversees rental use of the building space for community gatherings, such as wedding receptions, naming ceremonies for newborns, funerals and religious meetings. On Tuesday afternoons, girls come to play games, while on Saturday mornings, young boys commandeer the space for pick-up football. Residents bring discarded tyres to sit on when watching boy's football games, and construct street-side seating from cast-off cement blocks and discarded wooden planks. At the building's sidewalk space, which runs along High Street, local vendors set up stalls to sell drinks and cosmetics to passers-by.

The Old Kingsway Building's inclusion in the annual Chale Wote Street Art Festival in Ga Mashie has also brought new interest in the space. In early years, local artists would paint elaborate graffiti and mural art on the building's internal walls, channelling key aspects of the community's identity and heritage, such as its history as a fishing community and its local boxing traditions. Each year, festival programming features musical, theatrical and creative performances by local artists, performers and sportsmen in the buildings' walls and High Street, including bicycle stuntmen, tightrope walkers, boxers and dancers. With the building's popularity as a multipurpose venue enhancing its economic potential, the owner has increased rental fees and Ayittey's responsibilities. Ayittey has also involved local area boys to support management of the site. 'This place is for the community, but it's not free,' explained Ayittey. 'It's for somebody [privately owned], and you have to pay something in order to make improvements.' The returns from payments made by community residents have financed masonwork to fill in cracks along the building's walls; cement to smooth the pavement floor; carpentry work to fill in the open archways with wooden pallets; paying artists to paint new murals on the building's interior walls; and purchasing a football for the community kids to play their matches.

Bukom Square

Bukom Square is a 2.5 km² open dirt field bordered by densely packed streets, residential dwellings and street-based commercial activities. Over the course of a day, residents place a variety of demands on the space. In the early morning, homeless residents who have used the area as a sleeping space collect their belongings and relocate, while area residents dump and burn piles of household rubbish. Vendors set up kiosks and tables along the field's edge as the day starts and commerce begins. In the afternoon, the site is claimed by young boys and men for football matches and street boxing, while area entrepreneurs rent bicycles to young boys and girls to ride around the area. In the evening, further commercial vending takes place, along with meetings between neighbours and informal gatherings involving conversation, debates and leisure activities such as board games. At the weekend, the square might be set up with a stage for music concerts, performances or boxing – a highly popular sport in the neighbourhood.

Bukom Square has long been held up in the Ga imagination as a civic space – that is, a gathering place to discuss public matters. Historically, it has been used as a site to gather public opinion and arrive at collective decisions, whether through conciliation or confrontation (Osei-Tutu, 2000/2001). Today, Bukom continues to be a place of contestation due to the spatial practices of individuals seeking to impinge on the shared space. As a large open space in a dense, built-up neighbourhood, Bukom Square is continually subject to competing spatial claims by area residents. As long-term Ga Mashie resident Emmanuel Mark-Hansen observes: 'When you have an open space, you have to guard against people putting up new structures – from a table, to a stand, to a built structure. Over time, as the area becomes built up, then it will be a challenge to move them … it is a political issue, and we have to stop it before it starts.'[7] The fluidity and openness of the space, which enables residents to enter, occupy and use the space for their own ends, also poses a challenge to preserving the space's communal nature. In particular, mobile tabletop vending activities can quickly evolve into the use of permanent structures, such as built commercial spaces or even extensions of residential dwellings. Such incremental practices have already claimed parts of the square, reducing what was once a much more expansive space to its present day bounds.

In the absence of government regulation, it is residents themselves who protect the common area of Bukom from individual claims. Residents have become vigilant in monitoring vendors and other users who attempt to permanently claim available edges, first with tables, then kiosks, then cement structures. Street vending is the most proliferous activity, present throughout the day and seldom hemmed in except by the young area boys, who pushed out the night market to preserve the space for their football matches. Certain users' claims can prevent or constrain those of others, with young men and boys playing a particularly assertive role in claiming open spaces for their football activities. This ability to assert claims for football space over the claims of street vendors is a phenomenon seen not only in Ga Mashie but throughout the city of Accra.

Discussion

A wide gap exists between government authorities' dominant narrative of urban modernity in African cities such as Accra and the everyday spatial practices of urban poor and working-class residents. In Ga Mashie, evolving local conceptions of urban commons, alongside exclusion from decent labour, housing and other urban opportunities, have pushed residents into claiming public and shared lands. This use of 'marginal, vacant, underutilised or abandoned spaces' for necessary local commercial, social, recreational and cultural needs (Ayitio and Sarfoh, 2014) is grounded not only in urban development processes but longer-term histories of challenging, subverting and operating outside colonial and postcolonial plans, as the experiences from Ga Mashie's streets and alleyways, the Old Kingsway Building and Bukom Square show.

In Ga Mashie, residents' appropriations and transformations of space produce a collective understanding of spatial usage. Government planners, recognizing the high incidence of these spatial practices in Ga Mashie, rarely intervene. Government recognition of the Ga people as indigenes of Accra and Ga Mashie as an indigenous neighbourhood in the city affords these groups special rights and entitlements that structures political engagement and informs urban development approaches (Paller, 2019). In other areas of Accra, violent means have been employed to enforce city authorities' modern urban imaginary and control residents' appropriations of streets, open spaces and buildings. Through harassment, fines and demolitions, local authorities have threatened and dispossessed residents – mostly those operating in street vending, hawking or living in settlements developed outside of government oversight (Steel, Ujoranyi and Owusu, 2014; Gillespie, 2015; Falt, 2016).

While city authorities recognize the contradictions between state-sanctioned planning and residents' everyday labour to produce urban commons, they provide limited responses. The Town and Country Planning Department (TCPD) oversees the development of land in rural and urban areas. It determines land ownership and designates land use, and possesses the authority – subject to certain processes and procedures – to permanently or temporarily re-designate any space for uses other than its original designation. One TCPD official expressed great familiarity with the spatial appropriations common within Accra and Ga Mashie. While technical policy documents frame these spatial practices as illegal and informal encroachments, officials acknowledge they take place throughout the city regardless:

> A street space can be used as a playground on temporary basis, it can be used as a market on a temporary basis. We cherish celebrating dead people [such as through funerals]. We usually are not proactive as far as the dynamics of space reallocation, but you find that the users define the path, they tell us what they want to use it for, by closing the streets, putting large speakers there, perhaps for a wedding, naming ceremony or somebody has died [funeral]. There are certain experts saying that we should plan based on what people say they want the spaces used for, and not behave as if we are perfect – 'build here, market there, drive here' – and then when people aren't conforming, we can't get them to conform. We need to develop a smart use of space, unless it is a tight space. We have to learn to circulate, recycle and alter uses conveniently, just make sure the rule is clear, that there are no conflicts. You don't want to endanger somebody by asking them to use another space. Globally this is happening, but it's not really a defined policy here [in Ghana]. In Ghana, it happens informally a lot, but not through clear, definite policy pronouncements … For example, people pay and get permission from local authorities sometimes to do these activities. They are given a licence, which means it's possible to do that. So it's not a defined policy but it's happening in reality.[8]

Although much of the literature on commons has emphasized sites as grounded in collective agreements and practices, experiences from Ga Mashie demonstrate that not all forms of commons provide full and open access to all, and may still be regulated and policed by various actors (Harvey, 2012).[9] The absence of government requires residents, neighbourhoods and users of space to negotiate spatial usage. In the case of Ga Mashie, the street-level actors enforcing these regulations are neighbours, potential and competing users of the space, as well as legal owners and on-site guardians. Negotiations are informed by power dynamics, with access to space determined by one's status, gender, age, class or other identity marker. Streets, which are simultaneously regarded as belonging to everyone and no one, are the most frequently claimed of these open spaces. Enclosed open spaces, such as Bukom Square, though open to temporal activities, are frequently threatened by the construction of fixed residential and commercial structures by individual residents, which other residents seek to vigilantly regulate in order to maintain the space as a collective one. As a result, the extent to which Bukom is a fully open space is limited, with everyday negotiations and power dynamics producing an urban commons that is constrained by certain regulations. As a privately opened community space, the Old Kingsway Building is the least open, as its owner and managers balance its usage with user fees – particularly for adult gatherings, meetings and ceremonies – to maintain its upkeep.

Several threads tie these spaces together. In each of these spaces, street vending and small-scale patty trading are the most visible practice. This is an important income-earning opportunity conducted largely by women, and, following wider trends in urban Ghana, the spatial practice persists despite the colonial and postcolonial emphasis on fixed markets (Asiedu and Agyei-Mensah, 2008; Anyidoho, 2013). Through their activities, the vendors convert these sites – along High Street pavements and secondary street roadsides, in alleyways, and at the edges of Bukom Road and Old Kingsway Building – into important, economically productive spaces. These spaces are also essential resources for public life, with residents' daily social, leisure and recreational activities marking a consistent pattern of spatial usage and experience. As spaces for community gatherings and meetings, games and football matches, or just sitting around and hanging out, these sites are critical to promoting community interaction. Moreover, the spaces provide a platform for cultural festivals and events that sit at the centre of the community's identity, traditional spirituality and creativity. From the re-enactment of historic rituals, processions, food preparation and communal meals to the production of art and performances, these spaces enable the enactment of enduring connections between Ga Mashie's past and present.

The wide spectrum of activities that Ga Mashie residents engage in – some of which are contested, some of which are individualized and some of which are assembled – are spatial processes that employ and produce urban commons as a shared, material urban framework within which residents can dwell (Harvey, 2012: 74). Even within residents' individualized and disparate practices, their shared ways of operating – claiming, using, negotiating, transforming – represent common ways of being in the available space. Taken together, these everyday, intermingling spatial practices, undertaken by various publics manoeuvring within their own 'fields of operations', enable a mode of urban life enacted through the critical resource of space (Simone, 2012). In turn, by sharing affinities, resources, social and cultural experiences, residents can build and sustain networks that enable them to thrive in the city (Simone, 2004; Hunter et al., 2016).

Conclusion

Across much of the Global South, a tension exists in urban spatial development between profit-driven market opportunities supported by government modernist visions, and the needs and priorities of the urban poor, which are often absent from city planning and design (Watson, 2009). The spatial practices through which residents of the indigenous neighbourhood of Ga Mashie occupy and produce everyday space exist in stark contrast to the disembodied planning and design techniques employed by Accra's local authorities, both historically and currently. Accra's government authorities orient planning and design to 'planned' living, working and operating arrangements, such as private land tenure, regulated labour arrangements, infrastructure and service provision. Yet, as part of everyday life in Ga Mashie, residents claim, inhabit and adapt abandoned, vacant and unused spaces, making them available for commercial, recreational, leisure, social, religious and/or cultural activities. Thus, residents insert their needs, desires and priorities into an existent built environment, thereby disrupting the city's seemingly dominant colonial/postcolonial spatial order. In focusing on how residents occupy and transform three spaces in Ga Mashie neighbourhood, this chapter has highlighted the incremental nature of city-making as a process driven not just by government authorities but also residents. Through myriad and overlapping spatial practices, residents conceive, regulate and negotiate space. Such practices represent more than just a challenge to government orientations – they produce spaces grounded in other ways of being, relating and life-worlding (Osei-Tutu, 2000/2001; Vasudevan, 2015).

This chapter has traced the everyday spatial practices of urban commoning in Ga Mashie, mapping the trajectory of these practices in this historic neighbourhood. Regardless of the attempts of city planners, designers and urban managers to chart the future of Accra's modernity – including planned large-scale tourism projects, these small-scale practices will likely continue to dominate the urban landscape. Government plans and policies frame Accra's urban trajectory as a modern, world-class city, yet urban governance authorities struggle to manage the city's existing and expected growth. Thus, reflecting and learning from the ground – that is, the enduring spatial practices through which residents transform urban spaces into individual and communal resources, appropriating streets, pavements and other open areas for everyday essential activities – presents an alternative, inclusive path forward, centred on the lived experiences of an urban majority who are already in the process of remaking the city.

Notes

1   These settlements consist of Ga Mashie, Osu, Labadi, Teshie, Nungua (in present-day Accra Metropolitan Area) and Tema (in Tema Metropolitan Area).
2   Interview with N. N. Amarteifio, Accra, 16 December 2015.
3   Frantz Fanon (2001: 37–40) and AbdouMaliq Simone (2019) engaged the European colonization of Africa as the parcelling out of territories into colonized worlds, achieved through the 'appropriation' of African spaces and the violent imposition of colonial rule. Achille Mbembe writes that the colonization process was 'a matter of seizing, delimiting, and asserting control over a physical area – of writing on the

ground a new set of social and spatial relations' through the re-organization of border and territorial arrangements, property relations, resource extraction and spatial imaginaries (2003: 25–6).

4   British colonial authorities originally constructed the High Street, its major side roads and key buildings as part of Jamestown, the initial British administrative and mercantile quarter oriented around James Fort. The streets were designed according to European and modernist planning guidelines: straight, broad roadways for cars, with imposing commercial and governance buildings visible from the street. In 2012, the street was formally named after the late president John Evans Atta Mills, who had died in office that year. However, Accra residents continue to refer to it as 'Jamestown High Street'.

5   The corporation was an amalgamation of trading firms: F&A Swanzy trading firm (which had been trading since 1807), Millers Brothers of Liverpool (which began trading in Accra in 1859), and two other trading firms (Jackson, 2019).

6   Interview with A. Issaka, Accra, 13 June 2019.

7   Interview with E. Mark-Hansen, Accra, 27 March 2018.

8   Interview with Town and Country Planning Department, Accra, 3 December 2015.

9   Interview with E. Mark-Hansen, Accra, 27 March 2018.

Chapter 9

LEARNING FROM DIY URBANISM: LESSONS FROM FREETOWN

Federico Monica

Introduction

In Western cities or in contexts characterized by a long tradition of social awareness, DIY urbanism is usually linked to political protest movements and consists of demonstrative acts of resistance, or else provocative actions of a playful or artistic nature. However, within the complex reality that characterizes many African cities, DIY urbanism is not a deliberate means of struggle or a tool of protest, much less an act of creative expression. Rather, it is implemented unconsciously by many urban residents as the only possible means of finding shelter, protecting their family or community, or developing a more efficient micro-economy.

More generally, DIY urbanism comes into play where official urbanism has failed to provide answers, forcing residents to make the most of available resources and adapt in creative and resilient ways to the environmental context. Such strategies of adaptation and the creation of alternative urban systems offer new ways of conceiving planning and urban management, especially in fragile and complex realities.

This chapter examines how DIY urbanism manifests in Freetown, capital of Sierra Leone. In doing so, it attempts to highlight the perspectives and visions that may inspire more efficient and inclusive urban planning strategies.

Freetown – A DIY city?

DIY urbanism is not new to Freetown. On the contrary, it can be seen in the earliest origins of the city – while many West African coastal towns are physical expressions of colonial domination, Freetown has a completely different background. The city was founded on the basis of philanthropic rather than exploitative aims, and grew from several small villages built and administered by their inhabitants (Butt-Thompson, 1926).

A unique origin

In 1787, a British anti-slavery society led by the philanthropist Granville Sharp bought some lands on the shores of Sierra Leone from native leader King Tom and named the area 'Province of Freedom', creating a new settlement for several hundred liberated slaves. Following this, the promulgation of the 'Slave Trade Act' in 1808 allowed the British Navy to patrol Atlantic coastlines, freeing thousands of people from slave vessels. These liberated slaves – who hailed from every corner of West and Central Africa – were brought to Freetown, giving birth to a melting pot culture and lingua franca known as Krio (Alie, 1990). This multi-cultural atmosphere also influenced the urban pattern of the town, with each ethnic group founding their own village within it, creating a polycentric framework that can still be seen in neighbourhood names. The location of Sierra Leone, in the heart of French West Africa, led the British to declare it a colony in the mid-nineteenth century, resulting in Freetown's population growth and planning coming under strict control (Kandè, 1998).

Following independence in 1961, many people from Sierra Leone's inlands moved to the capital bearing hopes of a prosperous future. However, the newborn republic suffered several military coups and long years of dictatorship, leading in the early 1990s to the destructive civil war known as 'the diamond war'. Despite a large deployment of UN and African Union forces, Freetown was conquered and looted by RUF rebels three times. Thousands of people were killed or tortured, while ministries, the town hall and the cadastral archives were burnt down, and around 70 per cent of houses were damaged.

The civil war disrupted the city's appearance: in 1985, Freetown had 540,000 residents; by the end of the war in 2001 this had risen to more than a million, with most of the new inhabitants displaced from other areas. Since then, the city has continued to experience high growth rates, expanding rapidly without any strategic planning or infrastructural development. This has resulted in extensive urban sprawl and a number of environmental, sanitary and social issues.

Thus, Freetown's current urban form is the product of a series of 'global' factors, starting from the abolition of slavery, passing through colonialism and leading up to conflicts over exploitation of raw materials, climate change and, last but not least, epidemics. However, while these wider aspects have directly influenced the city's demographic and socio-economic evolution, the development of its urban environment also lies in local – and problematic – geographic factors: the town is crammed into a narrow strip of flat land situated between steep hills and the ocean. As a result, contemporary Freetown is an overcrowded, hemmed-in city with an extension of almost 50 km.

The city suffers from a variety of problems faced by many African cities, including lack of infrastructure; water and power shortages; inadequate waste management; an insufficient road network; and an unhealthy environment. Moreover, the Ebola epidemic in 2014 devastated the country's economy just as a process of development and transformation was underway.

Slums and informal settlements in Freetown

Contemporary African metropolises are ecosystems subject to constant transition, where everything is both connected and precariously balanced (Balbo, 1999). In such complex environments, defining the boundaries of what is formal or informal is a near-impossible (and probably pointless) task. Given the lack of clear division between official and unofficial – both in terms of economic and spatial organization (Bairoch, 1985) – any framing simplistic based on the parameters of legality risks not only blunting perceptions of a complex phenomenon, but potentially leads to a mere fraction of a town or city being considered 'real'.

In Freetown, such a framing would exclude the overwhelming majority of the city's built environment, preserving just the downtown and colonial neighbourhoods, as the government of Sierra Leone has still not approved normative parameters that would indicate informal settlements or slums. If, however, the standards developed by UN-Habitat were to be applied, most of the city could be defined as a slum, given the lack of basic infrastructure (mainly sewerage and road networks) and hydrogeological risk (UN-Habitat, 2012). Even the last census, carried out by Sierra Leone Statistics in 2015, cannot help, as it lacks specific indicators that would allow for the quantifying of informality.[1] Given this, the question remains: what level of DIY urbanism is present in Freetown today?

Utilizing historical aerial images of Freetown (2002–14), it is possible to draw an approximative map of urban informality involving areas not linked to the road network, steep lands, coastlines and river banks, and former 'green belt' areas (Figure 9.1).

Official documents, supported by various research, report seventy to seventy-five settlements defined as slums, most with populations that range from double

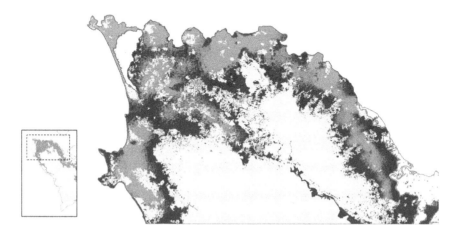

Figure 9.1 Diffusion of urban informality in Freetown.

Built surfaces are in dark grey; informal areas and slum are represented in black.
Source: Monica (2014).

figures to a few hundred. Fifteen are of a considerable size, hosting 5,000–10,000 inhabitants (Monica, 2014). However, as stated, the boundary between 'official' neighbourhoods and informal settlements is ill-defined, with the long-term absence of effective urban planning, uncontrolled expansion during the war, building speculation and lack of infrastructure having created an extremely fragmented patchwork. Moreover, the lack of a cadaster (burned during the war) and endemic corruption among public officers has resulted in widespread granting of permissions to build in unsafe areas, as well as false certificates of ownership.

Within these zones of informality, characterized by strong economic and social inequalities, there are marginal areas definable as 'real' slums: located in high-risk areas (within already hazardous zones), with high population densities and buildings constructed using extremely poor-quality materials. While the 'official' town developed along the major coastline roads, the informal settlements have emerged in places unsuitable for ordinary urban expansions: mainly on hills, in river beds and in swampy bays near the downtown.

It is possible to classify Freetown's informal settlements according to their location and the common features that characterize them. In particular, three macro-categories can be seen: 1) filling settlements; 2) expansion settlements; and 3) border settlements. Each of these incorporates a number of sub-categories:

- **Filling settlements**, located in the central districts of downtown, occupy dangerous and unhealthy land unsuitable for building, thereby filling the gaps left by the official city. They are characterized by overcrowding and consequent sanitary emergencies. Despite this, their proximity to the centre of the city provides microeconomic opportunities. Filling settlements can be further divided into sub-categories depending on their location: river areas settlements; coastal settlements; and settlements in environmentally hazardous areas (landfills, industrial areas).
- **Expansion settlements** are slums that extend the city's urban footprint, eroding surrounding green areas. They are not densely populated and are usually built on the slopes of hills too steep to build safe houses, in areas at risk of landslides, or in riverbeds. These settlements are far from the central areas and communication routes.
- **Border settlements** are located outside the administrative boundary of Freetown (Western Area Urban District), and are usually the first destination for those relocating to the city from the countryside. They can be divided into the following sub-categories: 'market' settlements (located near local markets, usually near the terminus of urban transport lines); occupied settlements (such as former refugee camps from the civil war); or relocation areas, whereby the government has attempted to transfer some slum-dwellers from central slums, who have then sub-leased concessions before returning to live in their communities.

These categories and subdivisions allow for deeper investigation of Freetown's informal settlements, highlighting their different characteristics, common aspects, and the threats and risks to which they are subjected. Examining the galaxy of

DIY urbanism through the typologies and common features of settlements can provide a more nuanced perspective, in turn facilitating guidelines, best practices and intervention modalities that are tailored to the specific urban context.

DIY urbanism and politics in Freetown

Despite the long tradition of self-building initiatives and DIY urbanism in Freetown, such activity rarely has strong political connotations or takes place within a collective awareness. This apparent absence of political consciousness among slum-dwellers cannot, however, be relegated to the total 'subalternity' of urban informality described by various authors (Roy, 2011; Simone, 2011; Choplin, 2017).

Although not as clear and self-conscious as in South American and Asian realities, the initiatives and resilience of DIY interventions in Freetown can partially be read as a confrontation with power regarding the affirmation of basic rights (Holston, 2009). These, though, are not insurgent realities, but concealed struggles, based on obstinacy and daily resilience rather than direct conflict. Instead of facing off, political power and popular action seem instead to ignore each other.

For years, politics at all levels has ignored the issue of slums, proclaiming the need for evictions while failing to take action. Urban improvement and service provision have been minimal and ineffective, while attempts at relocation – apart from a few failed pilot programmes – have been confined to small settlements near the main tourist areas (Montero, 2016). The process of decentralization, implemented between 2004 and 2010, signalled a further setback for citizen and slum-dweller involvement in urban policies, as local governments were not properly equipped to adopt effective and inclusive policies. Thus, from the perspective of slum-dwellers, politics is absent, distant and unreachable, and so all their creative energies are directed at multiplying the few resources available, both human and material (Simone, 2006).

In addition to the informal economy networks rooted in slums, the first slum-dwellers' organizations – such as the Federation of Urban Poor – have grown in strength over recent years and are starting to assume a fair degree of negotiating power with authorities (Johnson, 2009). Moreover, Yvonne Aki Sawyerr's election as major of Freetown in March 2018 has signalled a small turnaround, with Freetown City Council adopting some grassroot initiatives to prevent flooding and improve waste management. 'Operation Clean Freetown' and the 'Flood Prevention Plan' are city-wide programmes based on simple micro-interventions inspired by daily activities developed by slum-dwellers. Due to the cleaning and excavation of small drain networks in disaster-prone areas, rainy season flooding has been reduced.

So, can Freetown legitimately be termed a DIY city? In some ways, the answer to this is 'yes': it was developed directly by its founders and first residents; has demonstrated an ability to flexibly adapt to disasters and emergencies; and its recent growth is in large part due to the city's informal areas, which contain an extraordinary array of settlement typologies.

In the next section, we turn to the main elements and strategies of DIY urbanism characterizing Freetown's informal settlements.

Elements of DIY urbanism in Freetown slums

Although slums are commonly perceived as realms of spontaneity and confusion, the organization of space and community activities is never left completely to chance. Behind the apparently indecipherable chaos lie extraordinary systems and techniques facilitating resilience, exploitation of the few resources available, and the ability to adapt dynamically to a difficult and constantly changing environment.

Every settlement, slum and DIY urbanism experience – being the product of individual creative efforts to adapt to a particular context – represents a world unto itself, incorporating its own peculiarities and unique elements (Tranberg Hansen, 2004). Even so, it is possible to identify common aspects among settlements: generalizable experiences or good practice that can be exported, and that may act as an interpretative basis for the phenomenon.

This section therefore examines DIY urbanism in Freetown through both its physical elements (spatial solutions, types of built environment and infrastructure) and the system of rules (land use policies, planning and informal tenure systems) governing the independent development of informal settlements. These local and highly circumscribed actions have significant implications for alternative urban policies, not only in Freetown but also in many urban areas across the African continent. This offers a possible key to interpreting complex urban realities, in which the nominally 'informal' part of a city is recognized as being extensive, if not preponderant. Thus, we can go some way to understanding underground systems of self-organization that ensure the survival not only of the settlements in which they are used, but the entire urban ecosystem.

DIY planning and spatial organization

Planning and spatial organization are among DIY urbanism's most interesting themes, as they involve conscious strategies that have a time horizon and are supported by a system of rules. These strategies are in many ways similar to traditional planning, but are based on different assumptions and tools.

In official maps and planning documents, the areas occupied by slums are generally empty or without specific indications – normative black holes apparently lacking any authority or rules of development. The reality, however, is often very different (Roy, 2011), with the absence of national government and urban management policies compensated for by parallel organizational structures that lay down rules and decide on infrastructure investment and implementation.

The system of oral or unwritten traditions is still widespread in various cultures across West Africa, particularly in rural societies, and has been partially recognized in some post-independence constitutions, which have tried to reconcile a 'Western' approach with local traditions[2] (Freund, 2007). The most organized slums have internal hierarchies based on these regulations: informal governance structures in which traditional chiefs, religious and community leaders, elders or first settlers deal with issues ranging from security to the local economy to land use. Here, though, it is important to acknowledge that such systems can exacerbate inequalities, increasing the power of first residents and those holding property rights to the potential exclusion of, for example, rural–urban migrants and newcomers (Floris, 2007).

Kroo Bay offers an instructive example of DIY planning effectiveness – the slum, located in a marshy area at the mouth of the Alligator River, is one of the largest in Freetown. Since its foundation, the settlement has developed around a large empty area, which forms a central square used as a meeting place, market, sports field and entertainment area (Figure 9.2). Despite the number

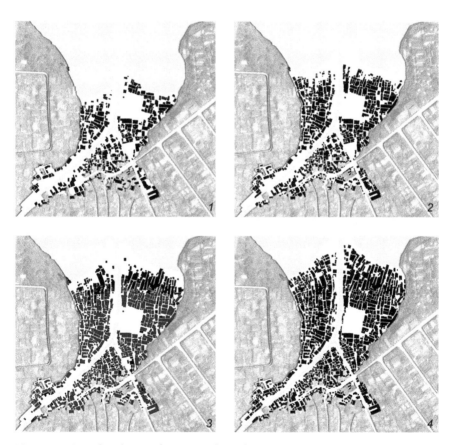

Figure 9.2 Spatial evolution of Kroo Bay slum: 1) 2000; 2) 2008; 3) 2012; 4) 2017.

NB. Note how the central square has been preserved, with new shelters located on reclamation ground along the coastline.

of residents almost doubling over the past ten years, the central square has not been built upon. Instead, space for new homes has been created by raising the land by the sea, a solution that required considerable work and economic outlay (Monica, 2017).

In a totally spontaneous settlement, it would be natural to assume that newcomers would occupy the areas where it is simplest and cheapest to build. Thus, keeping a large open space free from construction implies that rules and control systems are in force. Here, oral conventions act as a form of agreement among residents, allowing development of the community in order to ensure its survival and functionality. Similar systems of spatial organization are used in settlements, especially in relation to the management of open areas used for community purposes.

Urban elements

The term urban elements refers to the set of physical structures realized in the slums: the shape of buildings and their agglomeration in blocks, the role of unbuilt areas, and the relationship between the natural and built environment. Not being able to count on large-scale investment or infrastructure, the urban form of the informal districts has adopted the ancient (and wise) habit of adapting to its surrounding context, complying with local geography as much as possible and only utilizing ephemeral and reversible modifications.

The built elements that make up most of the settlements do not differ overly from classical urban forms: early detached buildings are replaced by compact blocks that form semi-regular grids in flat areas, and linear rows or irregular shapes as necessary to fit on steep or rough terrain. Thus, the layout of DIY urbanism areas usually resembles the remains of medieval cities, but with significantly smaller dimensions – a walkway may be less than a metre wide and a block of houses rarely more than few metres in width.

While major differences between traditional urban planning and its DIY equivalent may not be in evidence in terms of building, it is in the management and use of empty spaces that the most interesting DIY aspects are found, with each unbuilt area allocated a specific use in order to enhance the informal micro-economy or meet the community's needs. In coastal settlements especially, where space is limited, such areas cannot exist areas without a function. Moreover, empty spaces are rarely monofunctional, but are used flexibly according to requirements. Thus, depending on the time of day or day of the week, these areas may be used for cooking, meeting, playing or as small markets; they may at some point be completely empty, only to be filled a few hours later with ephemeral structures, narrowing or widening according to intended use. In the Old Wharf slum, the small beach is usually used to haul and repair boats. In the mid-afternoon, however, boats are removed to make room for a colourful fish market. The fishermen's canoes are docked a few metres from shore, with sellers carrying buckets of fish on their head to customers crammed on the shoreline.

The promiscuous use of space is a necessity practised not only for community activities, but also for the simplest of daily actions – the road, for example, becomes at certain times of day a natural extension of the home. Given houses are usually reduced to the minimum necessary to afford shelter during the night, meaning indoor comfort during the day is poor, each has an additional shared room: the section of street in front of it. This becomes a kitchen, parlour, playground, workshop, laundry and sometimes even a dancing hall.

With even the most absurd of objects recycled to build shelters or houses, any residual space is inevitably used and assigned a function – such is the case for drainage channels and dykes, which may become walkways during the dry season. In settlements such as Access Road and Granville Brook, which were built by terracing steep slopes, riverbeds have been partly converted to stone or concrete stairways connecting downtown to the hilltops.

DIY infrastructure

Infrastructure represents the strategic elements that usually mark the boundary between formal and informal, with one of the main characteristics of slums being the absence of infrastructure and, consequently, services, security and opportunities (Simone, 2014). Among the elements of DIY urbanism found in Freetown's slums, infrastructure is by far the most important. Firstly, it allows, through self-building, to compensate for the absence of planning and state intervention; secondly, it shows there are communities able to organize themselves in order to create useful resources for residents (Pushak and Foster, 2011); and, thirdly, it facilitates the creation of safer urban areas and efficient microeconomic systems.

DIY infrastructure located in Freetown's slums can mainly be seen in water defence works: rudimentary embankments aimed at containing river floods; levees preventing tides or marine erosion; and simple water management works, such as drain networks for rainwater and sewage.

Beyond defence and risk management infrastructure, there are many interesting examples of land development, including embankments made from recycled waste in order to raise land in alluvial areas, and even dams and fillings aimed at creating new empty areas for the expansion of settlements. Over the past ten years, the populations of Susan Bay and Kroo Bay slums have doubled, with this growth only made possible through reclamation lands. In Kroo Bay, a swampy river mouth, the coastline has been extended through extensive fillings, while embankments have been built on the steep shores of Susan Bay, as shown in Figure 9.3.

Some infrastructure, meanwhile, has been implemented by communities to support the local micro-economy. In slums such as Susan Bay a complex system of self-built wharfs and piers, small warehouses and laboratories has facilitated an informal wholesale market of fresh food and charcoal transported by boat from inland – a significant proportion of the goods that daily reach the central markets of Freetown come through the slum piers (Monica, 2018).

Figure 9.3 Expansion of Susan Bay slum over past ten years.

NB. The expansion of Susan Bay slum over the past ten years took place entirely on reclamation lands obtained through DIY infrastructures: a series of self-built embankments made from wood and recycled waste.

DIY tenure and rights systems

The system of property rights governing land and housing within the slums is an important issue: alongside DIY urbanism there is often an informal 'real estate' market, which has a number of implications for social cohesion. While in many settlements, a 'slumlord' may exercise great power over residents by imposing unfair rent prices, in other areas self-managed property rights systems have developed. These systems are rooted in local customs and traditions, and stand in contrast to the Western concept of private property as a permanent and absolute individual right (AlSayyad, 2004).

In many African cultures, including Sierra Leone, traditional conceptions of ownership apply not to the individual but to the community – a property may belong to an individual but must be managed in order to grant the survival and prosperity of the group (Johnson, 2011). This culture, which is often contrary to state laws (usually inspired by the constitutions of former colonial powers), affects local habits. This is mainly the case in rural districts, but can also be seen in some urban areas, such as slums (Fyfe and Jones, 1968).

In Freetown, most of the slums are on government land unsuitable for any construction likely to involve official ownership issues. Even so, many settlements have developed systems of informal property rights. In the slums of Kroo Bay and Susan Bay, the first settlers and their descendants specialized in activities such as land development and the building of DIY infrastructures. These families invest in clearing and developing new building areas inside the slum, and therefore receive a small monthly or yearly payment for each dwelling built on the plots they improved. In effect, it is a kind of informal urbanization fee.

Other residents have specialized as builders. Only a small number of buildings – usually just the most recent shelters, made of plastic sheets and cardboard – are totally self-built by residents. As soon as possible, more durable buildings made from zinc sheets or mud bricks are constructed by skilled workers. A builder usually owns part of the house they have constructed, becoming a resident landlord.

In many of Freetown's slums, however, more than half of families rent rather than own the shack in which they live. An even higher proportion sublet a room inside a larger building (CODOSHAPA and FEDURP, 2011). Against this background, the payment of rents becomes a complex system of fees: a family (the room tenants) pays rent to the house tenant, who must then pay a certain amount to the landlord (the one who invested in the building of the shelter), who in turn must pay a contribution to those who developed the land and the slum infrastructure. The role of 'land developers' is informally recognized even by the authorities, with some of them asked by Freetown City Council to pay a yearly fee for public land occupation.

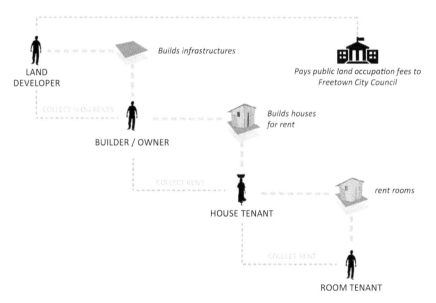

Figure 9.4 Scheme showing the informal system of rent, housing rights and financing of land development in Freetown's major slums.

DIY land use policies

Another notable aspect of the slums is the presence of productive buildings such as workshops, small craft factories and storage areas. Some workshops may have particular needs, such as appropriate accessibility, storage areas or proximity to transport routes or the sea. Others may produce noise or smoke, increasing environmental pollution and exposing adjacent dwellings to potential risks. In order to reduce pollution and discomfort to residents, workshops and ateliers are usually positioned at the margins of settlements, along the coast or in remote and isolated areas on the hills. However, due to the rapid growth of settlements, new shelters are soon built close to the workshops, until the latter are totally incorporated into the housing pattern, creating mixed-use areas.

In fast-growing slums such as Kroo Bay or Dworzak Farm, residents have addressed this problem in a creative way, elaborating a kind of informal land-use policy. When workshops become surrounded by houses, they are abandoned and converted to dwellings or community kitchens, with working activities transferred to new buildings far away from residents. In this way, informal land-use policies are applied in a flexible and continuously adaptable way, being subject to gradual revision in order to meet the needs of the community.

Learning from DIY urbanism, a new approach to planning

DIY urbanism – in the form of minimal, cheap, and extremely localized initiatives – works out of necessity. However, a set of many such interventions can also be integral to creating settlements, neighbourhoods and even entire areas of the city, with some metropolises delegating essential parts of their services to informal solutions. Despite this, informal settlements – and more generally the galaxy of DIY urbanism – are usually regarded as a disgrace by urban planners (Balbo, 1999), whose unavowable dream is of a 'machine city', which evolves according to predictable dynamics and is governed by immutable laws. In reality, this utopian (perhaps dystopian) dream cannot exist even in the most well-organized and technologically advanced countries.

This anxiety regarding control leads to informality being confused with illegality, and so a failure to recognize the opportunities offered by DIY urbanism in the short term, and to take inspiration from it in terms of strategic planning. Looking at DIY urbanism in a positive light is not a matter of turning a blind eye to difficult living conditions or serious exploitation dynamics, but rather involves analysis of complex phenomena that risk being trivialized or misunderstood if they are merely dismissed as 'poverty traps' (Robert, 2004).

Taking this approach, a number of measurable positive effects can be seen. These include: the reduction of sprawl, with the density of slums helping maintain a compact urban structure; the diversification of the housing market, which is often inaccessible to ordinary workers in central areas; and the promotion of alternative recycling and waste management practices. There can also be unexpected environmental benefits: in various coastal settlements, residents have constructed small-scale infrastructure such as piers in order to facilitate micro-economies linked to food and goods transported by boat, leading to considerable reductions in traffic and pollution on the roads leading to main markets (Monica, 2018).

In addition to these effects, DIY initiatives offer a number of insights into how new urban management and planning strategies may be developed.

Planning and infrastructure

As has already been described, the initiatives implemented by Freetown City Council in 2018 were inspired by the DIY urbanism approach of highly targeted micro-interventions. Beyond this, however, informality can help provide a new way of interpreting planning in critical areas, one that is not bound up in generalized, long-term strategies.

While the planning of spatial organization and the built environment in slums is rightly considered an oxymoron, we have nevertheless seen how the urban structure of many settlements is not left to chance. Perhaps, then, the problem is not the slums themselves, but the idea of planning – even in settlements where strong self-organization strategies are in evidence, long-term planning is perceived as a nonsense given the lack of certainty surrounding rights and property.

DIY urbanism shows how planning can be light-touch and flexible, while maintaining adequate levels of efficiency. Thus, one important – and perhaps revolutionary – insight is that planning need not necessarily be linked to a territory's faithful representation or written codes. Extraordinarily changeable installations require equally flexible tools, with the considerable time required for mapping and continuous updating at odds with the ephemeral reality of slums. Given this, the opportunity to study alternative tools, such as shared oral rules or simple guidelines, should be grasped. In such contexts, swift self-enumeration based on Google aerial views and a limited number of generic rules may be more effective than detailed maps or elaborated spatial plans (Appadurai, 2012). In addition, the challenges of climate change with the increased risk of sudden and unpredictable disasters require rapid, adaptable solutions that traditional infrastructure often cannot guarantee.

DIY urbanism offers economical and localized answers to wide-ranging problems. Above all, it manifests as concrete reality, in contrast to many dead letter strategies and guidelines that fail to make the transition from an inert set of principles to action. Moreover, the diffusion of self-built infrastructure, capable of significantly improving the lives of many people, calls into question the assumption that infrastructure must be 'public', or at least that it requires large and invasive interventions. Rather than planning massive transformations that are often unattainable or overly expensive, strategies for strengthening and incentivizing self-built infrastructures could be implemented. This might involve providing guidelines and introducing minimum standards, in the process expanding local micro-measures up to the urban scale.

Tenure rights and land use policies

Another area where lessons can be learned from DIY urbanism concerns permits and tenure rights, an issue that causes many upgrading interventions to fail (Davis, 2006). Here again, ephemeral realities require flexible tools, prompting residents to develop alternative and efficient methods of self-recognition.

Land law is based on the concept of real estate (immovable buildings and land). However, given land in informal settlements is public, the possibility arises of issuing permits not linked to any particular place, piece of land or building. Such generic permits could be used to establish the right to reside or build a shelter within a given neighbourhood (or it could apply to several areas), while temporary permits could be renewed or extended depending on the type of materials someone intends to use in building or consolidating their home – the more durable is the structure (e.g. meeting minimum building standards), the longer will last the permission.

The extreme flexibility that characterizes DIY urbanism – for example, the switching of a building's function or the relationship between productive and residential areas – also generates insights on the rigidity of traditional methods such as zoning. In contrast to informal areas, which must be able to adapt swiftly when different functions are called for, the zoning method relies on the relevant context remaining static over time. Is it then possible to imagine a form of 'provisional zoning' capable of adapting to a constantly changing environment?

Procedures such as those outlined above do not fit within the classical Western approach to planning, which is based on rigorous, irreversible and long-term solutions. As such, flexible DIY land use can offer inspiration when it comes to developing alternatives suitable for ephemeral contexts where traditional methods have failed.

Conclusions

The concept of 'do it yourself' is often interpreted as being in opposition to professionalism – derogatorily indicating work that is provisional, imprecise, cheap and ineffective. DIY urbanism is also subject to this stereotype, even taking on the stigma of illegality. Despite this, it should be recognized that such initiatives, even if temporary, make functional and liveable the places where 'professionals' (official planning strategies) have failed.

The bottom-up DIY urbanism solutions found in Freetown's slums are extraordinarily adaptive, and should lead urban planners to question the effectiveness of 'traditional' planning in enormous, constantly changing urban realities. The challenges cities currently have to face, especially in terms of climate change, are undermining not only infrastructural systems, but the very model of transformation and standardization of territory that underpins them. This model, if unaddressed, risks becoming too static to respond to such epochal changes.

At this juncture, the main lesson that should be drawn from DIY urbanism is the necessity of pursuing environmental adaptation – in the form of small-scale strategies that are cost effective, light-touch, flexible and reversible – rather than blindly chasing technical solutions aimed at environmental transformation. From the point of view of urban policies, the focus should be on defining new strategies and instruments of inclusion that challenge the orthodoxies on which traditional urban planning is based. Temporary building permits, tenure rights not necessarily linked to a particular plot of land, and unwritten or unmapped plans are potential tools that could be elaborated on when attempting to adapt to fast-changing urban realities.

In sum, rather than forcibly formalizing the informal, the perspective offered by DIY urbanism suggests the opposite – that the instruments of urban planning and management should, at least in part, be informalized.

Notes

1   For example, the 2014 housing census shows that 8 per cent of Freetown's dwellings are 'pan body' (temporary houses made of iron sheets or nylon) and 12 per cent are made of mud bricks. However, in many slums, concrete block buildings can be found alongside brick houses and makeshift shelters. Regarding tenure, only 3.2 per cent of residents claim to illegally occupy the building in which they live, but property rights in slums is a complex matter, with many dwellers unclear as to what legal or illegal tenancy means (Statistics Sierra Leone, 2016).

2   Even the 1991 Constitution of Sierra Leone, in article 170, states that: 'The law of Sierra Leone shall comprise … customary law: the rules of law which by custom are applicable to particular communities in Sierra Leone.'

Chapter 10

DIY URBANISM AS ECOTOPIA: THE CASE OF THE GREEN CAMP GALLERY IN DURBAN, SOUTH AFRICA

Antje Daniel

Introduction

Currently, half the world's population live in cities, with Africa being the continent with the fastest-growing urban population. This trend is often idealized by scholars and developmental agencies, who highlight changing living conditions in urban areas arising due to the emerging middle classes, and economic growth in countries such as Kenya and South Africa (Daniel et al., 2016). Such studies 'replace the usual motifs of hunger, diseases, environmental degradation, and conflict, with images of creative energy, entrepreneurship, and prosperity' (Beall 2013: 23). Even so, cities in Africa continue to be shaped by issues such as informal settlements, poverty, unemployment, insecurity, pollution, waste disposal and crime, which overshadow this enthusiasm for urbanization and exist despite economic growth. Thus, we see an ambivalence between the rising wealth and persistent socio-economic marginalization present in many African cities (Baell, 2013: 29). These problems, in combination with rising urbanization, pose a challenge to the South African state.

On a national and even municipal level, government's reaction to this has been through urban planning aimed at an inclusive city (Obrist, 2013: 10; Samara, He and Chen, 2013). However, despite the post-apartheid government prioritizing the provision of housing and public services within its anti-poverty agenda, these issues remain present in South African society (see Seeking and Nattrass, 2005; Vusi, 2015).[1] As Gillian Hart (2013: 5) argues, in the 2000s, local governments became the most important actors in managing poverty and deprivation. Politicians, though, are often unable to offer the country's rising urban citizenship the services they require, particularly in informal settlements. As such, those in informal settlers – as well as other citizens – are often forced to resort to public protest in their claim for social services and the right to the city (Alexander, 2010; Mottiar and Bond, 2012). Such public protests are a near daily occurrence, with several newspapers calling South Africa the 'protest capital of the world' (Runciman, 2017). The high number of protests is related to the particular way in which change within the country tends to be initiated. As political scientist Steven Friedman observes: 'If you want … change in South Africa, create a crisis – then stand by to negotiate a way out of it' (Friedman, 2018).

This approach to address a situation of discontentment is a consequence of South Africa's history, in which social and political problems have been solved through social movement pressure (see Colland, 2016).[2] Most practices and policies do not change until a crisis emerges, at which point citizens exert pressure on the government in the hope their problems will be solved, or at least addressed. While people are more likely to express their grievances through public protest, less noticed is how they organize themselves in do-it-yourself (DIY) activism. Generally, these collectively organized citizen groups receive less attention than social movements, as they are not as immediately visible to the public. However, such forms of self-organization show an alternative way – beyond visible public protest – of coping with crisis in growing urban areas. The Green Camp Gallery Project (Green Camp) in Durban is one these forms of self-organization, with its members aiming to initiate change by doing it themselves, irrespective of government intervention. The Green Camp exemplifies how change can be initiated by living differently, rather than simply claiming rights.

Localized in the industrial area of Durban, the Green Camp aspires to an alternative future shaped by green and post-growth thinking, as well as the spirituality of nature and the collective practices of *Ubuntu*. For Green Camp members, utopia is not merely a fiction to be imagined, but rather a form of practice in which the future becomes apparent in daily life. Following this understanding of utopia as a method of aspiring to an alternative future (Levitas, 2014), the Green Camp can be interpreted as utopian community in which ecotopism becomes visible in the do-it-yourself practices of its members.

Accordingly, the Green Camp questions a number of widespread assumptions about urbanization. *First,* the Green Camp contradicts the common perception that poor people are focused solely on their daily and material needs, and so protest in favour of state responsibility due to their being unable to problem solved by themselves or imagine an alternative future. Instead, in creating space with which to cope with situations of insecurity and marginalization, the Green Camp exemplifies peoples agency and creativity (Förster, 2013). As such, it may be viewed as a laboratory for an alternative – an ecotopian, do-it-yourself activism. It's imaginary of a sustainable, post-growth society that contradicts the existing market-driven political economy.

Second, the Green Camp overcomes popular preconceptions regarding awareness of climate change and the need for environmentalism, especially in areas such as Durban. Durban is the largest city in the South African province of KwaZulu-Natal, and, other than Johannesburg, the most important manufacturing hub in the country, with industry-related environmental pollution and health problems an ongoing problem for the city. Environmentalism in South Africa is often described as being an issue taken up by the middle and upper classes, with poor people lacking concern about environmental pollution or climate change.[3] The Green Camp, however, illustrates that sustainable living in an urban context is not necessarily linked to prosperity. In creatively responding to a situation of insecurity, marginalization and uncertainty, the Green Camp offers a pathway in which environmental consciousness, spirituality and *Ubuntu* play a fundamental role, and space is created to overcome the everyday segregation of South African society.

The exploration of the Green Camp Gallery Project in this chapter is the result of qualitative research conducted between 2016 and 2018, comprising biographical and narrative interviews with the founders, trustees and supporters, as well as informal talks and participant observation.[4] This research was further bolstered by analysis of social media reports and newspaper articles.

In the following, I will argue that the Green Camp Gallery Project can be interpreted as a do-it-yourself ecotopian activism. Building on this, I will introduce the reader to the Green Camp through reference to its creation, future imaginary and daily practices. Moreover, I will discuss the ambivalences of the Green Camp in terms of how open or closed off it can be in the context of its growing success, and the downsides this brings.

Do-it-yourself urbanism as utopia?

The literature on do-it-yourself (DIY) urbanism encompasses a broad range of urban projects, such as guerrilla greening, urban gardening, graffiti and other forms of street art or aspirational urbanism (Douglas, 2013; Iveson, 2013). These various activities can be regarded as micro-spatial urban practices that are reshaping the urban place, through which urban citizens are maintaining their agency. In independently solving problems, mostly on a limited budget and sometimes involving unauthorized use of public space, citizens are adapting creatively to the challenges of urbanity. Such ideas fit with the work of Henri Lefebvre (1972), who highlights the potential of citizens to 'inhabit' urban space and produce new meaning, thereby questioning urban development from below. Generally, DIY activist initiatives are temporally limited, created in an unauthorized urban place with the hope of creating a lively environment. Several studies argue that DIY urbanism represents citizens claiming their rights through resistance to urban bureaucratic development plans (Williams, 2004; Douglas, 2013; Talen, 2015). Beyond this, however, DIY urbanism can be perceived as a form of resistance, an alternative economy, personal or artistic expression, an urban sub-culture, vandalism, or self-help improvisation in response to crisis (Iveson, 2013).

While DIY is usually considered a temporary strategy to recreate space (Talen, 2015: 135), it is also possible to regard it as an expression of an utopian community. While the notion of DIY urbanism focusses on agency and creativity, the idea of utopia highlights the imaginary of the activists involved. Thus, the future-oriented dimension implied by utopia offers a means of enlarging the debate on DIY urbanism, making visible the norms and values of those actors practising alternative ways of everyday living and production. In this way, utopia need not be perceived as a normative aspiration or an imagined ideal society, but rather a method of understanding future imaginations through alternative practices and aspirations (Levitas, 2014).

This may be perceived as an unusual approach to take regarding urban planning in Africa, as utopia is generally regarded as either a literary genre or a description of an ideal society (see Wegner, 2002; Jamerson, 2005; Levitas, 2011; Schröderle, 2012). Research on utopia has its roots in critical examinations of state and society seen in political works such as Thomas More's *Utopia* (2011 [1516]), originally published in 1516. The utopian idea of a 'good life' or 'ideal society' can be found in almost every historical period and culture, whether in religious, spiritual, secular, literary or political form. Here, utopia can be regarded as utilizing the imagination to hold a mirror up to society, as well as a means of imagining a future society based on justice and harmony: 'Utopia is about how we would live and what kind of a world we would live in if we could do just that' (Levitas, 2011: 1).

While, historically, most utopian studies have presented a fictional depiction of what an ideal society should look like, the idea that utopia is not merely a dream has existed since the beginning of the nineteenth century. For instance, with his notion of 'concrete' utopia, Ernst Bloch (1985 [1959]) demonstrates that utopia can be a real aim developed through learning, emotional realization and hope. As such, utopia becomes a potentially realizable. More recently, Eric O. Wright (2010) has used the notion of 'real utopia' to describe a journey that realizes utopian imaginaries, while Ruth Levitas (2014) describes utopia as a method, analysing from an imaginary perspective how ideas about an ideal society are performed and transformed. These understandings of utopia have been used to understand different forms of self-organization, among them eco villages. Framed as utopian communities, these studies describe how utopia can become a real possibility, bridging the tension between future imaginaries and everyday life through 'alternatives' (Andreas, 2015; Daniel and Exner, 2020).

In relation to these studies, the Green Camp Gallery Project can be interpreted as a DIY ecotopian community. Here, the term utopian community is used to highlight the Green Camp's future-oriented practices, which aspire to an 'alternative' future in everyday life. These practices are visible in the behaviour of the founder and other supporting members of the Green Camp, exemplifying that an 'alternative utopian' future can be made possible through the daily practices of an eco-utopian community. The prefix 'eco' highlights the fact that green thinking and sustainability shape these future imaginaries, aspirations and daily practices.[5]

Utopian communities build upon a critique of society by offering ways of practising daily life differently based on future imaginaries of an ideal or good life. However, the possibility of living life differently is not a given, as it requires a certain kind of creativity to imagine an alternative life equal to the daily challenges of the urban context: 'Without an imagination of what we as actors aim for, what we intend to achieve, consciously or unconsciously we would not engage in any practice, neither individually or a social actor' (Förster, 2013: 245). Creativity builds on particular forms of agency and social practice, which are related to individual life experience. According to Till Förster (2013: 244), creativity in urban contexts is not only individual, but also social, as the city is a social space. Thus, alternative creative practices always follow an imaginary about how the broader society should be. The Green Camp exemplifies the agency of activists and contradicts widespread pessimism regarding how imaginaries and futures are being engulfed by the ongoing neoliberal crisis (see Goldstone and Obrarrio, 2016).

The Green Camp is not a coherent in itself – rather it integrates a variety of aspirations, imaginaries and forms of agency. However, it is in the daily practices of the founder and his partner that the future imagination becomes most clearly visible.

The Green Camp Gallery Project: Tales from the imperfect practices of an ecotopian community

As is the case for many South African cities, Durban is shaped by discrepancies, the divisions in its social, economic and spatial life rooted in the past segregation of the apartheid era. During apartheid, the Black majority was denied the right to democratic participation, and the population segregated between *non-whites* and *whites*, with the former group evicted to homelands. This restricted each social group to a particular quarter, hindering the emergence of an overbridging urban society. Even today, the segregation of society persists, despite the post-apartheid government's attempts at inclusion. Thus, the poorest population remains spatially excluded and socially marginalized (Haferburg and Huchzermeyer, 2014; Vusi, 2015).

Nevertheless, urban planning continues to follow the blueprint of a safe, clean, vibrant and inclusive city. By contrast, the Green Camp Gallery Project does not wish to overcome urban challenges through cleaning them up – rather, its approach is to accept the ugliness and brokenness of the area. The Green Camp is located in an industrial area, surrounded by small- and medium-sized enterprises and home to relatively few residents. Previously, the property was a place for vagrants, prostitution and illegal squatters. From the perspective of Green Camp activists, keeping the place untidy acts as a reminder of how society is, with the demolished house symbolic of the fact that spatial and social segregation is ongoing and requires long-term transformation. However, by planting flowers and vegetables they aim to show that a healing process is possible.[6] Thus, their objective is not to clean up the property and replace it with modern architecture – instead, by integrating the brokenness of the ruin as symbolic starting point, they aim to support citizens' creativity and self-help capacity in a healing process that overcomes spatial and social segregation.

The founder of the Green Camp initiated the Green Camp Gallery Project in 2013. Together with his supporters, he set up the Green Camp, and in 2016 was joined by his partner. Both live on the property, while others – for instance, the trustees, supporters and friends – have permanent residences. In line with the idea of the Green Camp as an 'ecotopian community', all future imaginaries are based on critiques of society and personal life experiences (1). Furthermore, the community demonstrate alternative future imaginaries (2), which activists aspire to in their daily practices (3). In aspiring to an alternative future, an ambivalence between opening up and closing off becomes evident (4). Through following these features, the sections below proceed to describe the Green Camp as an ecotopian DIY community.

Biographical approach to criticism

For the founder of the Green Camp, green and sustainable living represents healing – healing from a history of discrimination and healing from the exclusion he experienced in South African society:

> The reason why I am here today because of the burning need to tell my story as it is and tell my history as I want to. I realised that the social structures of our society – they have never allowed me to do that. ... My background is colonisation. It is somehow a loss of identity. Not by choice, but by technically implemented systems.[7]

The founder grew up in a township close to Durban where, as a Zulu, he experienced the shadow of the apartheid regime and the discrimination of a segregated society in the post-apartheid era. The experience of being forced to live at the margins of society and the difficulty of overcoming such structural discrimination led to deep frustration and a loss of identity. This loss of identity was also a response to daily life in an informal settlement, in which values, norms and family relations were being undermined.[8] The founder decided to express his feelings in a dance company, and so travelled to Sweden. Over time, his thinking changed:

> The idea for the Green Camp came about from the difficulties I witnessed in my travels of about 16 years in Europe ... Being there, you look at home through a different lens. ... All the wealth is over here. I felt homeless in Europe and homeless when I came back.
>
> (Sosibom, 2018)

He decided to create his own home place, which would bring together the green sustainable living he had experienced in Sweden with the spirituality he located in South Africa. Having experienced social marginalization and exclusion, the founder set up the Green Camp with the aim of overcoming societal constraints and offering a place in which alternative imaginations are possible, thereby giving hope to people and fostering their self-help abilities.

I realized that it is the system that is within our social environment that hasn't allowed any sort of true integration ... and never mind the ability for people to imagine. I saw that the system does not allow.[9] Thus, the creation of the Green Camp Gallery Project is a direct response to its founder's personal experiences and social criticisms.

The Green Camp's members and supporters do not necessarily subscribe to the founder's critique – rather, they share a general feeling of societal discontent and a desire to find alternative ways of living. This becomes evident in the life story of the founder's partner. Having had a prosperous upbringing in a well-educated Swedish middle-class family, she became increasingly frustrated at the competitiveness of her society and its fixed scheme of life, which is decoupled from nature. She decided to leave home and eventually found a way of realizing her future imagination by joining the Green Camp.[10] Beyond the narrow circle of the founder, trustees and supporters, the Green Camp offers a place for people who are discontented with society and are searching for a 'place of transition: a place to rest and which is healthy' (Green Camp Gallery Project, 2017).

Most members of the Green Camp do share the founder's criticism of an 'economised society'. As he observes: 'We are living in a world of success, with a lot of competition. We are trying to bring an alternative. ... It is about creating an alternative system for our city.'[11] The founder criticizes his society's dominant lifestyle, which is based on economic values in the form of success, competition and consumption. Thus, the Green Camp contests mainstream future imaginaries, which are built on ideas of economic growth: People are thinking it is the money that solves problems. They give everything, their brains, their dignity, their spirits to money. ... I didn't have money. I have a lot of wealth. I have a lot of wealth, but it's not in a form of money. So, nobody sees this wealth. That's sad. And so, I said okay, then I'm going to build a new institution, that's going to realize. That's going to be recognized. That's going to last for generations to come and that's going to be an alternative.[12] In sum, the critique not only addresses the discrimination, marginalization and loss of identity of 'Blacks' in South African society, but more widely its pattern of capitalist production, consumption and 'economised social behaviour'. Such arguments go far beyond the Green Camp Gallery Project, with aspirations towards a fairer, post-growth society growth arising in many places across the world (see Rosa and Henning, 2018). In South Africa, for instance, Rhodes Must Fall has highlighted discrimination against Blacks in universities, while the Abahlali base Mjondolo movement has made claims for social services in socio-economically marginalized areas. While these social movements usually try to initiate change by claiming government responsibility, the Green Camp addresses feelings of discontent by initiating change through everyday practices. In this, its outstanding features are the radical daily practice of living in a ruin and the degree of privation the founder and his partner accept in order that they can pursue their imaginary of a good life.

Imagining a society beyond economic exploitation and growth

Critique is the basis for developing an imaginary of what society should be – if we know what is wrong in society we can develop alternatives. The Green Camp's aim of establishing a sustainable and socially responsible form of living within a post-growth society is a response to the economic focus of South African society, as well as the segregation and discrimination that are a part of this. Self-reliant forms of production should fulfil daily needs. Partly, this imaginary is located in rurality, which allows for being close to nature.[13]

From the perspective of the Green Camp activists, contemporary South African society has severed the spiritual connection to nature, thereby preventing spiritual forms of living. This is because the value of nature is now mostly seen in terms of resources and exploitation, with its spiritual features ignored or even destroyed. As such, gardening and self-reliance offers a means of reconnecting with nature's spirituality, providing a source for 'traditional healing methods', as well as encounters with ancestors. Thus, the Green Camp intends to preserve nature in order to ensure such spirituality can be practised, and traditions carried over into the future. The founder explains:

> So if we can all do that, then this world would be a better place. So what I'm saying is that within Green Camp we really learn from the original. The natural ecosystem.[14]

Building on this insight, the imagined lifestyle should recognize the spirituality of nature and value the supposed spiritual knowledge of 'traditional' healers, namely the *sangomas*. According to this perspective, nature is not something to be exploited, but rather should be conserved as being part of human life and its cosmology. Similarly, nature is something that should form part of the Green Camp's urban architecture (Green Camp Gallery Project, 2017). Reconnecting to nature means symbolically intertwining urban life with 'tradition', thereby recreating a supposedly traditional identity and regaining dignity and respect.

Furthermore, the Green Camp aims at creating a space of otherness by referring to *Ubuntu*, a Bantu term for humanity towards others (see Mnyaka and Motlhabi, 2005; Praeg, 2014). *Ubuntu* builds on the idea of helping rather than competing with one other. While South African society remains highly fragmented, the Green Camp aims at giving misfits a welcoming space and encountering them with respect. The idea of the Green Camp as an inclusive space is in contrast to the spatial segregation of Durban's urban space.

Lastly, the Green Camp aims at opening up minds to change, and to embracing new ideas and imaginations. The Green Camp perceives itself as a laboratory for another society, with the founder stating: 'We want a showcase, that it is possible. And when people believe it, then there is going to be more hands and more numbers of community.'[15] The Green Camp aims at influencing broader society through acting as a role model. This is why it remains open to cooperation, as well as visitors from both Durban and further afield (Project Proposal Green Camp Gallery Project, 2017).

Aspiring to an alternative future: Daily practices

The Green Camp developed a ten-year plan for his future imagination of the Green Camp Gallery Project, based on a philosophy of three phases: *recycling*, *rehabilitation* and *stimulation*.

The first phase of *recycling*, which started in 2013 and lasted for three years, aimed at clearing up the property. Xolani Hlongwa and his friends used the materials left over from the demolished house: 'While many may rise from the rubble, we chose to work with it' (van Niekerk, 2016). A small flat was constructed in one corner of the property, where the founder and his partner live today. Likewise, vegetables – such as cassava trees – were planted amid the rubbish and ruins. The main aim was to create a living and working place for the project, and to do this without financial investment. From the founder's perspective, being independent from material needs and societal constraints paved the way for thinking and living differently, prompting him to interrogate if and how he fitted into society, as well as to question mainstream society more broadly.[16]

The second phase of *rehabilitation* intended to showcase the possibility of living differently. Firstly, the founder and his supporters run educational projects in order to share their knowledge on recycling, sustainable living, urban agriculture and organic food production. Through workshops on recycling methods, cooking classes and discussion forums, the Green Camp has begun spreading its vision and offering an inclusive space in which alternative forms of production and living become possible.[17] For instance, in collaboration with the non-governmental organization One Voice South Africa, the Green Camp conducts workshops for schools, teaching teenagers about recycling materials and methods, and introducing them to composting and an organic kitchen. These activities show how food can be grown in an urban environment, thereby demonstrating to the children a simple means of responding to food insecurity and rising food prices, while at the same time reconnecting with nature (van der Walt, 2016).

Secondly, the Green Camp regularly sells its harvest from gardening (and from organic farms) at Saturday markets. Its members want to promote the local economy by creating a platform that encourages small and creative enterprises, such as those selling second-hand clothing (Gazette Weekly, 2016). On market day, the property of the Green Camp turns into a lively place where people from different backgrounds gather. Upper-class youth drink coffee, artists paint on the walls, and homeless people drop in and relax.[18] In the context of South Africa's segregated society, the Green Camp manifests itself as an unusual but inclusive place. Today Green Camp no longer organizes market days but sells its products on other markets and occasions.

Thirdly, the Green Camp defines itself as a space for art, with almost every wall of the ruined house covered in graffiti. As the founder explains: 'Art is a message we choose to convey the message of greening and organic environment' (Green Camp, 2016).

The Green Camp offers a space for exhibitions, music, theatre and discussion forums. It is a space where people can connect and develop new ideas – in short, it is a space for creativity. The artist Jessica Pike, for instance, used found objects and photographs to create a public installation (van Niekerk, 2016).

The third and final phase (current phase) of *stimulation* aims at establishing the Green Camp and its imaginary as a role model. From the founder's point of view, South African society is suffering from a lack of space for social relationships and an unhealthy obsession with money. This phase is therefore intended to exemplify that a post-growth form of living based on *Ubuntu* and spirituality is possible.

Beyond this three-phase pathway, the everyday lives of the founder and his partner demonstrate that living without wealth in a ruin is possible, even healing. They practise a humble life in which food, nature, reflection and deep social relations play a fundamental role. Having time to reflect; taking care of nature; questioning existing values, norms and roles; and confronting and challenging unreflective social behaviour – this is the basis for how they elaborate their pathway. A conscious daily life and a willingness to challenge social behaviour that may be built on discrimination or hierarchies is, for the founder, a process of 'healing' from the experiences he faced in South Africa, as well as a means by which he and his partner can realize their future imaginary. The multicultural relationship between the two offers a space to reflect and build an understanding that circumvents racial stereotypes.

Imperfect tales: Ambivalences between openness and closure

Many people have been attracted by the idea of the Green Camp. While some are fascinated by the place itself and its symbolism, others admire its ethos of sustainable living and being close to nature. Some join the Green Camp for an art performance or simply value daily resistance to mainstream society of the founder and his partner. One of the trustees joined the Green Camp because it is a lively and creative space for environmental activists, breathing new life into the scene.[19] Another trustee argues that the Green Camp gives hope by showcasing how an alternative form of living can be practised: 'they believe in what they are doing and they treating people with dignity.'[20] Others just like the atmosphere, which allows for self-expression. Some citizens, however, are shocked by the fact that the couple is living in a demolished house, and feel threatened by their unusual and confronting lifestyle.[21] Thus, reaction to the Green Camp ranges from appreciation to dismissal.

Realizing dreams and practising an alternative daily life has its downsides. The partner of the founder reports that from time to time she gets the feeling that 'society works against us.'[22] For instance, the property owner tried to evict the Green Camp and cut off the electricity. Daily life is full of privations, as living in a demolished house means accepting insecurity. Among other things, several of the few items of value the couple owns have been stolen, while living on savings and self-reliant production requires austerity and abandoning privileges. Such consequences are accepted, though at times it can lead to friction in family life and among friends.[23] The Green Camp is also confronted with free-riders – people moving in and trying to take advantage through co-opting the project or using it as a springboard for contacts or other resources.

The idea of the Green Camp is spreading, making it increasingly important that the project is protected. As a consequence, an ambivalence has arisen between being open – in order to act as a role model – and the need to close up, in order to protect against co-optation. As a trustee explains, the Green Camp faces a number of problems and is at a crossroads.[24] Even so, the Green Camp remains a space that provokes enthusiasm and invites people to think and live differently, with the passion and persistency of the founder and his partner exemplifying how an uneven and sometimes confrontational existence may offer a pathway to a better life.

Conclusion

The Green Camp is not perfect, is not unique in its aspirations for a post-growth society, and cannot in itself solve such overarching problems in South African society as poverty or discrimination. Nevertheless, it offers an 'island' of hope amid a challenging environment, its members' persistent and challenging way of living offering an alternative to the constraints of mainstream society. The Green Camp also contradicts the argument that less wealthy citizens are solely focused on satisfying their material needs, with environmentalism restricted to the upper classes.

Based on a ten-year plan, the Green Camp aims at establishing a green and sustainable lifestyle hub. In doing so, the Green Camp emphasizes the agency and creativity of citizens. However, agency is not a given, and so the emergence of the Green Camp must be seen in the context of its founder's background. Based on feelings of being different, experiences of racism, exclusion from South African society and the drive to find somewhere where he could feel at home, the founder was inspired by different cultures to develop his own future imaginary. Arising from this, the Green Camp can be perceived as an ecotopian DIY community shaped by the idea of a post-growth society based on nature, spirituality and *Ubuntu*. However, adhering to this future imaginary can be challenging, and has led to the Green Camp being co-opted on several occasions. Even if the Green Camp is ultimately unable to fulfil its aim of being a role model, it has already inspired many people through showcasing the ideas and, more importantly, attitude of its founder and his partner: that aspirations to an alternative future are based on persistence and maintaining hope, and that future imaginaries must be practised in daily life regardless of the obstacles faced.

The Green Camp belongs to wave of self-organized citizen groups worldwide that are questioning the exploitive dimensions of the economy. Following this trend, the Green Camp has the potential to connect with other projects that aspire to a life beyond economic growth and marginalization. The Green Camp also has a part to play in the search for an alternative, post-growth future that is increasingly shaping academic and public debate in South Africa and beyond. However, contrary to a number of social movements, the Green Camp does not aim to initiate change by holding government accountable rather practice the imaginary of a post-growth society in everyday life in order to exemplify an alternative, ecotopian community future. In doing so, they demonstrate that utopia can be more than mere fiction, and that a future imaginary can be achieved under certain favourable conditions through daily practices.

Notes

1   For further information about the history of the South African metropolis, see Bickford-Smith (2016).

2   For further information about social movements in South Africa, see Ballard, Habib and Valodia (2006).

3   For further information about the environmental movement in South Africa, see Cook (2006); Müller (2017).

4   The Green Camp Gallery Project is one of the cases featured in the research project 'Towards a sociology of lived utopias. How the future becomes present in imaginaries and aspirations of lived utopias in South Africa'. The research project investigates various collective forms of resistance and their utopian imaginations (see Daniel and Exner, 2020; Daniel, 2022; Daniel and Platzky Miller, 2022).

5   We are witnessing an increasing number of eco-related projects around the world, such as gardening, eco villages and other forms of sustainable living. The Green Camp is part of this wave of reaction addressing ecological and economic crisis.

6   Interview, trustee, 24 September 2017.

7   Interview, founder, 25 August 2016.

8   Interview, founder, 25 August 2016.

9   Interview, founder, 25 August 2016.

10   Interview, founder, 24 September 2018.

11   Interview, founder, 25 August 2016.

12   Interview, founder, 25 August 2016.

13   Interview, founder, 24 September 2017.

14   Interview, founder, 25 August 2016.

15   Interview, founder, 25 August 2016.

16   Interview, founder, 22 September 2017.

17   Interview, founder, 22 September 2017.

18   Participant observation, 24 September 2017.

19   Interview, trustee, 15 September 2018.

20   Interview, trustee, 25 September 2018.

21   Interview, trustee, 25 September 2018.

22   Interview, partner of the founder, 14 September 2018.

23   Interview, partner of the founder, 14 September 2018.

24   Interview, trustee, 25 September 2018.

Chapter 11

DISABILITY AND URBANISM IN MALAWI

Jonathan Makuwira

Introduction

The current global trend for population growth, including in urban areas, is increasingly becoming a challenge that, if left unattended, is likely to become a costly worldwide phenomenon. Not only does this state of affairs set a policy conundrum, it creates a situation whereby the most vulnerable populations – especially people with disabilities in urban areas – will continue to be trapped in a vicious cycle of poverty. While the challenges faced by people with disabilities in cities across the world are many, so are the attempts to ameliorate them. This chapter aims to highlight critical issues of urbanism and disability in Malawi. First, the scene is set with a brief account of disability and the idea of 'do it yourself' (DIY) in Africa, with issues of disability and urbanism as a development issue analysed. Second, the policy context for people with disabilities in Malawi is set out through a snapshot of relevant issues, including accessibility, mobility, inclusion and exclusion, participation, and government support mechanisms. Building on this, using critical discourse analysis and disability-inclusive development theories, the chapter interrogates the dynamics of urbanization and its impact on people with disabilities. Third, the chapter aims at developing a better understanding of how disabled people's organizations (DPOs) support their constituencies in the context of growing urbanization. The central assumption of the chapter is that despite urban areas supposedly being accommodative of all citizens, people with disabilities often find themselves on the periphery of society. Furthermore, disability in urban areas has been – and continues to be – 'commodified' due to the limited services directed towards people with disabilities. This has created a yawning gap, which has been filled by alternative 'DIY' measures implemented by either DPOs or syndicates seeking to take advantage of the situation for their own benefit. Despite the growth in the number of DPOs in Malawi, there has been little attempt to engage with the DIY approach. The chapter concludes by suggesting a model that places people with disabilities in urban settings firmly within the mainstream development agenda.

Disability and DIY in Africa

The situation of people with disabilities in Africa is extremely complex. While statistics on the state of disability, as well as relevant organizations, are not always readily available, attempts have been made to highlight critical issues pertaining to the plight of people with disabilities, especially in urban settings. While Africa is typically seen as the least urbanized continent, its recent rate of urbanization – which between 2010 and 2015 was pegged at 1.4 per cent – actually makes it the second-fastest urbanizing continent behind Asia (Sow, 2015). The importance of this growth cannot be overemphasized, particularly in relation to vulnerable populations, such as people with disabilities. Back in 2011, I noted that there would be significant challenges due to this rapid urban expansion and the inevitable creation of megacities in Africa: in 2010, African's urban areas were host to an estimated 400 million people; by 2050, it is anticipated this figure will rise to some 1.26 billion people (Makuwira, 2013).

As it stands, cities such as Lagos, Cairo and Johannesburg are unable to adequately provide accessible and inclusive infrastructure, with the greater part of their infrastructure catering exclusively to 'able' residents while barely acknowledging the presence of people with disabilities (Agbo and Makuwira, 2019). Only a negligible percentage of public buildings and spaces are accessible to people with physical disabilities, denying them the use of the modern facilities and infrastructure these contemporary African cities take such pride in. As Lang et al. point out, while the Africa Union has made some inroads into ensuring access to education, health, employment and social protection, there remains a yawning gap in urban space design, as well as 'an apparent and discernible "disconnect" between the rights of disabled people and their inclusion enshrined and guaranteed through the ratification of the UNCRPD, and application of its principles in the actual process of policy development and implementation' (Lang et al., 2017: 2). This is echoed in a study by Munthali et al. (2017), who, in their analysis of healthcare provision for people with disabilities in Malawi, highlight severe limitations in both rural and urban areas. The implications of increased urbanization on country-specific challenges are immense, and will be turned to later in the chapter. Before this, though, the concept of DIY in Africa – which is critical to a country such as Malawi – requires further interrogation.

The practice that today – at least in the United States of America – is known as 'do it yourself' developed from roots in urban design (see Douglas, 2013). However, DIY is not a clear-cut concept from a development studies or sociological perspective, and its definition remains problematic. In general terms, though, it can be seen as 'small-scale, creative, unauthorised, yet intentionally functional and civic-minded "contributions" and "improvements" to urban spaces inspired by official infrastructure' (Douglas, 2013: 6). These contributions and improvements can be seen in, for example, Dhaka in Bangladesh, where – according to a Rockefeller Foundation report – people in slums, who thrive on informal economies, are directly integrated into city planning and priorities

(Swift, Sweeting and Magee, 2016). In Africa, such stories are not so common. Where they do exist, contributions and improvements are often carried out by non-governmental organizations (NGOs) or, in the case of people with disabilities, DPOs. This will be elaborated later in the chapter.

Before proceeding to an analysis of disability and urbanism in Malawi, it is necessary to examine how urban centres in Malawi are understood. Any discussion involving Malawi's population must, inevitably, be based on the official statistics provided by the 2008 National Population and Housing Census, which puts the country's overall population at 14.27 million (National Statistical Office, 2008). However, unofficial data for 2018 indicates this figure has grown by over 5 million in the interim, with Worldometers (2020) estimating that Malawi is now home to roughly 19 million people. The 2008 National Population and Housing Census found that 15.3 per cent of Malawi's population lives in urban areas of various sizes. While this may be viewed as a moderate level of urbanization compared to other countries in the developing world, Malawi's 5.2 per cent annual rate of urbanization is significantly higher than its annual national growth rate of 2.8 per cent. As such, the national urbanization level is expected to rise from 15.3 per cent to 30 per cent by 2030, and to 50 per cent by 2050.

To date, the definition of urban centres reflects the 1987 National Physical Development Plan (NPDP), which defines urban centres according to level of service provision in areas such as administration, commerce and business, health, education, and infrastructure. Malawi currently has four cities: Blantyre, Lilongwe, Mzuzu and Zomba. Rapid urbanization in these cities has resulted in the mushrooming of informal settlements, poor infrastructure and basic service delivery, with national projects being located in centres other than those suggested in the NPDP. According to Manda (2013), the influx of people from rural to urban areas has placed huge strains on urban authorities, which are constantly experiencing planning and management challenges related to urban development. This situation has been worsened by the rural focus of Malawi's development agenda and a lack of political will. As a result, urban areas tend to have insufficient funds and capacity, leading to inadequate basic services and weak accountability within governance structures. This, in turn, leads to deprivation of rights, lack of participation, and a failure to achieve national and international development goals. The resultant situation is characterized by a lack of control, guidance and regulation concerning development in both established and emerging towns.

Disability: An overview from a development perspective

The current global discourse on disability makes clear that disability is not only a human rights issue but also a critical development issue. Irrefutable evidence points to around 15 per cent the world's population (1 billion people) having some form of disability, of whom at least 80 per cent are estimated to live in poverty (World Health Organization, 2011). While, at its inception, the Millennium

Development Goals (MDGs) ignored issues of disability and development, the United Nations 2030 Agenda for Sustainable Development Agenda clearly states that disability should not prevent access to development opportunities or the realization of human rights and potential. The current Sustainable Development Goals (SDGs) framework – which addresses essential development domains, including education, employment and decent work, social protection, resilience to and mitigation of disasters, sanitation, transport and non-discrimination – stipulates seven clear targets, with explicit reference to people with disabilities. Alongside these are six further targets concerning persons in vulnerable situations, which include people with disabilities. Of particular importance in relation to the SDGs is the New Urban Agenda (United Nations, 2016), which specifically commits to promoting measures that facilitate equal access to public spaces, facilities, technology, systems and services for people with disabilities in urban and rural areas. These international instruments draw on the ongoing discourse concerning the link between poverty and disability, which for a time remained largely invisible in mainstream development literature. Underscoring this new focus is the argument that people with disabilities are not only poorer in economic terms, but also marginalized in terms of access to health care, education, employment and broader social inclusion. Groce (2015) maintains that people with disabilities often face stigma and prejudice, which severely constrains their voice in both households and communities.

Disability issues in Malawi

In order to understand the effects of urbanism and urbanization in Malawi, we need to first understand the broader situation of people with disabilities in the country. According to the Malawi Disability Act of 2012, disability is defined as 'a long term physical, mental, intellectual, or sensory impairment which in interaction with various barriers may hinder the full and effective participation in society of a person on equal basis with other persons' (Government of Malawi, 2012: 3). The stated emphasis on participation is of critical importance to current development thinking. Not only is participation a form of empowerment, whereby individuals and/or communities can influence relevant decision-making processes and policy, it is also about holding duty-bearers to account.

Statistics on disability issues in Malawi are scarce due to poor documentation and limitations in researching the field. However, Munthali (2011) has shed some light on the current state of affairs, noting that as of 2003 about 4.18 per cent of Malawi's population constituted people with disabilities. This is backed up by the 2008 Population and Housing Census, which showed that of the then 14 million people in Malawi, roughly 498,000 (4 per cent) were people with disabilities. Of particular concern is that children with disabilities constitute 2.8 per cent of the country's population (National Statistical Office, 2008). Furthermore, a study by Munthali et al. (2013) highlights, 'The 2008 Malawi Housing and Population Census found that the prevalence of disability among children was lower at 2.4% (159,878) than among the general population at 4% (498,122). Prevalence was slightly higher among males at 2.5% (84,721) than females at 2.2% (75,157)' (Munthali et al., 2013: iv).

The statistics above follow an earlier attempt to understand the living conditions of people with disabilities in Malawi, which – despite being reliant on now outdated data – provides a number of important insights, including:

- The percentage of people with disabilities who have never been to school is twice that of the general population;
- The percentage of people with disabilities who are unemployed far exceeds that of the general population;
- Women with disabilities are more disadvantaged than men;
- Only 5 per cent of people with disabilities who need occupational training or welfare services actually receive such services or training; and
- Only 25 per cent of people with disabilities have access to medical treatment, technical aids, counselling or education (Leob and Eide, 2004; Wazikili et al., 2011).

The indications are clear: there is a marginal gap between people with disabilities and non-disabled people. Beyond the prejudice and discrimination suffered by people with disabilities in Malawi, this data points to the structural violence directed against them.

Having a disability in Malawi puts people at a disadvantage for the reasons highlighted earlier: lack of medical care, discrimination, higher chance of unemployment and, for women, gender-based violence. In addition, the way in which society constructs disability and frames the term itself is often disabling rather than enabling. Oppression, discrimination and other negative attitudinal traits are prevalent in Malawian society. Despite this, Chapter 4, Section 20, Subsection (1) of the Constitution of Malawi clearly stipulates: 'Discrimination of any person in any form is prohibited and all persons under any law guaranteed equal and effective protection against discrimination on grounds of race, colour, sex, language, nationality, ethnic or social origin, disability, property, birth or other status.'

This aside, the 'rurality' of disability in Malawi is where many challenges lie. According to the 2008 Population and Housing Census, the majority of people with disabilities (90.1 per cent) live in rural areas, where poverty is rampant and entrenched cultural practices against disability inclusion are equally prevalent. It is against this background that rural-to-urban migration – not only for people with disabilities, but more broadly – has increased over recent years (Makuwira, 2010). Thus, it can be seen that poverty constitutes an overarching issue when looking at why people with disabilities may be forced to beg on the streets of Malawi's cities.

Government efforts in Malawi

Over the past three decades, the government of Malawi has made attempts to put disability issues on the agenda. Part of this has involved developing an enabling environment through which other actors have been involved (see next section). As a point of departure, issues of access and support for people with disabilities are clearly articulated in the Constitution of Malawi, with Section 13(g) clearly stating:

> The State shall actively promote the welfare and development of the people of Malawi by progressively adopting and implementing policies and legislation aimed at achieving the following goals:
>
> g. Persons with Disabilities
>
> To enhance the dignity and quality of life of persons with disabilities by providing:
> i.   adequate and suitable access to public places;
> ii. fair opportunities in employment; and
> iii. the fullest possible participation in all spheres of Malawian society.

Similarly, Section 20(1) stipulates that:

> Discrimination of persons in any form is prohibited and all persons are, under any law, guaranteed equal and effective protection against discrimination on grounds of race, colour, sex, language, religion, political or other opinion, national, ethnic or social origin, disability, property, birth or other status or condition

Urbanism, people with disabilities, and disability people's organizations in Malawi

Whether we consider urbanism as the creation of place identity at a citywide level or more generally a way of life for city dwellers, there is cause for concern regarding people with disabilities worldwide, and particularly so in the case of Malawi. The fulfilment of city life requires equalization of opportunities, with an attendant reduction in inequality and poverty. However, lack of reliable data on disability issues in Malawi has compromised the extent to which disability-inclusive development can be mainstreamed in poverty reduction efforts, as well as in national development plans, such as the Malawi Growth and Development Strategy I, II and now III.

The issues pursued by DPOs in Malawi gravitate around 'equity', 'equality' and 'wellbeing'. While these issues are not unique, they are central to both human rights conventions and urbanism discourses. Equity, according to Jones (2009: iv), 'comes from the idea of moral equality, that people should be treated as equals'. Similarly, equality is about equal treatment of those presumed to be equal. Equity recognizes pre-existing disadvantages, and so the focus is on correcting these, thereby achieving *equality of outcomes* – elements such as equal life chances, concern for people's needs, and meritocracy are fundamental to achieving equity. Wellbeing, on the other hand, is extremely hard to define, as how the concept is understood is context specific. According to White (2010), there are three dimensions critical to the wellbeing debate. First is the *material aspect*, which is concerned with practical welfare and standard of living; second is the *social aspect*, which is concerned social relations and access to social goods; and third is the *human aspect*, which is concerned with human capabilities, attitudes to life and personal relationships (White, 2010: 7). It is on the basis of these three interrelated issues that DPOs in Malawi have sought to advance the voices of people with disabilities by forming associations and networks whose common themes are underpinned by equal rights and equalization of opportunities. More broadly, these entities use the idea of DIY to engender human wellbeing.

Since the advent of multi-party political pluralism in 1992, Malawi has made significant gains on the political front, reflected by an increase in the number of NGOs established to fill the gaps left by government. In terms of disability, the most significant change has been the formation of the Federation of Disability Organisations in Malawi (FEDOMA) as an umbrella organization for the country's DPOs. FEDOMA's aim is to provide a unified voice through:

- Promotion and advocacy for the rights of people with disabilities;
- Advocating for and monitoring equalization of opportunities for people with disabilities, as stipulated in the United Nation's Standard Rules; and
- Coordinating, and strengthening the capacity of, affiliated DPOs (FEDOMA, 2006).

FEDOMA currently has eight affiliate organizations, as shown in Table 11.1.

As can be seen from Table 11.1, DPOs in Malawi respond to various social, political and economic issues pertinent to the urbanism debate. More importantly, the issues these organizations tackle are political in nature, hence their push for policy dialogue and civic engagement.

Table 11.1 FEDOMA membership organizations

Member organization	Year formed	Major objective/Focus	Number of members
Malawi Union of the Blind (MUB)	1984	Cater for the needs of the visually impaired	1,762
Malawi Disability Sports Association (MADISA)	1998	Promote sporting activities for people with disabilities	562
Disabled Women in Development (DIWODE)	1996	Women's social, political and economic empowerment	300

(continued)

Member organization	Year formed	Major objective/Focus	Number of members
Association of the Physically Disabled (APDM)	1999	Enhance participation and self-reliance of people with disabilities in social life and development	1,000
The Albino Association of Malawi (TAAM)	1995	Inclusion and promotion of albinos' interests in social issues	Data not available
Parents of Disabled Children Association in Malawi (PODCAM)	2005	Promote interests and voice regarding the rights of children with disabilities	3,214
Malawi National Association of the Deaf	1990	Cater for the needs of the hearing impaired	2,396
Disabled Widows and Orphans Organisation in Malawi	Data not available	Enhance voices of widows and orphans in social and development issues	Data not available

Source: Makuwira and Kamanga (n.d.: 6).

Civic engagement and equalization of opportunities for people with disabilities in Malawi

Civic engagement is a difficult concept to define, but as a basic premise can be understood to mean community service, collective action, political involvement and social change (Diller, 2001; Adler and Goggin, 2005). It is the latter two aspects that are directly relevant to this chapter. While people with disabilities in Malawi are, by and large, engaged in community service through collective action, one can argue, from a Malawian perspective, is a form of DIY – the challenges they encounter are political in nature, hence the emphasis here on political involvement and social change. Social change is a complex process, as development, which is not only complex but political (Makuwira, 2013). Thus, *equalization of opportunities* not only means engaging in political processes in order to change power structures in favour of the vulnerable, it is also a social process in which the complex interplay of politics, society, resource transfers and agency must be acknowledged.

The preamble to Malawi's National Policy on Equalisation of Opportunities for Persons with Disabilities acknowledges that the country's people with disabilities are amongst the poorest of the poor (Braathen and Kvan, 2008). Furthermore, the policy's emphasis on 'inclusion' and 'creating an enabling environment' is an acknowledgement of the systematic and cultural marginalization suffered by people with disabilities (which runs contrary to the definition given above of urbanism as being the fulfilment of city life), with Chapter 1 of the policy stating that: 'Persons with disabilities in Malawi … face numerous challenges that result in their exclusion from the mainstream society. Many make their way through life … abandoned … neglected and vulnerable'

(Government of Malawi, 2006: 9). The existence of systematic marginalization is further authenticated by the statement: 'This means that there must be integration of disability issues in all government development strategies, planning and programmes' (Government of Malawi, 2006: 9).

Over the past twenty-five years, Malawi has implemented a number of national development policies, including Vision 2020, the Malawi Poverty Reduction Strategy Paper (MPRSP), the Malawi Economic Growth Strategy (MEGS), and the Malawi Growth and Development Strategy (MGDS I, II and now III). MGDS III is the current overarching strategy for the country's development vision, serving as a reference document not only for policymakers in government, but also the private sector, civil society organizations (CSOs), donors and other relevant stakeholders (including the general public).

The processes leading to the development of these documents merits attention, as they highlight the limitations imposed on people with disabilities regarding civic participation and DIY in Malawi. A comprehensive study on 'Social Inclusion of People with Disabilities in Poverty Reduction Policies and Instruments' (see Wazikili et al., 2011) observes how the process of MPRSPs was:

- Conceived and dominated by international donors, especially the IMF and World Bank;
- Initially not consultative, with most CSOs and DPOs excluded;
- Government-dominated, with the organisational structure having very little CSO and/or DPO presence.

While it may be argued that Wazakili's study is now somewhat out of date, it should nevertheless be noted that the current state of affairs for people with disabilities continues to fall short of the standards required by the SDGs (UN, 2015) envisaged as lifting people out of poverty by 2030.

DIY urbanism as a moral response to spectatorship of the commodification of disability

This section of the chapter takes a different approach to what has preceded it. Here, rather than simply writing academically, I intend to offer personal insight into the link between DIY as a concept and what I call 'spectatorship of the commodification of disability' (Chouliaraki, 2006). Thus far, I have argued that insufficient support for people with disabilities in Malawi has helped push a particular form of urbanism (as a way of life). This lack of attention has created another layer of DIY, with those people who support people with disabilities forced to make tough choices – which in some instances may appear wrong or misguided. For example, attempting to garner public support by parading people with disabilities along the streets of Lilongwe city is a form of DIY urbanism. Such actions are not necessarily initiated by people with disabilities, but rather by those who are either sympathetic to their situation or simply want to take advantage of them (exploitative syndicates). Two scenarios are apparent: first, there is the spectatorship of the commodification of people with disabilities (the inability of structures of power to do something about people with disabilities) and, second, there is the 'commodification of disabilities' (the parading of people with disabilities for money which 'they' have no control over). In articulating the meanings behind spectatorship and commodification, the utmost consciousness must be applied to the role of 'pity', as explained below.

Here, I wish to acknowledge Lilie Chouliaraki's critical media studies masterpiece *The Spectatorship of Suffering*, which has had a great impact on me – working in a seemingly distant field of scholarship – in terms of unravelling the hidden. In the opening of the book, Chouliaraki (2006: 1) expresses disquiet at television images of people's suffering, posing the following questions: 'How do we relate to television images of distant sufferers? Do we switch off, shed tears or get angry and protest? Do we forget about them or seek to do something about their suffering?' Like Chouliaraki, I have questions that trouble me in this regard. How do we relate to the men and women with disabilities who are paraded on the streets of Lilongwe? Do we pause for a moment and ask ourselves what is going on? Do we shed tears or get angry and protest at the lack of care? Are we socially responsible enough to intervene and demand that authorities show human decency for people with disabilities? Such questions underpin this chapter, and stem from my personal belief in what forms the basis of our common humanity – that is, caring for one another through any form of DIY that does not dehumanize the other.

The term 'spectatorship' implies standing aloof – watching without taking part. Imagine, for example, watching a soccer match or sporting event, our interest in the events unfolding before us serving to thrill or delight us. However, if our expectations are not met or our favourite team loses, we may end up leaving the stadium in a low mood or with high blood pressure. Either way, despite the fact we were merely a spectator to the 'event', we have experienced a profound emotional effect, which serves to reaffirm our completeness as human beings. Likewise, pity – the feeling of sorrow and compassion caused by the suffering and misfortunes of others – can trigger emotional reactions, one of which is a desire to 'do something' about it. Before proceeding down this line of enquiry, it is first necessary to explore the process of commodification.

Commodification or seeking help?

Commodification as a process of transforming things into objects for sale (Gilbert, 2008) is not a new phenomenon. At the most basic level, a commodity is anything intended for exchange, or any object of economic value. While this may not be problematic when applied to goods, services or ideas, numerous moral and ethical issues arise when humans – especially people with disabilities – are turned into economically valuable commodities. An example here can be seen in the grey line dividing commodification and seeking help through begging.

As in other parts of Africa, street begging has long been a feature of Malawi (see Maart et al., 2007; Rugoho and Siziba, 2014). In fact, it is not only common among people with disabilities but also able-bodied persons, with official documents issued by the District Commissioners office endorsing, as it were, an individual's legitimacy in begging for 'good' reasons. Such reasons may range from seeking money for tuition fees to seeking money for food. However, the practice has now come under intense scrutiny and is now highly discouraged, with the government and DPOs intensifying their advocacy for an alternative approach to supporting people with disabilities.

Street begging and the commodification of disability in Malawi can be understood as a multidimensional issue. While 'street begging' is, as alluded to above, a common phenomenon, the solicitation of alms by people with disabilities in Malawian cities can be understood from two vantage points. First, societal attitudes towards people with disabilities are largely defined in terms of abandonment. This problem emanates from overdependence which, in turn, invites a self-designed logic of rescue – the very heart of DIY. While some beg because they want to survive, others do so because they are ignorant of how abnormal the practice is. It is possible that some beg due to learned behaviour, while others beg due to psychological predisposition.

The behavioural practices described are individual-centred – that is, under normal circumstances, individuals with disabilities would engage in one or more of these alone. However, this chapter focuses on the second vantage point, which is the intricate level, with more than one beggar involved in the process of alms solicitation. This dimension sits well with the practice of DIY. Here, it should be stated that the 'additional beggar' (or 'escort') must be carefully understood within the context of self-interest, as illustrated in Figure 11.1.

While there is no question that people with disabilities beg because there is a 'good' reason to do so (because of the various limitations), the dynamics between

Disability

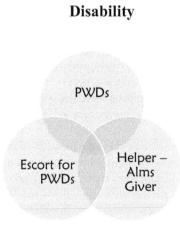

Figure 11.1 Dynamic nature of the spectatorship of the commodification of disability.

the beggar (in this case, the person with disability) and their 'escort' (the person who begs on behalf of the 'actual person with disability') invites closer scrutiny of who is in charge of the process, as well as what the escort's motivations might be. Moreover, the question of what motivates the 'giver' should also be posed. Are the actions of the escort and giver driven by the nature of disability? This question leads me into the final part of this chapter.

It is important to single out visual impairment, physical disability and albinism – what I term the 'problem body' – for analysis (see Chivers and Markotić, 2010). Due to the attendant stigma, the majority of people with disabilities (the real people who draw peoples' attention) have one or more of these forms of disability. Leaving albinism aside, if one is physically and/or visually challenged, it seems justifiable to help. While such help is not, in itself, a bad thing, when it emanates from a syndicate – people with a common motive to parade a person in order to generate money that the 'helped' has no control over – it becomes problematic. This is where the issue of 'commodification' comes in.

A 2014 survey in Lilongwe (Makuwira, n.d.) revealed some of the subtle methods of DIY urbanism conducted *for* people with disabilities. Anecdotal evidence describes a group of people who have organized themselves to act on behalf of people with disabilities, promising good returns that, according to many sources, never materialize. Such revelations prompt a number of inferences, one of which is that the structural failures of both the public and non-state institutions supposedly responsible for providing safety nets have contributed to this situation. The yawning gap left by these institutions creates fertile ground for a form of unorthodox DIY. Given that disability is not inability, the practice of acting 'on behalf' of people with disabilities – who might otherwise be able to develop the self-reliance and survival skills needed to live a decent life – in fact disempowers and demeans them.

Conclusion

There is no doubt that, as an emerging area of inquiry, the discourse of disability and urbanism requires further investigation. This chapter has argued that there is a link between disability and poverty, with stigmatization and other forms of stereotyping offering fertile ground for people with disabilities to be marginalized. While attempts are made to support people with disabilities, the manner in which such forms of DIY are conducted leaves a lot to be desired.

There exists a power play between people with disabilities and their escorts and/or helpers. The helper or escort is in a position of power, and the more they parade the 'problem body' of their disabled companions, the more power they wield over them. This disempowerment results from the helper performing actions 'on behalf of' the person with disability – in other words, it stems from pity. In other words, the 'escorts' are performing such actions for self-enrichment rather than 'pity' (though they are exploiting the 'pity' of the alms-givers). As has been discussed, disability is presented in urban areas in a problematized fashion, despite the fact that the problem may not be as presented. This draws the attention of onlookers who, in turn, express pity and render help. The help that ensues is, however, not empowering in any way, and ultimately leaves people with disabilities in a more precarious position. If we are to call this DIY, then perhaps a new model is needed that takes account of the complicated social fabric. Thus, more research into disability and urbanism can be seen as both inevitable and necessary.

Chapter 12

THE BIOPOLITICS OF DO-IT-YOURSELF URBANISM ON THE ZAMBIAN COPPERBELT

Patience Mususa

Introduction

Scholars concerned with environmental sustainability, resilience and life in fragile settings face a number of questions regarding how best to get by with scarce or limited resources, how to organize life in the absence of the infrastructures regarded as necessary to underpin contemporary modern life and how to live with uncertain futures.

Ash Amin – in his article 'Surviving the turbulent future' – is among the scholars pondering these topics, asking 'how the relationship between practices of situated dwelling, human response and infrastructural capability shapes the capacity to address ambient and unexpected adversity' (2013: 141). Amin's response to this is not only to elucidate the neoliberal condition and its iterations, but also to explore the possibility of a politics beyond it. When most of the industrial workers in Zambia's copper mining region, the Copperbelt, were laid off following a prolonged economic downturn and the privatization of key industries, it catalysed a major socioeconomic crisis. During this time, the country was experiencing a radical restructuring, transitioning from a semi-socialist to a free market economy. This saw the withdrawal of social services and drastic cuts in spending on public infrastructure and services, which in turn spurred urban residents in previously serviced neighbourhoods to rely on their own devices to organize health and infrastructure services. This chapter draws on do-it-yourself (DIY) as a methodological framing to explore how Copperbelt residents have organized their lives and livelihoods within a shifting political-economic environment characterized by periodic booms and busts (Fraser and Larmer, 2010), and how this has gone on to shape people's relationships with one another, their sense of wellbeing and their politics.

The Zambian Copperbelt provides an interesting example with which to explore the broader political nuances and implications of DIY practices. This is because the region – an industrial mining hub from the 1920s until the mid-1990s – was, from the mid-1950s at least, dominated by an industrial welfare approach led by two private mining corporations; then, from about five years after Zambia gained independence in 1964 (following progressive mining sector nationalization), by the welfare largesse of the state mining company, Zambia Consolidated Copper Mines (ZCCM). Thus, prior to the privatization of ZCCM (and other national industries) in the mid-1990s, social and economic life revolved around these companies, which often provided subsidized housing, access to healthcare, education, recreation and other services such as water and energy (see Mususa, 2021). This also entailed regulation of residents' lives, with state and company welfare officers mediating domestic life. For mineworkers and their families, therefore, reprivatization brought an abrupt end to what has been described as a 'cradle to grave' (Lungu, 2008: 545) mode of social organization.

Given this contraction of state service provision, Copperbelt residents were forced to rely on their own resources. Self-reliance had been pursued as a development policy in the country's semi-socialist past (until 1991), and was linked to communitarian notions of charting a path for the country's economic independence (Martin, 1972). This policy, which was state-led and concerned with food self-sufficiency, saw the emergence of state farms (Scott, 1985) and 'back to the land' policies for urban retirees (Ferguson, 1999). While the contemporary situation on the Copperbelt reveals continuities with the past, it also diverges in a number of ways, with self-reliance pursued not only as a survival strategy, but an individualized entrepreneurial pursuit. This chapter therefore aims to demonstrate how the past and present inform private and public self-provisioning processes on the Copperbelt, as well as how the prevailing economic situation informs DIY strategies. Here, the ultimate objective is to not only illuminate the practical aspects of making place and life in distressed settings, but – as Amin (2013) makes a case for – highlight the political dimensions arising. In asking how Copperbelt residents organize goods and services in the context of an austere state, the chapter also considers how power and agency is deployed in situations where people struggle to thrive. What kinds of social institutions are being created or mobilized? How are they being materialized?

The background context for this chapter, which draws on ethnographic research conducted periodically between 2008 and 2021, can be seen in the housing provision and agriculture self-help/self-reliance narratives and policy push that emerged following Zambia's economic crisis beginning in the late 1970s. The chapter focusses on two cases. The first, which addresses the major labour retrenchments and cutbacks on social spending that occurred during the height of the HIV/AIDS epidemic, looks at how Copperbelt residents attempted to organize healthcare amidst severe austerity and the psychosocial stresses of job loss and death. The second looks at how residents who had subsidized access to treated piped water during the ZCCM era now face significant water bills, and as a consequence are increasingly self-provisioning water and organizing access through other means. For Copperbelt residents, both health and water had previously been public goods, provided by ZCCM and the state. Through these cases, I posit that there is a biopolitical dimension to self-provisioning, and in turn DIY urbanism. Shifts in the political economy, such as a restructuring of the economy and periodic booms and busts, play out on an experiential basis. For example, in terms of the increasing reliance of manual labour – what Copperbelt residents would refer to as 'working with one's own hands' – we should consider not only the practical and political skills deployed in self-provisioning processes, but individuals' physical and mental wellbeing while engaged in these activities. The state's retreat from service provision, which in turn necessitates its relegation to private individuals, literally places responsibility on the bodies of citizens. This directs us towards an ontological framing of DIY urbanism that spotlights what exactly may be afforded people by the social, economic, political and material elements of their environment, and how this in turn shapes people and their experiences.

From informal urban to DIY urbanism

There is a rich literature on informal urbanism in Africa (Simone, 2001; Hansen and Vaa, 2004; Lindell, 2010). Particularly notable in terms of Zambia are the influential studies of anthropologist Karen Tranberg Hansen (1997, 2000) who, against a context of economic decline, describes the empirical realities of neoliberal urbanism from the perspective of the country's traders, youth and women. Hansen's book *Keeping House in Lusaka* (1997) – which focuses on how the residents of a township organized their housing and livelihoods, and the social, economic and political implications of this – paints a nuanced picture of the practices and politics underlying the processes of place making. It also indicates, as argued by Paul Jenkins (2004), the difficulty of making a distinction between formal and informal spheres of life in African cities. In recognition of this, Keith Hart, with whom the term 'informal economy' (1985) is associated, now prefers to refer to it as the 'human economy' (2013), which he argues better describes the plurality of people's engagement with economic life. Rather than a value-based judgement of what is formal or not, the 'human economy' focuses on what people do to get by and get on. In urban studies, this focus facilitates exploration of the self-provisioning/DIY processes that have emerged as the dominant driver for place making in African cities – for wealthier as well as poorer residents. Given that Zambia urban residents, whether individually or collectively, must seek retrospective planning permission for the material and social infrastructures they create in order to counter the threat of demolition or the demobilization of services, DIY urbanism in this context more closely resembles Duarte's (2016) understanding of such processes as a *de facto* sanctioning of formal planning regimes. This departs from the DIY processes described in Global North cities, which are best defined by LaFrambois as 'unauthorised, grassroots, and citizen-led urban interventions that are small scale, functional, temporary, creative, and place specific; are focussed on reclaiming and re-purposing urban spaces; and take place outside formal urban planning structures and systems' (2017: 421). In the cases described in this chapter, the majority of Zambian Copperbelt residents are not attempting to create some kind of 'voluntary city' (Beito et al., 2002), asserting their freedom from the state's regulatory control. Instead, they are at best surviving, their DIY place-making activities pointing to a state apparatus that has relegated its service provision and infrastructure obligations to neoliberal market forces. Thus, in the Zambian context, DIY can be seen as state sanctioned, a requirement placed on citizens to fill in the service provision and infrastructure gaps that have opened up due to the state's incapacity and/or retreat. The following describes how these DIY processes became institutionalized through self-help programmes.

From state provision to self-help

In the 1970s, a critique of big government informed by free market ideology (Hayek, 1948) and ecological concerns (Schumacher, 1973) became globally institutionalized when it was adopted by the World Bank as a development framework for Third World countries (World Bank, 1981). Notably, three practical policy perspectives emerged, later adopted by Third World countries such as Zambia. The first was that efforts should be made to regularize the informal economy, thereby allowing developing countries to collect rents from the sector. The second, influenced by Hernando de Soto (2001), advocated the titling of informal land. While ostensibly this was aimed at increasing tenure security for the poor, another key objective was releasing the monetary value of land, allowing it to be transacted and used as collateral to procure credit. The third, which is of primary concern to this chapter, involved the promotion of self-help. This perspective was pushed by John Turner (1976), who, in the face of the housing deficits and financial constraints experienced by developing countries, made the case that the responsibility for housing provision should be shifted from the state to individuals, who could use their own labour and resources to meet their housing needs and thus lower housing costs.

In Zambia, this latter change was no more apparent than in the shift in responsibility for housing provision from the state and employers to individuals that occurred around fifteen years after independence. Faced with declining commodity prices, the country struggled to meet urban housing demand, which – following independence – had been catalysed by the removal of colonial restrictions on Africans residing in cities. Thus, in the late 1970s, Zambia's housing policy shifted from state- and employer-provided housing to a form of state-facilitated self-help housing. It was not just housing that the Zambian state, with the support of the World Bank and other development agencies, encouraged urban residents to provide for themselves, but other essential services and infrastructures as well – for example, development programmes were run to demonstrate how to build improved pit latrines in densifying urban settlements, and how to build protected water wells (Glennie, 1982). Such self-help programmes were directed not only towards individual projects but also towards community management, with committees later created to collectively run urban communal water stands and to mobilize resources for building and maintaining community roads and drains. While these institutionalized DIY urban processes essentially signalled a shift in responsibility for the provision of services and infrastructure away from the state towards individuals or groups, such processes remained within the state's planning purview.

Economic crisis and self-reliance on the Copperbelt

As a result of the policy shifts described above, Zambia became a site of experimentation for self-help initiatives spearheaded by municipalities and state corporations alike. It was hoped that voluntary labour and community resources would fill the welfare, service and infrastructure gaps that the state was unable to meet. Thus, prior to reprivatization in the 1990s, the state mining corporate ZCCM adopted policies promoting self-reliance in its operations and among its staff. At an operational level, ZCCM pursued self-sufficiency through adopting a policy of industrial substitution. This meant that rather than importing spare parts, the company, through its various subsidiaries, started fabricating its own machinery replacement parts and components. For staff, the company offered retirees training programmes in agriculture and aquaculture. ZCCM social welfare programmes directed jobseekers – often family members of mine employees – towards agricultural colleges and apprenticeships in the region's state farms.

The removal of food subsidies – in particular the maize meal coupon in the late 1980s (Simutanyi, 1996), part of the International Monetary Fund (IMF)'s prescribed economic structural reforms – pulled the rug on the safety net cushioning Zambian families from hunger during the economic crisis. For workers in the Copperbelt's mining sector, who had been among the most protected, reprivatization of ZCCM and the loss of their jobs meant the complete loss of social protections, including food rations and child grants. This forced mine workers and their families into self-reliant livelihoods, including urban agriculture. While miners' wives had been encouraged to take up farming on the urban peripheries to supplement wages by mining corporations during the early establishment of industrial mining in the twentieth century (Chauncey, 1981), and though such farming was promoted by the state as a nationwide policy for getting 'back to the land' in the 1980s (Ferguson, 1999: 123–65), it was the massive labour layoffs following privatization in the mid-1990s that pushed the majority of Copperbelt residents to urban farming. Since then, it has become a core livelihood strategy, alongside other economic pursuits – including, for some, artisanal mining.

It is in agricultural activities that Copperbelt residents adopted the *modus operandi* of DIY more visibly. Subverting municipal and state regulations stipulating what one can do in the city and its wider environs, including protected forests, many Copperbelt residents took up the growing of food and the rearing of poultry/livestock in these spaces. While some were able to purchase land or acquire it from traditional authorities in the urban peripheries, a significant number – such as the residents of the Copperbelt town of Luanshya – literally 'showed themselves' pieces of land, squatting in forest areas, mining reserves and public parks. It was also in urban farming that the associational dimensions of a self-organized economy could be seen, with urban agriculture not only pursued at an individual and household level, but through group cooperatives (Chishimbi, 2010; Musaba and Bwacha, 2014) that allowed members to take advantage of pooled resources and link up with commercial farming and agribusiness out-grower schemes.

In the context of state retreat, and a policy push towards entrepreneurship, another economic sector emerged: agriculture middlemen. The shrinking of support provided by the country's state cooperative, the Zambia Co-operative Federation (ZCF) (Moen, 2003: 22), to farmers had catalysed an even worse crisis in rural areas (see Gould, 2010). This, however, created an opportunity for former miners, who used their retrenchment package to buy trucks and become agriculture commodity traders, travelling to remote rural areas to buy grain from small-scale farmers who did not have the means to transport their goods to urban markets. Some, such as the Bwalya family from the Copperbelt town of Luanshya, made a significant sum of money transporting grain – enough, after a few years, to buy two more trucks and thus expand their reach and the volume of goods they could being to market in cities and border regions with the Democratic Republic of Congo. Urban middlemen thus reached small-scale producers in the countryside that ZCF could no longer reach. However, rural farmers interviewed in 2008 in Kasempa, North Western province, where many Copperbelt residents travelled to buy rice, maize and beans for resale, complained that the margins they were getting were low. In addition, a futures trade in agricultural produce had emerged: Mrs Bwalya, who was key in managing the buying of produce, often bought small-scale farmers' harvests in advance, which she readily admitted placed the rural families she was buying from at risk of food insecurity should they have a smaller harvest than anticipated. The retreat of the state cooperative thus also ushered in a more speculative and exploitative side to the agricultural sector, indicating the potential economic and spatial inequalities arising from these self-organization processes.

The fact that many former workers gained a house as part of their severance package made houses and backyards a key site of DIY experimentation. Given that retrenchment payments were in many cases not paid for several years, if at all, the house and land owned or appropriated by former employees became key to livelihoods. Previously, under the tight administration of ZCCM, mine employees and residents were limited as to what livelihood activities they could conduct from their homes. Now, economic crisis and deregulation became visible in the material manifestation of DIY activities: in self-built housing extensions for the rental market or for schools; in small out-buildings for poultry keeping; in makeshift front-yard stores; and in small brickmaking enterprises. In yards and Copperbelt neighbourhoods there was also visible growth in urban agricultural activity – not just gardening, but the keeping of poultry and small livestock (see Mususa, 2021). Less visible, however, was the emergence of new social, often voluntary, institutions to cope with the HIV/AIDS epidemic and other endemic diseases, amid cuts in public health spending and rising individual healthcare costs. Given that all this occurred when urban residents were struggling to access water following the removal of water subsidies highlights how important self-provisioning for food, health and water had become in maintaining the integrity of life. Across several fieldwork trips involving ethnographic participant observation, it became clearly apparent how much effort – physical and social – was required to organize food, water and health. The energy expended in life-sustaining activities, and the endurance required to do so, lent a visceral quality to the DIY urban activities Copperbelt residents were engaged in.

Much of the Copperbelt's agricultural and other economic activity is increasingly reliant on individual, unpaid family labour and low-paid occasional workers. Most Copperbelt residents spoke of the physically taxing nature of agricultural work and how 'each had to do their part' to eat. Beyond the physical demands of 'working with one's hands', Copperbelt residents explained the constant calculations they had to make to get by, including making cuts to health-related expenses. This reflected the general precarity of their economic situation, which required that they be constantly inventive and on the look-out for opportunities and support. It is this that points to a biopolitical understanding of DIY, which was expressed in residents' popular narratives around self-reliance. One such narrative, which could be interpreted as a critique of austerity, involved speaking of a resource-depleted body and society in need of the creative resources and physical energies to survive and possibly make it. Another narrative, addressing the withdrawal of state welfare and the perceived collapse of the extended kin system, stated that one had to rely on oneself rather than the state, which in the eyes of citizens had become corrupt due to the rent-seeking that had accompanied privatization and the state's facilitation of investment. Moreover, one could not solely rely on one's kin, as they were either also hard up or at risk of exploitation, given that in many cases the household as entrepreneurial site tended to rely on unpaid family labour (Manje and Churchill, 2002: 8). In the new political-economic dispensation prescribed by a small state and 'free market', people were urged towards self-reliance. Despite an awareness of the myriad difficulties facing the many micro-enterprises operating on the Copperbelt, a harsh narrative ascribing 'laziness' or lack of entrepreneurial spirit to those whose businesses had failed could sometimes be heard. This narrative emerged alongside a critique of selfish individualism, noted by Ferguson (1992: 80) as a link to the collective moral ethos embedded in customary notions of belonging and Zambia's socialist past. Nevertheless, for the majority, this keen awareness of how difficult it was to survive spurred people to keep on trying and not give up (Mususa, 2021).

This moral ethos inflects the efforts made by Copperbelt residents to get by and provide services and infrastructure for themselves in the context of a diminished state. As such, urban DIY initiatives fluctuate between self-serving and altruistic, cooperative and rogue – either way, they are largely dependent on what kinds of resources people have access to.

DIY water provisioning

It is not uncommon in Zambian Copperbelt towns to see children and women carrying large plastic containers of water drawn from their neighbours' supplies or occasionally burst municipal water pipes. This has become a feature of these towns and points to the difficulties a significant number of urban residents have in meeting their water bills. Water provision was one of the key services to be restructured following the reprivatization of the mines. Previously, mine township residents had enjoyed a free treated water supply for domestic use, as well as treated wastewater from the mining process for use in their gardens. As the new mining companies where unwilling to take on responsibility for services such as water provision, water and sanitation services now fell to reorganized municipal services, with consumers required to pay for the service (Kazimbaya-Senkwe and Guy, 2007). However, a combination of factors negatively impacted the efficient provision of piped domestic water and the ability of people to afford it. Many Copperbelt residents – such as those in the town of Luanshya, who were hard hit by massive retrenchments and a poorly executed layoff process following the bankruptcy of the town's reprivatized mine – were unable to pay water bills on a consistent basis, often leading to them being cut off. Interviews with the Kafubu Water and Sewerage company, a joint venture between the Copperbelt's Luanshya, Ndola and Masaiti local authorities, indicated several other problems. The company has struggled to meter water supply in its medium- and low-income neighbourhoods, and thus collect revenues. This in turn has affected the company's ability to fund other operational costs, such as the treating raw sewerage and replacing damaged or vandalized pipes. Given that these old and often dilapidated water and sanitation systems could no longer meet the demands arising from the urban growth catalysed by copper commodity price rises, development loans and grants have since 2014 been procured to replace them – for example, from bilateral partners such as the Danish International Development Agency (DANIDA).

Water scholars have for some time been anticipating major water crises in African cities, with Kate Showers arguing in 2002 that while studies of water provision have tended to focus on such aspects as pricing and water supply distribution, little attention has been paid to where the water is to come from, and how this not only impacts rural and urban landscapes, but how they are planned (2002: 621). This raises the question of how residents of cities in financial distress will go about providing themselves with water once the state and its municipal authorities are no longer able to do so. Or, alternatively, in a context of privatized public services, how people will go about provisioning for water when commercial water suppliers consider it not worth their while building up water and sanitation infrastructure for low-income residents who are unlikely to pay. Chileshe's (2005) comprehensive study on water scarcity in Zambia reflects these concerns, noting that while those in rural and peri-urban areas predominantly used shallow hand-dug wells for their water, urban residents in the mining town of Kabwe (formerly part of ZCCM) were reportedly drawing water from wells on their own premises. In my own fieldwork in the Copperbelt town of Luanshya I encountered several residents in newly established neighbourhoods – both high- and low-density – who had dug wells in their yards. For the most part, these wells were shallow, unlike some of the (relatively few) wealthier residents, they could not afford to sink a borehole with a water storage tank.

This DIY provisioning for water is not out of place, even for the Copperbelt's older established neighbourhoods, which have access to piped water. Here, reduced incomes following retrenchment and higher water costs following the removal of subsidies meant that even where residential piped water infrastructure existed, a failure to pay bills meant a significant number of households did not have running water. Thus, across the urban landscape, people sank both deep and shallow wells, with the water used not only for daily domestic activities such as cleaning, but also for a variety of livelihood activities, such as vegetable gardening, poultry keeping and, in a few cases, fish farming. The combined push for agricultural self-sufficiency – with related activities expanding following the layoffs of former mineworkers – and economic activities such as brick moulding created greater demand for water beyond domestic residential use. While rainfed agriculture still dominated urban farming cycles, DIY water provisioning from groundwater wells and experimentation with low-cost irrigation solutions came to be used outside the rainy season. Copperbelt resident Mr Mubita, for example, created his own DIY irrigation system in order to grow tomatoes throughout the year and have an orchard (Mususa, 2021: 90–2). DIY water access in Copperbelt towns has also involved the hijacking and retrofitting of municipal water and sewer pipes. For instance, a burst sewer pipe – such as those I encountered in the Copperbelt towns of Kitwe, Ndola and Luanshya – may have its sewerage runoff channelled towards a series of vegetable gardens, allowing them to be irrigated and fertilized (despite the risk of pathogens from faecal matter). In other situations, such as in the Copperbelt town of Chingola, pipes carrying water pumped from underground mining have been vandalized, with the continuously gushing water then becoming a place where nearby residents wash their clothes and socialize. All this, according to the region's municipal services, has made their operations less efficient and more costly.

The commercialization of municipal water on the Copperbelt has also gone hand-in-hand with water becoming a tradeable commodity. At one end of the scale, large commercial vendors sell bottled mineral water, while at the other end, small vendors package up water in recycled plastic bottles or small freezer bags and sell it at bus stops and markets. Due to constrained resources, regulators have struggled to monitor the quality of water sold by the larger commercial vendors, and even more so that of the water sold by the myriad small water vendors. A water quality study that included analysis of commercial bottled water in Zambia's capital, Lusaka, found that few of these water vendors met acceptable water quality standards, with most failing to check for or filter heavy metal contamination (Banda et al., 2021). In Lusaka, the concomitant use of ground water wells and pit latrines within a dense urban setting has resulted in periodic outbreaks of dysentery, typhoid and cholera. Meanwhile, though the Copperbelt towns are not as densely populated as Lusaka, improperly treated water has led to a higher risk of groundwater contamination from heavy metals (von der Heyden and New, 2004). The weak regulatory context has also seen water supplied by municipal services periodically contaminated with toxic wastewater from mining activity. For example, UK newspaper *The Guardian* reported in August 2015 that residents of the Copperbelt town of Chingola had sued the London-registered mining company Vedanta for polluting their water sources (Vidal, 2015). For Copperbelt residents, such incidences of water contamination have led to concerns over tap water quality, prompting some wealthier residents to spend considerable sums (US$1,500–3,000) sinking their own boreholes based on the assumption this will provide safer water. Despite this becoming a growing practice, groundwater quality tests are often not conducted. The sinking of private boreholes also reflects a trend towards autonomy in how those with more money deal with public services they are unhappy with. Rather than press for better services, or in their absence attempt to pool resources for communal facilities, those with the financial means tend to go it alone in highly individualized DIY practices. In lower-income Copperbelt neighbourhoods, such as Mpatamatu in Luanshya, there is, to an extent, greater collective use of resources. Here, for instance, residents with more productive shallow water wells are willing to share with a greater number of neighbours, who – when I visited – could be found lining up with containers ready to draw water from someone's backyard well.

For those residents with less resources, who struggle to pay water bills, a social moral economy has emerged. In these cases, residents are forced to turn to neighbours, often sending children laden with containers to ask for water. Some residents I interviewed who were concerned about rising costs due to sharing their water resources had switched off their garden taps, thereby extinguishing the possibility of neighbourhood children playing in their backyard gardens or domestic staff offering water to those who ask. Requests for and denial of water were seen in social-political terms, with water, despite its cost, seen as belonging to the sphere of goods where one cannot morally decline a request. To do so would be regarded as an act of selfishness, and people were disinclined to do so, partly due to the fact that no one person can guarantee their long-term water security, meaning that at some point they are likely to find themselves in a position of asking for water. Access to water thus gives rise to a politics of conviviality, contesting its commercialization.

From the ease of being able to afford clean running water to the insecurity of unreliable and unaffordable supplies, water provisioning has become an effortful activity in the Copperbelt's former mine townships. A social and moral economy has emerged around it, which includes begging for water, selling water and digging wells. The growth of agriculture and fish farming micro-enterprises and small-scale construction has generated demand for water beyond domestic consumption, placing pressure on the existing infrastructure and landscape. This, writes Jessie Smart (2015: 42), necessitates consideration of the water and infrastructure demands of activities such as urban farming. There are also biosocial implications: the physicality needed for children and women to lug large containers of water, or for (mainly) men to dig shallow wells, draws attention to the integrity of the body and its ability to keep up in a context of significant health burdens and diminishing healthcare. Copperbelt residents increasingly conceive of the body as a vehicle that must be maintained and given fuel given the primacy of its role in the varying DIY activities people are engaging in. This highlights Copperbelt residents' concerns regarding their ability to go about their activities in debilitating circumstances characterized by precarity, physically demanding work, and epidemics arising from diminished access to clean water and healthcare. In the following section, I therefore turn to how Copperbelt residents are re-organizing health and wellbeing following the systemic collapse of healthcare in the wake of mine reprivatization.

To look after oneself: DIY health provisioning

'Miners' wives were being kept nicely by ZCCM. They would provide free baby napkins for up to six children.'[1] Prior to its sale, ZCCM operated a cradle-to-grave welfare policy (Lungu, 2008; Straube, 2021) best reflected in the health and welfare schemes offered to women and children. In addition to comprehensive healthcare coverage addressing antenatal and maternal health, various social and recreational schemes geared towards creating a healthy family life were set up. These programmes were part of a company ethos of paternalistic industrial welfarism that was in sync with the Zambian government's developmental state approach prior to the introduction of economic market reforms in the early 1980s. Privatization of ZCCM brought an end to these industrial welfare policies and saw mine owners divest from social provisioning, preferring instead to focus on 'the core business of mining' while running noncommittal corporate social responsibility programmes, such as malaria control.

Following the sale of the first ZCCM mine (the Roan Antelope Copper Mines in Luanshya), its new owners, Binani, struggled to run not only the mines, but also the social services ZCCM had operated. These included several clinics and the town's two mine hospitals: Roan Hospital, which served the higher-density suburbs of the mine township; and Luanshya Hospital, which severed the lower-density suburbs where managers and other higher-skilled employees lived. The new mine owners struggled to pay its workers, culminating in an exodus of medical staff, several of whom left the country. In addition, the mine hospitals started falling behind on their payments to suppliers, resulting in frequent shortages of drugs and medical supplies. This forced residents of Luanshya's mine township to turn to the single government-run hospital in town, Thomson Hospital, which served the areas administered by the municipality.[2] This in turn stretched the capacity of Thompson Hospital, which was operating at a time when the country's resources were stretched thin due to large public debt. Moreover, the residents of Luanshya's mine townships of Roan and Mpatamatu – who had previously had easy and free access to Roan Hospital and its clinics – faced increased costs, partly due to the distance they now had to travel to access healthcare. Healthcare costs also increased for the residents of the lower-density mine township, who had previously used Luanshya Hospital at a subsidized rate. These subsidies were removed, and following major worker retrenchments from 1999, most former mineworkers and their families could no longer afford healthcare there. Between 1999 and 2004, operations at Roan Hospital were effectively suspended, leaving the place to fall into ruins until – following an upward turn in the economy (which also saw the mine resold to new investors) – the government took over and reopened the hospital's operations. The scaling back of health services in Copperbelt towns such as Luanshya occurred at a time when the HIV/AIDS pandemic was raging in Zambia. The Copperbelt has consistently had the highest HIV/AIDS prevalence rates in Zambia: according to a 2018 demographic health survey, around 15.4 per cent of the region's population were living with HIV/AIDS (CSO, 2018: 262). Limited access to testing due to budgetary constraints, let alone treatment or palliative care, made it difficult to constrain infection and save lives. That the HIV/AIDS epidemic was raging around the same time that people were losing their jobs and healthcare facilities were being closed or scaled back had terrible consequence for the Copperbelt's residents. It was amid this context of a limited and overwhelmed state that community care groups emerged to provide a scaffold for health support and public health messaging. According to Grace, a former ZCCM nurse who had initiated one such community healthcare network, the situation was 'bad in the mine areas. We had never seen hunger, but that time it came. There was a lot of depression, a lot of disease and a lot of deaths, a lot of everything … all you see is a bad ending, a gloomy picture'.[3]

Both the state and the management of state industrial corporates such as ZCCM were aware of the dire health situation wrought by the HIV/AIDS epidemic, but acknowledged that they alone could not mobilize an effective response without voluntary associations. This was well illustrated by Grace, who helped establish a network of voluntary caregivers in Luanshya. She told me how she and her colleagues, who at the time were still working for the mine hospitals, went about trying to mobilize support for the pregnant wife of a mine worker who had died following an HIV/AIDS-related illness. According to Grace, the woman had been left destitute when relatives of her husband grabbed all the household property following his death, and was facing eviction from mine company housing. Drawing on this woman's situation, Grace and her colleagues elicited support from ZCCM to help her, while also drawing attention to what they saw as a looming social catastrophe: 'We wrote to the general office [ZCCM's general management] and gave them a picture of what was happening to mine workers. We were seeing one miner dying after another, that was around 1997, 1998.'[4] However, the ongoing reprivatization of ZCCM and the new owners' decoupling from welfare interventions limited the scope of what the state mines – which were in process of being sold – could do.

Aware of these challenges, Grace mobilized a group of nurses and colleagues from her church to create a care network that would provide support to HIV/AIDS patients, many of whom were sick at home. 'Ten of the patients I was visiting died in one day – I was shaken,'[5] she observed of her lowest point in 1998. For Grace, this highlighted both the scale of support needed in terms of volunteer numbers, as well as the limited resources they had to provide appropriate training in psychosocial counselling. To address this, she turned the Copperbelt Health Education Project (CHEP), a pioneering health education initiative aimed at addressing information gaps concerning the HIV/AIDS epidemic. The project had been established by a medical doctor, who was working with one of the biggest public hospitals on the Copperbelt, along with the Rotary Foundation of Kitwe. Supported by Zambia's Ministry of Health and funded by an initial grant from the Norwegian Agency for Development Cooperation (NORAD), CHEP had been innovating public information communication strategies on HIV/AIDS prevention and care (Mouli et al., 1992). They also trained counsellors, including those from various associations that approached them for help. Given that no treatment for HIV/AIDS was available until around 2005, community caregivers had become the key scaffolding to an epidemic that had been running since the mid-1980s. Volunteer caregivers visited homebound patients, providing nutrition information, advice on palliative care, and counselling to patients and their family members. They also became key to HIV/AIDS prevention campaigns.

The twin crises of job losses and the HIV/AIDS epidemic on the Copperbelt amid state retreat thus catalysed DIY health provisioning, which had a strong inclination towards solidarity given the sheer number of people in the region facing these crises together. Also key to its emergence was the support that voluntary associational groups received from both the state and tertiary organizations (such as bilateral donors and non-governmental organizations), which, given the scale of the public health crisis, encouraged this collectivist approach. Maintenance of these health associations requires significant time, resources and energy on the part of members, who themselves are caught within a precarious socioeconomic situation and face similar health challenges. As such, people such as Grace are driven to note that it was better when ZCCM and the state provided decent universal healthcare. The lack of state investment in affordable healthcare, even when the economy has periodically bounced back, has served to underline the growth of voluntarism in healthcare provision in places such as Zambia, and tangentially the privatization of such provision.

The privatization of healthcare on the Copperbelt, and in Zambia more generally, has manifested in a proliferation of unconventional health purveyors promising not only physical health but also spiritual wellbeing. Among the alternatives on offer is traditional African medicine, which has always been practised, sometimes combined with Christian divinatory practices. Moreover, Chinese medicine has grown apace alongside Chinese investment in the country. Whereas in the ZCCM past, Copperbelt residents would have readily sought healthcare from state mine company or public hospitals and clinics, in the reprivatized context they are inclined to 'try out' various options due to cost, inconsistency of service, and the wider range of operators. The dire health and economic burdens have also had a psychosocial effect on the region's urban residents, who are acutely aware of the precarity and fragility of life. As such, they are willing to experiment with a variety of health and wellbeing options, including membership of associational networks – such as church groups or group savings schemes – that provide settings for emotional wellbeing in times of generalized societal stress. Many of the informants I spoke to were also prone to self-medication, buying self-prescribed (or recommended by family and friends) medicine directly from pharmacies – some of the pharmacies are regulated and others not. Several financial pyramid schemes have also emerged that involve participants selling health supplements and devices in order to earn money. The fact that this has left many people with unsold stocks of often unproven health products has not deterred new members from joining. I draw attention to these various examples of DIY health provisioning to highlight the syncretic and experimental approach people have been forced to undertake in order to ensure their health and wellbeing, even survival.

In conjunction with the above, there has been a rise in healthcare tourism amongst the relatively small number of wealthy citizens, who travel to South Africa and India for treatment. On top of this, there is a growing number of small private clinics, some of which are run by doctors who also work in the public system. This is occurring against a backdrop of two-tier – low-cost vs. high-cost – care in public hospitals. High-cost care in public hospitals requires a pricey membership fee and higher consultation costs, which grants access to speedier care and cleaner hospital facilities. Those with less resources receive slower service when it comes to consultations, but are still required to pay for tests and medication. Regardless of the public hospital services available, patients and their families must do much of the care work themselves, as medical staff are few and/ or moonlighting within the private sector. As a result, both in public hospitals on the Copperbelt and in Zambia more broadly, it is not uncommon to find patients being tended to predominantly by family members. These family members will run around looking for medication, organize recommended tests, take samples from surgery to the pathology department, and even look for blood donors. In hospital and domestic settings, against the backdrop of the HIV/AIDS epidemic and tuberculosis, women and children have become the key carers (Hunleth, 2017), filling the space left by the state's absence in order to ensure the survival of their kin. Given the protracted nature of these illness, the care provided by children in particular entails taking on economic responsibility for the household. This means, for some children, going out alone to sell goods, returning home to prepare meals and clean the house, and nursing a parent. As Jean Hunleth notes in her study on child caregivers in Zambia, this is something that children want to do, being only too aware of the fragility of being orphaned (2017: 5–8). In a context of depleted resources, both within the home and beyond, people have urged each other to survive through a collective mobilization of labour. This is reflected in the popular mobilization of survival narratives that find expression in songs and slogans (Burja and Baylies, 2012; Mususa, 2012). This helps ensure that even when individuals are attempting to deal with their own healthcare issues within a privatized setting, their struggles link into a wider collective condition, making visible groups – such as widows and orphans – who though worst affected might otherwise be invisible.

Conclusion

Since the 2000s, Zambian Copperbelt residents have sought to make a life while riding the turbulent economic waves of boom and bust, wavering always between hope and despair. An awareness of the fragility and precariousness of their setting has led residents to adopt a variety of self-provisioning and DIY healthcare approaches. This has entailed people learning new skills, some gained from state-sanctioned self-reliance policies facilitated by state industries, such as ZCCM, and later non-governmental organizations. These have expanded people's practical skills in agricultural production, which is now key to the Copperbelt urban economy. It has also catalysed political learning regarding processes of social mobilization and health provisioning: against a backdrop of pandemic and state retreat, a variety of healthcare and wellbeing initiatives – ranging from the individual level to the solidaristic – have of necessity sprung up. The self-provisioning of services, such as for water, has also seen an assertion of what can be described as a politics of conviviality among those with the least resources. The politics of conviviality, to draw from the work of Francis Nyamnjoh (2002) on the Cameroonian grass fields, emphasizes interdependency, showing persons how they are bound by a shared common humanity – often referred to in African philosophical terms as *ubuntu*. A denial of this shared sense of belonging can be seen in cases where those with more money literally extract themselves from the masses, a practice noted by Martin Murray (2009) in his writing on urban inequality in Johannesburg. On the Copperbelt, this is visible in wealthier residents erecting high concrete walls and impenetrable gates that preclude the possibility of passers-by asking for water. Meanwhile, in the case of healthcare provision, the few with means enclose themselves in private hospital wards or go abroad for treatment.

As Nyamnjoh (2015) notes, however, there is a 'cul de sac' to *ubuntu*, whereby this assertion of interlinked humanity is either denied or exploited. This points to the moral economy of inequality in the context of a laissez faire state: in trespassing on property to grow food, Copperbelt residents assert the moral right of maintaining life's integrity and the utilization of 'common' land to do so. A similar point is made when residents vandalize municipal water pipes to draw water for everyday domestic use. In both cases, residents show their willingness to trespass on the conventions of private ownership in order to access services within an austere state. This propensity to trespass is, in their view, implicitly sanctioned by a state that continuously urges them towards self-reliance and self-help. As a consequence, a dialectic has arisen between the state and its citizens, and residents, whereby the state occasionally comes down hard on vandalism or trespass, but is unable to sustain these sanctions due to its unwillingness to provide its citizens with universal services. On the Copperbelt, this plays outs as people doing their own thing while accepting the risk of occasional sanction from state authorities. To counter this risk, those with less resources mobilize others in a similar situation to politically sanction the state for its neglect. At the heart of Copperbelt residents' DIY is survival, something that can be clearly seen in the cases presented here: How can residents eat when they don't have stable work? How can they gain access to water when the service is unaffordable? How, in a context of significant illness, can they survive when state healthcare is inadequate? The displacement of service provision onto Copperbelt residents themselves, who must rely on their own labour and resources to gain access to essential goods on services, directly links to the biopolitics of state retreat. The Copperbelt's reprivatized landscape means that the state sees its role as facilitating the entry of new capital players, who are then free to divest themselves of any responsibility for maintaining the welfare of residents, as had previously been the case under ZCCM. At the same time, the state absolves itself of any key role in the welfare of its citizens, instead urging them to take primary responsibility for the provision of services. Thus, the state pushes a policy of self-reliance and entrepreneurship, but within formal bounds. Previously, state-facilitated agricultural cooperatives, trade schools, adult-learning initiatives and welfare centres sought to build the organizational and skills base necessary for a self-reliant society in the face of Zambia's subordinate position in global economic system – what remains are loose fragments of these projects, devolved to the bodies of Copperbelt residents.

Notes

1   Female participant comment at group discussion conducted in Luanshya on 1 June 2007 with Copperbelt Health Education Project volunteers on welfare and health services following the reprivatization of ZCCM.
2   Most Copperbelt towns had been governed by the mines and the municipalities under a dual administrative system.
3   Interview with Grace Mtonga in Luanshya on 30 May 2007.
4   Ibid 30 May 2007.
5   Ibid.

CONCLUSION: DIY URBANISM AS POLITICS OF INTERRUPTION

Stephen Marr and Patience Mususa

The future of DIY politics

In the closing pages of this volume on the practice and politics of DIY urbanism, we seek to engage with some of the questions and themes that have thus far remained under-answered. As such, the intention is more one of provocation than attempting to pronounce definitive conclusions. Towards the conclusion of Chapter 1, Marr posed a series of questions about the kinds of politics generated by DIY practices. Of particular urgency, in our view, is the question of whether the politics of DIY practice can engender an alternate form of political and civic participation – one which can serve as both source of collective action and bulwark against the state's failings, absent infrastructure, and the pervasive spatial and socioeconomic precarities common across Africa's cities. If so, what lessons might these possibilities portend for cities and citizens(hips) in urban contexts inside and outside Africa? Ongoing debates about the form and function of politics in the 'post-political' city make any answers given to these questions increasingly salient. Emplacing DIY politics within the frame of the post-political city illustrates the utility and – perhaps even more so – the limitations of such a conceptual apparatus.

Erik Swyngedouw, an influential advocate of the post-political orientation, has elsewhere (2017) described the concept of DIY politics as a condition where politics has not so much disappeared, but been transformed, with space for regular citizens' democratic participation reduced to the point that the very possibility of its realization becomes masked. Instead, politics manifests as 'stakeholder-based governance … whereby politics is reduced to expert management, based on accounting practices, and its rituals and choreographies of power to be found in city hall, a military barrack, a classroom or a concentration camp' (Swyngedouw, 2017: 58). Politics thus described takes on theatrical or kabuki-like attributes: widespread participation is mimed while rarely putting in doubt outcomes that reflect the corporate interests of technocrats and capital. Rather than providing evidence of an absence of politics, such a situation points to a politics drained of vitality and gamed out with a loaded die.

In an earlier essay, Swyngedouw contrasts these dynamics with what may be understood as a more authentic form of democratic politics, with a key point being that this ideal-type form of political action disturbs administrative and distributive orders (2009: 606). Given that justice and equality are foundational to politics, rather than normative objectives to be realized in the future, 'democratic politics is, therefore, always disruptive and transformative' (Swyngedouw, 2009: 607). Such an account hints at the inherent irrepressibility of democratic politics in an era of post-politicization, borne out by episodic 'eruptions of discontent' in recent years, ranging from Occupy Wall Street style-protests to Climate Strikes, to perhaps even the farmer-led street occupations now underway (at the time of writing) in India (Swyngedouw, 2017: 56). These intersectional protests – melding a wide range of interest groups from across society and societies – give credence to the idea that messy, heterogenic democratic politics lurks beneath the surface, separated from the space of action and appearance by homogenous veneers of managerial and corporate technocracy.

A politics characterized by high drama and eruptive moments of mass, perhaps even heroic, action(s) in which outcomes are no longer preordained is certainly not without its attractions – there is a reason the mass outbursts of the late 1960s continue to cast such a spell on the production of popular culture artefacts and social science theorizing alike. At the same time, such a politics is not without its problems. Beveridge and Koch, for example, take on some of the assumptions made by post-political advocates, which foreground the straitjacket placed on urban activism by 'global capital' and the outsized role played in municipal governance by a managerial class of technocrats (2017: 32–3). True political action therefore only 'finds – exasperated – expression in urban political violence from the margins' (Beveridge and Koch, 2017: 33). If such a claim is accurate, Beveridge and Koch argue, democracy across all levels of government is decimated, with democratic politics existing as a façade to obscure the inexorable furtherance of elite interests (2017: 33). And certainly, in an era characterized by conspiracy theories propagated by such entities as QAnon, involving apocalyptic narratives about leftist cannibalistic cabals and the oppressive influence of 'globalists', these ideas resonate.

Conspiracy theories aside, Beveridge and Koch's concern stems from the fact that this characterization suggests an atrophied vision of political action that forecloses the possibility of a wide array of political acts. What Beveridge and Koch instead advocate is not a wholesale refutation of the post-political city, but rather a more 'plural understanding of politics and depoliticization … [and the] multiplicity of political agency in cities' (2017: 32). Here, they seek to carve out a space that recognizes the role of social movements, unions and other civil society actors who participate in a slow and grinding urban politics that encompasses battles big and small. The result is a middle ground in which it is necessary to 'adopt a more open view of the potential of the city as a place of struggle and a site of (radical) political agency' (Beveridge and Koch, 2017: 39). While this move towards pluralism is welcome, we would argue it does not go far enough, as even this more expansive conceptualization tends to privilege a narrowly bounded understanding of politics and the actors who exercise agency. That is, it articulates an urban politics that operates primarily through formal organizations and Habermasian ideas of public spheres and discourses, and which is embedded within the institutional framework of a reasonably well-functioning state apparatus – even one with a reduced footprint under the drive to privatize public goods – that is willing to negotiate. Such an account of politics appears quite specific to cities of the Global North, meaning that while pluralism is acknowledged it remains geographically restricted.

The politics of DIY urbanism and the African urban environments in which they occur open an important pathway along which these debates can be carried beyond such myopic epistemic framing. DIY politics forces us to consider how politics unfolds, the actors involved, and the ends to which it is directed. In other words: how actually existing politics occurs, rather than the extent to which it adheres to an ideal-type model. Swyngedouw argued that politics carries with it the transformation of 'mere life into the possibility of more life' (2017: 58). While this is of course true, it is also true that the politics of *mere* life – of coping, of getting by, of making it from one day to the next – is no less consequential, and indeed no less political. Thus, a full accounting of the urban political requires embracing Southern perspectives of the DIY practices that lie therein.

There are several reasons for this. Broadly, as the gradual shift in attention paid to postcolonial and non-Eurocentric approaches over the past two decades has shown (see Robinson, 2002; Roy and Ong, 2011; Parnell and Robinson, 2012; Schindler and Silver, 2019), any attempt to identify a uniform model of either 'Southern urbanism' or a universal set of globally applicable standards is misguided. In part, this is because such efforts gloss over the vast diversity present in contemporary urbanism processes. More than that, however, postcolonial and non-Eurocentric perspectives call into question the idea that both Northern and Southern cities can be understood and analysed according to discrete, geographically bounded criteria. Instead, we – academics, practitioners and policymakers – ought to acknowledge the myriad empirical realities, processes and trends that arise from cross-regional comparison: in a similar way to how ideal-type conceptualizations of the urban North have been applied (largely uncritically) to the South, the cities of the Global South offer insights into the urban dynamics of their Northern counterparts. If these new trajectories of understanding are to be opened up, theorists must take seriously 'the idea of thinking with an accent' (Caldeira, 2017: 4) and the inevitable ambiguities and messiness this entails. For theorists, policymakers and practitioners, the time for urban purity contests is over.

'Thinking with an accent' is not merely an invitation to reconsider an epistemological or methodological stance, but involves illuminating important on-the-ground political realities. Bearing the imprint of Ernst Bloch and Mark Ritter's (1977) view that humans inhabit a world of multiple presents, Partha Chatterjee suggests that 'the real space of modern life is heterotopia' (2004: 7), implying that each person understands, conforms to and reacts to ideas and processes –

capitalism, inequality, citizenship or democracy – differently. 'Politics', Chatterjee writes, 'does not mean the same thing to all people' (2004: 7). In part, this is because in the states and cities of the Global South the machinery of statecraft has reproduced colonial logics of power and administration, focusing more on technocratic approaches to governance where 'populations ... had the status of subjects not citizens' (Chatterjee, 2004: 35). Of course, the notion that the state has worked and functioned differently in sub-Saharan Africa (among other places) is a well-made point in the literature (see Ekeh, 1975; Hyden, 1980; Young, 1994; Bayart, 2009). What makes Chatterjee's idea of heterotopia relevant for thinking about DIY in African cities is that it opens up the possibility of conceiving of these practices, and the politics they engender, as an (in)voluntary escape or separation from the state's administrative reach – comparable with Hyden's (1982) evocative idea of the 'uncaptured peasantry'. DIY can function either (or sometimes both) as a necessary action in response to state failure, economic precarity and infrastructural deficiency, or as a conscious choice made by rational, thinking individuals. Contra to theorists of post-political approaches, DIY politics therefore occurs in a variety of unexpected venues, driven by diverse (mixed) motivations and undertaken by actors who *do* politics differently from what convention suggests. These dynamics call into question the very idea of what counts as politics. Such a conclusion builds on Simone's (2010) argument that we must consider what people are actually doing in Africa's cities, rather than merely assessing the multiple ways in which people are failing to live up to expectations or ideal types. Thinking with an accent can also mean to think 'from below'.

Indeed, the post-political condition described above requires the presence of state institutions and managerial class(es) well-equipped to exercise authority and implement policy across the municipal landscape. However, in the (African) cases described elsewhere in this volume, such capacities are at best unevenly (if at all) present. As de Souza explains, in many Global South cities there is persistent and widespread 'low-intensity state dissolution' (2006: 339) at the local level of municipal governance, coupled with a pervasive enclave-ization of the urban spatial environment that both separates city sectors and provides the insulating space for challenges and alternatives to incubate. Thus, in the interstitial gaps of the state, embedded within its absences and inefficiencies, it is possible for both communities and individuals to conceive of and – keeping in mind the distinction between the act and the outcome – potentially implement something new. De Souza illustrates the argument by pointing to Brazil's *favelas*, in which criminal gangs may supplement or challenge, but not fully replace, the state.

Further, even where urban experiences in the Global North and South intersect, as in their deep intertwinement with neoliberal financial processes, an authentic politics is not exhibited solely in crescendos of mass Occupy-style outbursts. DIY practices, prompted by limited state capacity and the pressures of neoliberalism, push politics into the smallest capillaries of urban space and infrastructure in ways that are both invisible and everywhere. These practices occur parallel to and beneath, colliding and intersecting with, the formal realms of state and capital. Through infrastructure especially, the 'acting-in-common' demonstrated by Swyngedouw's mass public that is 'of necessity interruptive, transgressive, and rebellious' (2017: 59) takes on a different, no less political, form. (Infrastructural) practice is, in some sense, the politics.

The oftentimes small acts of DIY manifest a call for the infrastructural justice necessary to create new, or open up existing, forms of inclusion, citizenship and spatial belonging. DIY practices as a form of politics highlight the need to engage the realities of (political) power wherever they may be found, and that 'strategies to overcome forms of hegemony must engage with visible nodes of power' (Chantal Mouffe, quoted in Beveridge and Koch, 2017: 37). Indeed, there are few demonstrations of power more visible than that of absent, failing and/or decrepit infrastructure. In her essay on 'peripheral urbanization', Teresa Caldeira speaks to the responses of individuals on the margins – whether spatial, demographic or socioeconomic – noting that the processes they initiate 'generate new modes of politics through practices that produce new kinds of citizens, claims, circuits, and contestations' (2017: 4). Sites and processes of DIY infrastructure creation, renewal and innovation are crucial in this regard.

Arendt, action and the DIY

In support of the above argument, we would here like to introduce Hannah Arendt to the discussion. Specifically, we invoke her conceptualizations of politics, power and action in order to emphasize the oppositional and progressive potential of DIY practices and politics undertaken by those on the (urban) margins. Arendt is perhaps best known for her work on totalitarianism (1953), thought and judgement (1971, 1989), and the many crises confronting post-War Western civilization (1998 [1958], 2006). Given the debt Arendt's work owes to the classical tradition in Western political philosophy – with influences ranging from Aristotle to Kant – it may seem an unusual choice with which to anchor reflections on DIY urbanism in African cities, especially when framed through a progressive or participatory (democratic) politics lens. Indeed, critics have pointed to a running thread in Arendt's writing that is both elitist and anti-democratic. While Wolin, for instance, notes the leftward shift in her writing in response to the anti-establishment and anti-war uprisings of the 1960s, he also observes, 'it is difficult to exaggerate either the severity with which she drew boundaries around the political in order to separate it from the banality and low concerns of ordinary life' (1983: 7). In practice, critics have taken this walling off of public and political life to mean that Arendt argued only those capable of leaving behind their private material concerns can or should act politically (Honig, 1988: 81). This scepticism towards the poor points to an ostensibly impossible-to-bridge breach between politics and necessity (Dikeç, 2013: 84; see also Beltrán, 2009: 599). Indeed, Arendt herself helped feed these conclusions through relentlessly emphasizing the calamitous impact on society and politics arising from private interests first infiltrating, then ultimately overwhelming, public space(s) and common good(s) – what she characterized as the rise of the private and social at the expense of the public and (political) action. Writing approvingly of the ancient Greeks early in *The Human Condition*, for example, Arendt notes, 'no activity that served only the purpose of making a living, of sustaining only the life processes, was permitted [by the Greeks] to enter the political realm' (1998 [1958]: 37). Politics could never be for the sake of life alone.

At the same time, Arendt's writing invites a more nuanced portrayal of these concepts. An alternate reading of her innovative depiction of politics, power and the conception of *action* linking them illuminates that the lines running between the lives of politics and necessity are perhaps fuzzier than expected. Resolving these running tensions within Arendt's work perhaps comes down to a question of prioritization – essentially, what one chooses to elevate within her writing on freedom, politics and action. In her essay 'What Is Freedom?', Arendt identifies the prerequisite to freedom: 'in order to be free, man must have liberated himself from the necessities of life' (2006: 147). What might freedom mean, then, for those individuals whose lives are mired in pervasive socioeconomic insecurity? At the same time – in fact, in the very next sentence – Arendt states that freedom is not automatic or inevitable following liberation from necessity: 'Freedom needed, in addition to mere liberation, the company of other men who were in the same state, and it needed a common public space to meet them – a politically organized world … into which each of the free men could insert himself by word and deed' (2006: 147). Do we, in other words, emphasize everyday structural constraints and lack (of, e.g., food or steady employment) or the procedural and practical aspects of coming together, exemplified by action collectively taken in public? This tension nods to a broad tradition in social science and philosophy. Indeed, there is a lengthy literature ranging across disciplines advocating for recognition of marginalized people's agency. These studies variously investigate peasant communities (Scott, 1977; Scheper-Hughes, 1992), resistance (Gaventa, 1982; Scott, 1985), and moral (Thompson, 1971) or informal (Hart, 1973) economies. Each of these diverse perspectives requires the reader to see vulnerable populations as more than the sum of their impoverishments.

Although Arendt preceded much of these debates in contemporary scholarship, the manner in which she defines her key concept 'action' throughout *The Human Condition* appears to both anticipate and respond to them. Time and again Arendt returns to the idea that action is revealed in moments where individuals come together to act in concert (1998 [1958]: 188). Ultimately, then, 'to act' means to initiate, to set something in motion (Arendt, 1998 [1958]: 177). The conclusive outcome of these initiatory moments – that is, what an act produces – is to Arendt both unknowable to the doer, and perhaps even irrelevant. It is the doing itself that is key. This focus on the procedural mechanics of action, rather than the specific products of it, is crucial for linking the concept to practical acts of DIY urbanism. As such, there is perhaps connective tissue linking Arendt's writing on politics and action to the everyday work and practice of individuals/communities living on the urban margins in precarious circumstances.

In his introduction to Arendt's essay collection, *Between Past and Future*, Jerome Kohn argues that alienation and crisis are recurrent themes throughout Arendt's body of work (2006: xvi, xviii). Questions of crisis intertwine with concerns that range from totalitarianism to the rise of automation and rationalism at the cost of individuality and free thought. More consequential, however, is the attention Arendt paid to more foundational experiences undergirding the experience of what it is to be human. Namely, alienation from the world as exemplified by the existence of nuclear weapons and the onset of the space race – she even begins *The Human Condition* with a discussion of the pioneering space probe Sputnik's significance. Never before in human history have Earth's inhabitants had the power to either destroy the world or leave it. For Arendt, these possibilities are symbols that portend profound and lasting consequences.

In her introduction to *The Human Condition*, Margaret Canovan explains the phenomenological approach at the heart of this line of thought:

> At the heart of her analysis of the human condition is the vital importance for a civilized existence of a durable human world, built upon the earth to shield us against natural processes and provide a stable setting for our mortal lives ... Only the experience of sharing a common human world with others who look at it from different perspectives can enable us to see reality in the round and to develop a shared common sense.
>
> (1998: xiii)

The world shapes us, and we the world, through natural processes, labour, work and artifice. While humans would remain biologically human whether they traversed interstellar distances on a generational rocket ship or scraped by on an Earth scarred by nuclear holocaust, our *human condition* would be very much altered. Arendt describes 'the earth [as] the very quintessence of the human condition, and earthly nature, for all we know, may be unique in the universe in providing human beings with a habitat in which they can move and breathe without effort and without artifice' (1998 [1958]: 2). In some ways, Arendt anticipates current debates about environmental degradation and climate change, as ecological collapse transforms humans' interrelationships with the natural world and our place in it. Whereas the alienation generated by a space-faring civilization or nuclear destruction was characterized by its potentiality, the world alienation wrought by climate change and the Anthropocene is ongoing – and accelerating – in the here and now.

At the same time, Arendt's efforts to think through the conditioning effects of our surroundings helps (re)frame how we might think through questions of infrastructure, urban (spatial) precarity and DIY practices. As Canovan (1998) points out, however, Arendt's attraction to and approval of, for example, mass action directed against the Vietnam War specifically and establishment politics more generally during the 1960s, demonstrates that she was not immune to directing concern towards more grounded moments of crisis. Reading Arendt as a theorist of crisis, more broadly defined, allows us to think in a different light about the DIY politics and practices that occur amidst urban conditions characterized by extreme, everyday spatial, infrastructural and socioeconomic insecurity. Indeed, DIY as an exemplification of Arendtian action shifts the locus, site and actor-based nature of politics.

Drexler suggests that there is a need to abandon conventional understandings of politics, power and those who should wield it – that is, what counts 'as proper, legitimate, political, reasonable, even sensible', as they reflect a 'game that is rigged in favour of the maintenance of the very processes the actor wishes to disrupt' (2007: 2). In the current moment of multiple crises – socioeconomic, environmental, an ongoing pandemic, widespread democratic erosion – and uncertainties, DIY becomes a key form of politics utilized by those on the margins, sometimes by choice, oftentimes by necessity. For Arendt, and later, people like Iris Marion Young, (DIY) action and the disruptive force of politics 'improper' is driven by those who have been cut out of processes establishing the 'rules' of the status quo (Drexler, 2007: 5). Through acting outside, within, at cross-purposes or in opposition to established nodes of power, DIY practitioners, infrastructure builders and those navigating networks of people-as-infrastructure (Simone, 2004) and the gaps, angles and fissures within communities, insert themselves – or, at least, attempt to do so – into the urban spatial and political fabric. The DIY construction of infrastructure and the persistent efforts to make oneself visible such acts entail – what we might term 'platforming' – is characteristic of the kinds of actions (and actors) Arendt valorizes.

These challenges, as intimated above, now take on an increased urgency. In her essay 'Freedom and Politics', Arendt writes that 'today, more may depend on human freedom than ever before – on man's capacity to turn the scales which are heavily in favour of disaster which always happens automatically and therefore always appears to be irresistible' (1960: 46). The times are, though, not without hope, with Arendt reminding us that 'the capacity to act is present even in unlikely circumstances' (Canovan, 1998: viii). Such circumstances can arise in (among other places) unauthorized housing developments, amidst auto-constructed shacks, on the streets, and in community halls. When we talk about DIY as action, and vice versa, the importance of infrastructure becomes clear. For individuals resident on the margins, infrastructure – both physical and social – is not merely about the provision of basic services, but about building a solid and stable world from which to perform livelihoods, politics and citizenship. Moreover, the construction of connective platforms to elsewhere and each other have the potential to make otherwise unheard or unseen individuals/communities heard and present.

These activities are, then, never just about the concerns of daily life and getting by – though they are about that too – but come wrapped up within wider and more weighty concerns. AbdouMaliq Simone, who has written powerfully about life in sub-Saharan African cities in particular and Global South cities more generally, has consistently argued this point (2004, 2006, 2010). In *Improvised Lives*, for instance, Simone notes that economic activities can be a way 'of signaling, of making visible a willingness to explore collaborations that go beyond the function of these activities themselves' (2018: 59). While this is perhaps true for urban residents across class, gender and citizenship divides, it is more consequential for those on the urban spatial and socioeconomic fringes. Here, then, the intersection between thinkers such as Arendt and Simone, between action and DIY, becomes a bit clearer. Ring, for example, argues that the key figure for Arendt is the pariah, or 'history's outsider' (1991: 433), who must intrude on the places and communities from which they have been excluded in order to make themselves seen and heard.

Identifying the connection between DIY and action furthers understanding of what (urban) outsiders are 'actually doing', as well as recasting how we might conceive of Simone's idea of African cities as 'half built' (2003) platforms to elsewhere. DIY infrastructure(s) become a form of 'platforming' that can connect disparate people and places, thereby acting as a counter to alienation and marginalization. At the same time, the aggregation of individuals facilitated by these platforms disrupts established powers and publics, while simultaneously incubating new ones in ways that enable outsiders to engage both politics and necessity. The politics of presence engendered by these processes points to a multidimensionality inherent in African urban life that belies strict distinctions between public and private or labour and action (as Arendt would frame it) (see, for example, Ekeh, 1975; Lund, 2006; Meagher, 2012). To further develop these linkages between DIY and action, and the concept's connection to urban Africa, we below elaborate on a few key characteristics identified by Arendt, namely: 1) natality and boundlessness; 2) unpredictability and acting together; and 3) disruption and the politics of presence.

DIY action and inaugurating a politics of interruption

Arendt's interlocutors flag the importance of natality, the ability to initiate or begin, to her idea of action. Indeed, Honig succinctly states that in the public realm, 'the doing is everything' (1988: 88). The emphasis on doing, Wolin suggests, underpins an action-centred idea of 'the political', which is best understood as 'a mode of experience rather than a comprehensive institution such as the state' (1983: 18). For her part, Arendt argues in 'Freedom and Politics' that the key to freedom – exemplified by (political) action – is the simple but profound ability to conjure into being something that did not previously exist (1960: 32). Arendt makes an explicit connection to the moment of birth, in which each newborn, unique in human history, carries within itself the ability to start something new: 'in this sense of initiative, an element of action, and therefore of natality, is inherent in all human activities ... action is the political activity *par excellence*' (1998 [1958]: 9). All individuals, even the poor or paperless, possess these capabilities (Beltrán, 2009; Dikeç, 2013: 86).

The mechanics of doing are fairly straightforward: it should be done in public and with others. Outcomes are unforeseeable and unpredictable, to the degree that we ought to be 'prepared for and to expect "miracles" in the political realm' (Arendt, 2006: 169). Often, these undertakings fail to work or work in ways that generate unintended consequences. Moreover, they are frequently only comprehensible well after the fact – and even then, only by an external observer capable of tying together the myriad narrative threads, events and consequences: 'Action revels itself fully only to the storyteller, that is, to the backward glance of the historian, who indeed always knows better what is was all about than the participants' (Arendt, 1998 [1958]: 191). Perhaps, though, one thing the actor is aware of is the interruptive or disruptive potential of action. Arendt describes action as an injection into 'historical processes' (2006: 169) that shift trajectories in a different direction – we might narrow down this definition by applying it to actions that interrupt convention, routine or broader political/socioeconomic norms governing a given society. These initiatives come in all manner of forms, reflective of the infinite capabilities of individual actors working together (even if perhaps they aren't aware of it at the time).

We return to an incident detailed in Marr's earlier chapter, 'Comparative DIY Urbanisms'. In the chapter, Marr describes a moment during his ethnographic fieldwork in Gaborone, Botswana's central plaza – or Main Mall, as it is locally known. Main Mall is roughly rectangular in shape, surrounded by hotels, local businesses and government offices. Amidst these structures, street hawkers and informal traders wander about or set up table-top shops in the central open-air courtyard. The diversity of economic activities and people that traverse or daily occupy the square make it a vibrant hub within the city centre, and accordingly a site in which encounters with individuals across the economic and social spectrum are possible. It was here that Marr, as a graduate student early on in his PhD fieldwork, was called over to talk by an unemployed male in his twenties. The main thrust of the conversation involved the twentysomething man attempting to gather information, in particular a possible idea for a business or scheme through which he could improve his livelihood prospects in Botswana. For outsiders conducting fieldwork in sub-Saharan Africa and elsewhere across the Global South, similar types of interventions – requests, often from strangers, for marriage proposals or to be taken 'back to America' – are relatively commonplace. Though difficult to make sense of at the time, this particular request stuck with Marr through the intervening years.

We recall it here because it illuminates the unexpected ways in which DIY urban practice(s) and Arendtian forms of (political) action overlap and reinforce one another. Some characteristics of this encounter, in light of what we discussed earlier, are straightforward. For instance, the interaction occurred in public and was conducted by the two participants together, even if one of them was unclear as to what was actually happening or why. Further, the effort on the part of the unemployed twentysomething represented an attempt to initiate something new and disrupt the status quo. The question of whether this was successful or not is secondary to that first moment of action. Two additional points merit mention.

First, consider the expertise required to navigate the urban environment. Filip de Boeck, for instance, often refers (2014, 2015, 2016) to the diverse skillset required to steer a path through the flux and flow of African urban spaces and social relationships. This speaks to an everyday expertise necessary to take advantage of, or mitigate, risk(s). As in the preceding example, this could mean an individual grabbing hold of moments of possibility and subsequently assembling these disparate urban parts into something useful, conjuring from nothing a chance to create, call forth or embark on a new endeavour. The creative capabilities of the individual navigating these conditions not only intersect with

Arendt's notion of natality, but the expertise required to do so resembles another definitive characteristic of action: virtuosity. Echoing Machiavelli and his idea of *virtú*, Arendt's virtuosity highlights the 'excellence with which man answers the opportunities the world opens up before him' (1960: 33). Freedom and (DIY) action become a matter of performance, rather than being measured according to outcomes.

Seen from this perspective, virtuosity – acting when situations present themselves – carries both private and public consequence. From the point of view of the pariah, the urban poor or, in the above case, a guy asking for an idea, taking action amidst conditions of uncertain, fragmentary or contradictory information suggests a necessary willingness to make things happen in order to make a place for oneself within the city's urban fabric. In such a way, these seemingly mundane, superficially self-interested acts of building (ephemeral) bridges or scaffolding between individuals become a means of actualizing a politics of presence in conditions of urban uncertainty or exclusion. The virtuosity of DIY action offers a way of transforming, perhaps even wielding, risk and uncertainty in order to remake the social, spatial and political worlds. When paired with the idea of DIY, the vocabulary offered by Arendt provides a basis for rethinking, or thinking more broadly, about our idea of politics and what counts as political action. Sheldon Wolin writes that freedom for Arendt existed in a 'political realm where men could experience choice' (1983: 8). We could add to this idea that within DIY practice it is not only the experience of choice, but also the fact that it is possible to make one at all, however small or seemingly inconsequential. For many living in precarious urban circumstances, where state institutions and/or economies are riven with injustice, dysfunctionality and vastly imbalanced power relations, these everyday choices may be the only venue of action available. Beltrán describes these dynamics as shifting 'our attention toward present-day acts of freedom' in the everyday (2009: 598). The politics of DIY action functions as an expression of and reaction to state failure; as a critique of institutional/infrastructural absence or neglect; and as a subsequent attempt to force inclusion, connection or recognition by whatever – however temporary or improvisational – means necessary. Initiating a (small, potentially transitory) moment of disruption in order to break the chains of exclusion or marginalization speaks to a politics that, though born of desperation and often ignored or overlooked, is practicable by anyone.

The tactics employed to avoid public invisibility lead to the second point. The importance Arendt places on acting together in 'the space of appearance' echoes the view that DIY practice facilitates enactment of a politics of presence, with both perspectives highlighting the disruptive potentialities of action and DIY. Arendt uses the idea of the 'space of appearance' to argue that the space for politics – Arendt deploys the term '*polis*' – exists in any location where people act together, and in which 'I appear to others as others appear to me' (1998 [1958]: 198). During a key passage in *The Human Condition*'s chapter on 'Action', Arendt calls attention to the labour movement's emergence into the public realm in the latter nineteenth to mid-twentieth centuries, and the transformative consequences that arose. Through sustained and collective action, a set of economic and political aspirations running counter to the status quo forced its way into the mainstream. Economic concerns were, according to Arendt, incidental to their political force, as they sought to establish a 'new public space with new political standards' (1998 [1958]: 219) that would be available to all citizens.

'The calamities of action' that 'arise from the human condition of plurality', exemplified in Arendt's telling by the labour movement, eroded the protective shield within which the status quo was, and continues to be, ensconced (1998 [1958]: 220). Although Arendt developed this illustration to demonstrate the importance of acting together in public to combat the depoliticizing isolation common in the mid-twentieth century (1998 [1958]: 202) – a cause and consequence of the era's tyrannies – it carries significance for thinking about the role of the poor and the struggle against more structural or everyday inequities. Indeed, Beltrán suggests this was an intentional point made by Arendt, inspired by John Adams's argument that the poor lack not only bread, but 'voice and visibility' (2009: 605). Action for Arendt was a means of getting them both. The implications for DIY are significant, especially if we conceive of DIY as a platform for (social) infrastructure-making as politics under conditions of precarity or pervasive state absence. We see these dynamics manifest, for example, in recent writing on the fight to access sanitation facilities in marginalized urban settlements in Ghana (Chalfin, 2014, 2017) and India (Appadurai, 2001). Public struggles for basic private needs spark a solidarity born of persistent, everyday crisis, whose local 'depth and [cross-border] laterality become joint circuits along which pro-poor strategies can flow' (Appadurai, 2001: 43).

Action functions as a disruption of routine or established processes (Arendt, 2006: 167–8). Within a conventional view of politics, such action takes familiar forms – for instance, a protest or an act of collective resistance – but in the context of DIY it takes on a different character. DIY infrastructure-making, for example, becomes an oppositional, interruptive act that can operate outside formal politics to disrupt social, political, economic or spatial marginalization. The power of action is thus found in the interruption (Drexler, 2007: 11). Oppositional in the way it counters convention or marginalization, DIY action also engenders a politics of presence through which the poor or other vulnerable groups can claim a space in the city. The performance of this everyday politics 'shifts the boundaries of the possible' (Drexler, 2007: 13) for marginalized groups and communities. For the poor or marginal, it is often impossible to disentangle ordinary livelihood, survival or subsistence needs from politics. Indeed, these arenas tend to become the central site of political struggle, as urban 'pariahs' must publicly intrude and cause discomfit if they are to garner attention or recognition in the struggle for change (Ring, 1991: 443).

Coda: DIY, Covid and climate change

The concluding chapter has situated DIY urbanism within an ongoing debate about the nature of the post-political city. This has been done in order to argue that a broader frame be applied to understanding politics in contemporary cities

– in particular, recognizing the smaller, everyday practices deployed by vulnerable urban dwellers as an important site and form of politics. While technical systems and rule by experts certainly exist, it does so amidst a terrain fertile with political contestation. Such a perspective allows for a more inclusive understanding of the wide variety of politics practised every day by urban residents, perhaps most especially in cities of the Global South. At the same time, the chapter has deployed Hannah Arendt's conceptualization of action to theorize the nature of DIY politics and practices, thereby opening up pathways to develop a politico-urban theory that spans diverse intellectual traditions and geographies, both North and South. More than that, framing DIY practice as a form of Arendtian action demonstrates that these tactics – undertaken amidst conditions of insecurity and precarity – (can) possess an emancipatory potential capable of advancing a politics aimed at equity and inclusion, in doing so mounting a challenge to the status quo.

There are, of course, limitations to DIY politics and practices. Arendt herself exhibited some scepticism towards do-it-yourself – emphasis on *yourself* – endeavours. Writing in *The Human Condition,* for instance, Arendt states, 'whoever, for whatever reasons, isolates himself and does not partake in such being together, forfeits power and becomes impotent, no matter how great his strength and how valid his reasons' (1998 [1958]: 201), while in *Between Past and Future* she notes, 'if men wish to be free, it is precisely [individual] sovereignty they must renounce' (2006: 163). This perspective isn't altogether surprising for such a strong advocate of acting together and in public as a means to power, or conversely, a critic of the individuating isolation that feeds tyranny and represents a turning inward and away from the problems of the world. It is not hard to imagine Arendt being especially dismissive of liberty-espousing Doomsday survivalists, busy prepping their underground bunker or island fortress to ride out the crises of the day behind closed doors.

Indeed, further difficulties with DIY urbanism emerge in the context of two of the present moment's greatest emergencies: climate change and the Covid-19 pandemic. These challenges become even more apparent if we shift the focus to outcomes (what does DIY actually *do*?) rather than process (how does it *unfold*?). The imminent threats of severe climate change and the ongoing pandemic, which shows only spasmodic signs of abating, darken the view of DIY, especially as both processes continue to have the most debilitating impacts on those least capable of navigating them. In these final lines, we thus flag some of the most consequential challenges in order to help light the way for future research trajectories and academic considerations of DIY urbanism.

First, what can DIY urbanism conducted at the city, neighbourhood or household level accomplish when confronted with a global challenge such as climate change? It is a fact that the most devastating impacts of climate change occur in areas with limited access to financial, technical or infrastructure capabilities, despite its causes being located elsewhere. Given these imbalances, can locally based DIY urbanism deliver anything more than reactive responses that bounce from one emergency to the next, let alone transformative change that produces more durable, long-term and equitable solutions? A partial answer, well beyond the scope of the discussion here, can perhaps be found in work conducted on behalf of transnational civil society (see, for instance, Keck and Sikkink 1998), which illuminates how grassroots activists network and cooperate with one another.

In his work on democracy in India's slums, Arjun Appadurai (2001) suggests a model for how this might unfold: for grassroots activists to be successful at implementing pro-poor policies, organizations must be both deeply rooted and laterally connected. What, then, does this mean for DIY urbanists grappling with climate change adaptation and mitigation? One possibility could be to facilitate cross-border sharing of best practices to deal with climate-induced issues, such as heat island effects, vernacular architecture and urban flooding. Groups such as Slum Dwellers International attempt this already, and may therefore serve as a model illustrating these exchanges. Even so, significant challenges stand in the way of cooperation between organizations and local communities operating on their own. Lack of financial resources or institutional support often limits the ability to scale-up grassroots innovations. There is therefore a potential need to bring the state in as a willing partner. In this scenario, DIY approaches collaborate with the state, rather than functioning in parallel to or repudiating it. The catch here is that in the places where DIY is most needed or practised by urban communities, the state is not readily capable of fulfilling that role.

Second, under conditions of heightened resource-scarcity and impending environmental calamity, to what extent do DIY approaches overlap with nationalist politics? That is, does the emphasis in DIY increasing fall on the 'yourself', foreshadowing an exclusionary hardening of community boundaries at the local, national or regional level? Instead of strengthening resilience through expanding horizontal cooperative linkages, DIY conducted under the weight of the climate crisis may instead engender a zero sum autochthony along the lines described by Peter Geschiere (2009) or of Fred Cooper's 'Gatekeeper State' (2002; see Chapter 7 in particular). In this scenario, the various approaches, perspectives and motivations driving DIY urbanism veer away from moments of cooperation and competition to a more sustained conflict dynamic, as each DIY grassroots actor scrambles for whatever resources remain. Of course, these possibilities have always been present, but risk being amplified amidst accelerating climate change. While literature exists on the links between right-wing nationalism and climate scepticism (Lockwood, 2018; Kulin, Sevä and Dunlap, 2021), little has been written about what happens when the far right begins to take climate change seriously. This stands out as an urgent area of investigation given its relevance to DIY urbanism during the climate crisis.

Finally, turning to the Covid-19 pandemic, sustained lockdowns, social distancing and the closure of public (and private) spaces tangibly limits the possibility of people 'coming together' to act in concert. Withdrawing into the home bears significant impacts on the functionality of community and civil society, with the consequences arising almost certainly unevenly distributed due to differences in class, access to healthcare, and stable work and family support structures. For the most vulnerable – indeed, for anyone living during the pandemic – what this implies is a real need for a trusted state with resources, institutions capable of providing services, and widespread technical expertise wielded by technocrats (Marr and Mususa, 2020). When confronted with an event such as the Covid-19 pandemic, localized, informal or everyday expertise will only take you so far. What this suggests is that rather than simply thinking about the possibilities of DIY beyond the state, we must also consider how to reinvigorate the state. In much the same way as a vibrant civil society requires a solid, stable and functioning state, the practices and politics of DIY urbanism may require something similar. This applies doubly so in localities where the state has previously demonstrated little interest in inclusion or civic engagement. These challenges become ever more urgent as democracy frays around the world (Lührmann and Lindberg, 2019). The progressive potential of DIY will surely be limited if the states in which these tactics and politics are practised turn ever more hostile to citizen innovation and civic participation.

REFERENCES

Introduction

Annamraju, S., Calaguas, B. and Gutierrez, E. (2001). 'Financing water and sanitation: Key issues in increasing resources to the sector'. Water Aid briefing paper. London: Water Aid Prince Consort House.

Bond, P. (2019). 'Neoliberalism, state repression and the rise of social protest in Africa'. In Berberoglu, B. (ed.), *The Palgrave Handbook of Social Movements, Revolution, and Social Transformation*. Cham: Palgrave Macmillan.

Boone, C. (2011). 'Politically allocated land rights and the geography of electoral violence: The case of Kenya in the 1990s'. *Comparative Political Studies* 44(10), 1311–42.

Carmody, P. and Owusu, F. (2016). 'Neoliberalism, urbanization and change in Africa: The political economy of heterotopias'. *Journal of African Development* 18(1), 61–73.

Chitonge, H. and Mfune, O. (2015). 'The urban land question in Africa: The case of urban land conflicts in the City of Lusaka, 100 years after its founding'. *Habitat International* 48, 209–18.

De Boeck, F. and Plissart, M. F. (2014). *Kinshasa: Tales of the Invisible City*. Leuven: Leuven University Press.

Devisch, R. (1996). '"Pillaging Jesus": Healing churches and the villagisation of Kinshasa'. *Africa* 66(4), 555–86.

Douglas, G. C. (2014). 'Do-it–yourself urban design: The social practice of informal "improvement" through unauthorized alteration'. *City & Community* 13(1), 5–25.

Finn, D. and Douglas, G. (2019). 'DIY urbanism'. In Talen, E. (ed.), *A Research Agenda for New Urbanism*, 20–34. Cheltenham: Edward Elgar Publishing.

Fraser, A. and Lungu, J. (2007). *For Whom the Windfalls?: Winners & Losers in the Privatisation of Zambia's Copper Mines*. Lusaka: Civil Society Trade Network of Zambia (CSTNZ).

Fyfe, N. R. and Milligan, C. (2003). 'Out of the shadows: Exploring contemporary geographies of voluntarism'. *Progress in Human Geography* 27(4), 397–413.

Hamdi, N. (2014). *The Spacemaker's Guide to Big Change: Design and Improvisation in Development Practice*. London: Routledge.

Harris, A. S. and Hern, E. (2019). 'Taking to the streets: Protest as an expression of political preference in Africa'. *Comparative Political Studies* 52(8), 1169–99.

Jiménez, A. C. (2017). 'Auto-construction redux: The city as method'. *Cultural Anthropology* 32(3), 450–78.

Kesselring, R. (2017). 'The electricity crisis in Zambia: Blackouts and social stratification in new mining towns'. *Energy Research & Social Science* 30, 94–102.

Kinder, K. (2016). *DIY Detroit: Making Do in a City without Services*. Minneapolis: University of Minnesota Press.

Lawrence, D. L and Low, S. M. (1990). 'The built environment and spatial form'. *Annual Review of Anthropology* 90, 453–505.

Marr, S. (2016). 'Worlding and wilding: Lagos and Detroit as global cities'. *Race & Class* 57(4), 3–21.

Mattes, R. (2019). 'Democracy in Africa: Demand, supply, and the dissatisfied democrat'. Afrobarometer Policy Paper No. 54.

Mkandawire, T. (2001). 'Thinking about developmental states in Africa'. *Cambridge Journal of Economics* 25(3), 289–314.

Munalula, M., Kanyamunya, V. and Kanenga, H. (2018). 'State–civil society relationship in Zambia'. *International Journal of Humanities, Art and Social Studies (IJHAS)* 3(4), 17–26.

Murray, M. J. (2015). 'Waterfall City (Johannesburg): Privatized urbanism in extremis'. *Environment and Planning A* 47(3), 503–20.

Mususa, P. (2021). *There Used to Be Order: Life on the Copperbelt after the Privatisation of the Zambia Consolidated Copper Mines.* Ann Arbor: University of Michigan Press.

Myers, G. (2016). 'Remaking the edges: Surveillance and flows in sub-Saharan Africa's new suburbs'. In Loeb, C. and Luescher, A. (eds.), *The Design of Frontier Spaces.* New York: Routledge.

Myers, G. (2020). *Rethinking Urbanism: Lessons from Postcolonialism and the Global South.* Bristol: Bristol University Press.

Olukoshi, A. (2004). 'Property rights, investment, opportunity and growth: Africa in a global context'. In Quan, J., Tan, S. F. and Toulmin, C. (eds.), *Land In Africa: Market Asset or Secure Livelihood?* London: Church House.

Parnell, S. and Pieterse, E. (2016). 'Translational global praxis: Rethinking methods and modes of African urban research'. *International Journal of Urban and Regional Research* 40(1), 236–46.

Pieterse, E. (2011). 'Grasping the unknowable: Coming to grips with African urbanisms'. *Social Dynamics* 37(1), 5–23.

Pitcher, M. A. (2018). 'Entrepreneurial governance and the expansion of public investment funds in Africa'. In Harbeson, J. W. and Rothchild, D. (eds.), *Africa in World Politics: Constructing Political and Economic Order.* New York: Routledge.

Potts, D. (2006). '"Restoring order"? Operation Murambatsvina and the urban crisis in Zimbabwe'. *Journal of Southern African Studies* 32(2), 273–91.

Robinson, J. (2016). 'Comparative urbanism: New geographies and cultures of theorizing the urban'. *International Journal of Urban and Regional Research* 40(1), 187–99.

Udelsmann Rodrigues, C. (2022). 'Where is the state missing? Addressing urban climate change at the margins in Luanda and Maputo'. *Urban Forum* 33(1), 35–49.

UN-Habitat (2022). *World Cities Report 2022: Envisaging the Future of Cities.* UN-Habitat.

Victor, H. (2019). '"There is life in this place":"DIY formalisation," buoyant life and citizenship in Marikana informal settlement, Potchefstroom, South Africa'. *Anthropology Southern Africa* 42(4), 302–15.

Watson, V. and Siame, G. (2018). 'Alternative participatory planning practices in the global south: Learning from co-production processes in informal communities'. In Knierbein, S. and Viderman, T. (eds.), *Public Space Unbound,* 145–57. New York: Routledge.

Chapter 1

Amin, A. and Graham, S. (1997). 'The ordinary city'. *Transactions of the Institute of British Geographers* 22(4).

Arendt, H. (1968). 'Introduction'. In Benjamin, W., *Illuminations,* 1–55. New York: Schocken Books.

Baudelaire, C. (1995). *The Painter of Modern Life and Other Essays* [Jonathan Mayne (ed.)]. London: Phaidon Press.

Benjamin, W. (1968). *Illuminations.* New York: Schocken Books.

Benjamin, W. (1978). *Reflections: Essays, Aphorisms, Autobiographical Writings* [Peter Demetz (ed.)]. New York: Schocken Books.

Berman, M. (1982). *All That Is Solid Melts into Air: The Experience of Modernity.* New York: Simon & Schuster.

Beveridge, R. and Koch, P. (2017). 'The post-political trap: Reflections on politics, agency, and the city'. *Urban Studies* 54(1).

Biehl, J. G. (2005). *Vita: Life in a Zone of Social Abandonment.* Berkeley: University of California Press.

Bindé, J. (2000). 'Towards an ethics of the future'. *Public Culture* 12(1).

Comaroff, J. and Comaroff, J. L. (2000). 'Millennial capitalism: First thoughts on a second coming'. *Public Culture* 12(2).

De Boeck, F. (2005). 'The apocalyptic interlude: Revealing death in Kinshasa'. *African Studies Review* 48(2).

Demetz, P. (1978). 'Introduction'. In Benjamin, W., *Reflections: Essays, Aphorisms, Autobiographical Writings* [Peter Demetz (ed.)]. New York: Schocken Books.

Devisch, R. (1995). 'Frenzy, violence, and ethical renewal in Kinshasa'. *Public Culture* 7(3).

Diouf, M. (2003). 'Engaging postcolonial cultures: African youth and public space'. *African Studies Review* 46(2).

Ferguson, J. (1999). *Expectations of Modernity: Myths and Meanings of Urban Life on the Zambian Copperbelt.* Berkeley: University of California Press.

Gandy, M. (2006). 'Planning, anti-planning and the infrastructure crisis facing metropolitan Lagos'. *Urban Studies* 43(2).

Glaeser, E. (2011). 'How skyscrapers can save the city'. *Atlantic* (March). www.theatlantic. com/magazine/archive/2011/03/how-skyscrapers-can-save-the-city/8387/

Harrison, P. (2006). 'On the edge of reason: Planning and urban futures in Africa'. *Urban Studies* 43(2).

Kohn, M. (2009). 'Dreamworlds of deindustrialization'. *Theory & Event* 12(4).

Marr, S. (2016). 'Worlding and wilding: Lagos and Detroit as global cities'. *Race & Class* 57(4).

Mbembe, A. (2004). 'Aesthetics of superfluity'. *Public Culture* 16(3).

Mbembe, A. and Nuttall, S. (2004). 'Writing the world from an African metropolis'. *Public Culture* 16(3).

Mumford, L. (1989 [1961]). *The City in History: Its Origins, Its Transformations, and Its Prospects.* New York: Harcourt.

Mumford, L. (2003). 'What is the city?'. In LeGates, R. T. and Stout, F. (eds.), *The City Reader*, 3rd edition. New York: Routledge.

Norton, R. J. (2003). 'Feral cities'. *Naval War College Review* 56(4).

Packer, G. (2006). 'Megacity: Decoding the chaos of Lagos'. *The New Yorker* (13 November). www.newyorker.com/magazine/2006/11/13/the-megacity

Pieterse, E. (2010). 'Cityness and African urban development'. *Urban Forum* 21(3).

Robinson, J. (2002), 'Global and world cites: A view from off the map'. *International Journal of Urban and International Research* 26(3).

Russell, C. (2002). 'Against dead time'. *Time & Society* 11(2/3).

Sennett, R. (1976). *The Fall of Public Man.* New York: W. W. Norton & Company.

Simone, A. (2003). 'Moving towards uncertainty: Migration and the turbulence of African urban life'. Paper prepared for the Conference on African Migration in Comparative Perspective, Johannesburg, South Africa, 4–7 June.

Simone, A. (2004a). *For the City Yet to Come: Changing African Life in Four Cities.* Durham: Duke University Press.

Simone, A. (2004b). 'People as infrastructure: Intersecting fragments in Johannesburg'. *Public Culture* 16(3).

Simone, A. (2006). 'Pirate towns: Reworking social and symbolic infrastructures in Johannesburg and Douala'. *Urban Studies* 43(2).

Simone, A. (2010a). *City Life from Jakarta to Dakar: Movements at the Crossroads.* New York: Routledge.

Simone, A. (2010b). 'A town on its knees? Economic experimentations with postcolonial urban politics in Africa and Southeast Asia'. *Theory, Culture & Society* 27(7–8).

Simone, A. (2019). *Improvised Lives: Rhythms of Endurance in an Urban South.* New York: John Wiley & Sons.

Swyngedouw, E. (2009). 'The antinomies of the postpolitical city: In search of a democratic politics of environmental production'. *International Journal of Urban and Regional Research* 33(3).

Swyngedouw, E. (2017). 'Unlocking the mind-trap: Politicising urban theory and practice'. *Urban Studies* 54(1).

Zeiderman, A. (2008). 'Cities of the future? Megacities and the space/time of urban modernity'. *Critical Planning* (Summer).

Chapter 2

Adams, D. and Hardman, M. (2013). 'Observing guerrillas in the wild: Reinterpreting practices of urban guerrilla gardening'. *Urban Studies* 51(6), 1–17.

Adams, D., Hardman, M. and Scott, A. (2013). 'Guerrilla warfare in the planning system: Revolution or convergence in sustainable development discourse?' *Geografiska Annaler: Series B, Human Geography* 95(4), 375–87.

Adler, P. and Kwon, S. W. (2002), 'Social capital: Prospects for a new concept'. *Academic of Management Review* 27(1), 17–40.

Anjaria, J. S. (2016). *The Slow Boil: Street Food, Rights and Public Space in Mumbai.* Palo Alto: Stanford University Press.

Appadurai, A. (2000), 'Spectral housing and urban cleansing: Notes on millennial Mumbai'. *Public Culture* 12(3), 627–51.

Bayat, A. (1997). 'Un-civil society: The politics of the "informal people"'. *Third World Quarterly* 18(1), 53–72.

Bishop, P. and Williams, L. (eds.) (2012). *The Temporary City.* New York: Routledge.

Boltanski, L. and Chiapello, E. (2005). *The New Spirit of Capitalism.* London: Verso.

Daskalaki, M. and Mould, O. (2013). 'Beyond urban subcultures: Urban subversions as rhizomatic social formations'. *International Journal of Urban and Regional Research* 37(1), 1–18.

Day, A. (2017). 'Introduction: Creative play and collective imagination'. In Day, A. (ed.), *DIY Utopia: Cultural Imagination and the Remaking of the Possible*, VII–XIX. Boulder: Lexington.

De Boeck, F. and Baloji, S. (2016). *Suturing the City: Living Together in Congo's Urban Worlds.* London: Autograph ABP.

DeSilvey, C. and Edensor, T. (2013). 'Reckoning with ruins'. *Progress in Human Geography* 37(4), 465–85.

Deslandes, A. (2013). 'Exemplary amateurism: Thoughts on DIY urbanism'. *Cultural Studies Review* 19(1), 216–27.

Dotson, T. (2016). 'Trial-and-error urbanism: Addressing obduracy, uncertainty and complexity in urban planning and design'. *Journal of Urbanism* 9(2), 148–65.

Douglas, G. (2014). 'Do-it-yourself urban design: The social practice of informal improvement through unauthorized alteration'. *City & Community* 13(1), 5–25.

Dovey, K. (2014). 'Review of the temporary city'. *Journal of Urban Design* 19(2), 261–3.

Fabian, L. and Samson, K. 'Claiming participation: A comparative analysis of DIY urbanism in Denmark'. *Journal of Urbanism* 9(2), 166–84.

Ferreri, M. (2015). 'The seductions of temporary urbanism'. *Ephemera* 15(1), 181–91.

Finn, D. (2014a). 'DIY urbanism: Implications for cities'. *Journal of Urbanism* 7(4), 381–98.

Finn, D. (2014b). 'Introduction to the special issue on DIY urbanism'. *Journal of Urbanism* 7(4), 331–2.

Frank, T. (1998). *The Conquest of Cool: Business Culture, Counterculture and the Rise of Hip Consumerism*. Chicago: University of Chicago Press.

Gamez, J. and Sorensen, J. (2014). 'No more waiting for Superman: Teaching DIY urbanism and reflexive practice'. *Journal of Urbanism* 7(4), 333–50.

Gandy, M. (2006). 'Planning, anti-planning and the infrastructure crisis facing metropolitan Lagos'. *Urban Studies* 43(2), 371–96.

Gillick, A. R. (2017). 'Stitching the city: Continuity, urban renewal and grassroots action in late-twentieth century Glasgow'. *The Journal of Architecture* 22(2), 188–224.

Holston, J. (2008). *Insurgent Citizenship: Disjunctions of Democracy and Modernity in Brazil*. Princeton: Princeton University Press.

Hou, J. (2010). '(Not) your everyday public space'. In Hou, J. (ed.), *Insurgent Public Space: Guerrilla Urbanism and the Remaking of Contemporary Cities*, 1–18. New York: Routledge.

Iveson, K. (2013). 'Cities within the City: Do-it-yourself urbanism and the right to the city'. *International Journal of Urban and Regional Research* 37(3), 941–56.

Jabareen, Y. (2014). '"Do it yourself" as an informal mode of space production: Conceptualizing informality'. *Journal of Urbanism* 7(4), 414–28.

Jones, J. (2010). '"Nothing is straight in Zimbabwe": The rise of the Kukiya-kiya economy 2000–2008'. *Journal of Southern African Studies* 36(2), 285–99.

Kinder, K. (2014). 'Guerrilla-style defensive architecture in Detroit: A self-provisioned security strategy in a neoliberal space of disinvestment'. *International Journal of Urban and Regional Research* 38(5), 1767–84.

Kinder, K. (2016). *DIY Detroit: Making Do in a City without Services*. Minneapolis: University of Minnesota Press.

Kinder, K. (2017). 'DIY urbanism in shrinking cities: Or, what neighbors are left with when markets withdraw and governments contract'. *Metropolitics* (27 March). www.metropolitiques.eu/DIY-Urbanism-in-Shrinking-Cities.html

Lydon, M. and Garcia, A. (2015). *Tactical Urbanism: Short-term Action for Long-term Change*. Washington, DC: Island Press.

Marcuse, H. (1965). 'Repressive tolerance'. In Wolff, R. P., Moore, B. and Marcuse, H. (eds.), *A Critique of Pure Tolerance*, 81–117. Boston: Beacon Press.

Marshall, W., Duvall, A. and Main, D. (2016). 'Large-scale tactical urbanism: The Denver bike share system'. *Journal of Urbanism* 9(2), 135–47.

Martinez, L., Short, http://www.sciencedirect.com/science/article/pii/S02642751163075 08?via%3Dihub - ! J. R. and Estrada, D. (2017). 'The urban informal economy: Street vendors in Cali, Colombia'. *Cities* 66, 34–43.

Mould, O. (2014). 'Tactical urbanism: The new vernacular of the creative city'. *Geography Compass* 8, 529–39.

Pagano, C. (2014). 'DIY urbanism: Property and process in grassroots city building'. *Marquette Law Review* 97, 336–89.

Pieterse, E. (2013). 'Introducing rogue urbanism'. In Pieterse, E. and Simone, A. (eds.), *Rogue Urbanism: Emergent African Cities*, 12–18. Auckland Park: Jacana.

Rao, V., De Boeck, F. and Simone, A. (2007). 'Invisible urbanism in Africa'. *Perspecta* 39, 78–91.

Simone, A. (2003). 'The visible and invisible: Remaking cities in Africa'. In Ewenzor, O. et al. (eds.), *Under Siege: Four African Cities: Freetown, Johannesburg, Kinshasa, Lagos. Documenta 11_Platform4*, 23–43. Stuttgart: Hatje Cantz Publishers.

Spataro, D. (2016). 'Against a de-politicized DIY urbanism: Food not bombs and the struggle over public space'. *Journal of Urbanism* 9(2), 185–201.

Sundaram, R. (2010). *Pirate Modernity: Delhi's Media Urbanism*. New York: Routledge.

Talen, E. (2015). 'Do-it-yourself urbanism: A brief history'. *Journal of Planning History* 14(2), 135–48.

Thieme, T. A. (2018). 'The hustle economy: Informality, uncertainty and the geographies of getting by'. *Progress in Human Geography* 42(4), 529–48.

Vasudevan, A. (2015). 'The makeshift city: Towards a global geography of squatting'. *Progress in Human Geography* 39(3), 338–59.

Zeiderman, A. (2008). 'Cities of the future? Megacities and the space/time of urban modernity'. *Critical Planning* 15, 23–39.

Chapter 3

Abdoul, M. (2005). 'Urban development and urban informalities'. In Simone, A. and Abouhani, A. (eds.), *Urban Africa: Changing Contours of Survival in the City*, 234–60. Dakar/London/Pretoria: CODESRIA Books/Zed Books/University of South Africa Press.

Aluko O. E. (2011). 'Sustainable housing, population growth and poverty: The implications on Lagos mega city'. *Journal of Sustainable Development* 4(4).

Andreasen, J. (1990). 'Urban rural linkages and their impact on urban housing in Kenya'. In Baker, J. (ed.), *Small Town Africa: Studies in Rural Urban Interrelation*. Seminar Proceedings No. 23. Uppsala: The Scandinavian Institute of African Studies.

Augustine, B. (2010). *Post Modernism Encyclopaedia of Sociology*, 2nd edition, vol. 3. Macmillan Reference.

Bayat, A. (2000). 'From dangerous classes to "quiet rebel's": Policies of urban subaltern in the Global South'. *International Sociology* 15(3).

Binns, D. (1977). *Beyond the Sociology of Conflict*. New York: St. Martins Press.

Bradley, K. (2015). 'Open source urbanism: Creating, multiplying and managing urban commons'. *Delft Architecture Theory Journal* 16. http://footprint.tudelft.nl/index.php/footprint/article/view/901/1065 (accessed 22 November 2017).

Caminos, H. and Goethert, R. (1978). *Urbanization Primer*. Cambridge, MA: The MIT Press.

Cohen, B. (2006). 'Urbanization in developing countries: Current trends, future projections, and key challenges for sustainability'. *Technology and Society* 28(1–2).

Dowd, D. F. (1977). *The Twisted Dream: Capitalist Development in the United States since 1776*, 2nd edition. Cambridge, MA: Winthrop Publishers, Inc.

Duruzoechi, N. F. and Duru, M. N. (2015). *Land Use Planning, Design and Control*. Nigeria: Tropical Publishers.

Farah, J., Cabrera, J. E. and Teller, J. (Undated). 'Bridging the gap between do it yourself urban practices and urban systems: Insights from Bolivia and Lebanon'. https://orbi.ulg.ac.be/bitstream/2268/172501/1/ (accessed 22 November 2017).

Ferguson, J. (1992). 'The country and the city on the Copper Belt'. *Cultural Anthropology* 7(1), 88–92.

Gans, H. J. (1968). *People and Plans: Essays in Urban Problems and Solutions*. New York, NY: Basic Book Inc.

Gheris, M. (2005). 'Formal and decentralized financing of housing: Operation 200,000 Houses, Marrakesh'. In Simone, A. and Abouhani, A. (eds.), *Urban Africa: Changing Contours of Survival in the City*. Dakar/London/Pretoria: CODESRIA Books/Zed Books/University of South Africa Press.

Gugler, J. and Flanagan, W. G. (1978). *Urbanisation and Social Change in West Africa*. Cambridge: Cambridge University Press.

Hanna, W. J. and Hanna, J. (1971). *Urban Dynamics in Black Africa: An Interdisciplinary Approach*. Aldine-Atherton. New York: Transaction Publishers.

Jain, A. K. (2015). *Smart Cities: Vision and Action*. New Delhi: Discovery Publishing House.

Jelili, M. O. (2012). 'Urbanization and future of cities in Africa: The emerging facts and challenges to planners'. *Global Journal of Human Social Science* 12(7).

Kaplinsky, R. (2013). 'Environment, inequality and the internal contradictions of globalization'. In Butcher, M. and Papaioannou, T. (eds.), *New Perspectives in International Development*, 149–58. London: Bloomsbury Academic.

Keeble, L. (1969). *Principles and Practice of Town and Country Planning*, 4th edition. London: The Estate Gazette.

Kent, T. J. (1964). *The Urban General Plan*. Chicago: Chardler Publishing Company.

Levy, J. (2009). *Contemporary Urban Planning*, 8th edition. London: Pearson and Prentice Hall.

Little, K. (1974). *Urbanisation as a Social Process*. London: Routledge and Kegan Paul.

Mabogunje, A. L. (1968). *Urbanisation in Nigeria*. New York, NY: Africana Publishing Corporation.

Macionis, J. J. and Plumber, K. (2014). *Sociology: A Global Introduction*. Harlow: Pearson Education Ltd.

McGee, T. G. (1975). *The Urbanisation Process in the Third World*. London: G Bell and Sons Ltd.

Nordhag, M. (2012). 'Urbanization in sub-Saharan Africa: A study of contemporary urban population growth in a less developed region'. BA thesis. Linneans University, June 2012.

Pacione, M. (2009). *Urban Geography: A Global Perspective*, 3rd edition. London: Routledge.

Pagano, C. (2013). 'DIY urbanism: Property and process in grassroots city building'. *Marquette Law Review* 97(2).

Rae, D. (2003). *City Urbanism and Its End*. New Haven, CT, and London: Yale University Press.

Roy, A. (2011). 'Slumdog cities: Rethinking subaltern urbanism international'. *Journal of Urban and Regional Research* 35(2).

Silver, C. (2008). *Planning the Mega City: Jakarta in the Twentieth Century*. New York, NY: Routledge.

Simpson, C. (2015). 'An overview and analysis of tactical urbanism in Los Angeles'. Urban and Environmental Policy, Occidental College. https://www.oxy.edu/sites/default/files/assets/UEP/Comps/Simpson%20Final%20-%20Copy.pdf.

Spreiregen, P. D. (1965). *Urban Design: The Architecture of Town and Cities*. London: McGraw Hill Book Company.

Therborn, G. (2017). *Cities of Power: The Urban, The National, The Popular, The Global*. London: Verso Books.

Vanderschueren, F., Wegelin, E. and Wekwete, K. (1996). 'Policy programme options for urban poverty reduction: A framework for action at municipal level'. Urban Management Programme 20, Washington, DC.

Weber, M. M. (1969). 'Order in diversity: Community without propinquity'. In Wingo, Jr., L. (ed.), *Cities and Space: The Future Use of Urban Land*, 23–54. Baltimore/London: Johns Hopkins Press.

Wendler, J. (2014). 'Experimented urbanism: Grassroots alternatives as spaces of leaning and innovation in the city'. PhD Thesis. University of Manchester.

Wirth, L. (1938). 'Urbanism as a way of life'. *The American Journal of Sociology*, 44(1).

Yunusa, M-B. (2004). 'Urban development policies and infrastructure in Nigeria'. In Aina, T. A., Chachage, C. S. L. and Anna-Yao, E. (eds.), *Globalisation and Social Policy in Africa*. Dakar: CODESRIA.

Yunusa, M-B. (2005). 'Life in a high-density urban area: Anguwar Mai Gwado in Zaria'. In Simone, A. and Abouhani, A. (eds.), *Urban Africa: Changing Contours of Survival in the City*. Dakar/London/Pretoria: CODESRIA Books/Zed Books/University of South Africa Press.

Chapter 4

AFDB (2017). *African Economic Outlook*. Abidjan: African Development Bank.

AFDB (2018). *African Economic Outlook*. Abidjan: Africa Development Bank.

Agbo, M. (2017a). 'Letter from Abuja: The Fading Sheen of Nigeria's capital city'. https://commonedge.org/letter-from-abuja-the-fading-sheen-of-nigerias-capital-city/ (accessed 8 August 2017).

Agbo, M. (2017b). 'Tale of two cities: Unravelling the brutal backstory behind Africa's emerging megacities'. http://commonedge.org/tale-of-two-cities-unravelling-the-brutal-backstory-behind-africas-emerging-megacities/ (accessed 27 June 2017).

Bamidele, R., Joseph, A., Ake, M. and Raji, A. (2017). 'God fatherism and political patronage in Nigeria: A theoretical overview'. *Political Science Review* 8(1), 77–101.

Budgit (2017). 'How much does Nigeria make from oil?'. www.yourbudgit.com/oil/ (accessed 25 December 2017).

Duncombe, S. (1997). *Notes from the Underground: Zines and the Politics of Underground Culture*. New York: Verso.

Echessa, G. (2010). 'The role of residents' association in urban service delivery: The case of Nairobi city, Keny'. Masters Thesis. Kenyatta University, Nairobi.

ECOSOC (United Nations Economic and Social Council) (2014). 'Sustainable urbanization in Africa, Addis Ababa': UNECA, united nations economic commission for Africa.

Furness, Z. (2010). *One Less Car*. Philadelphia: Temple University Press.

Gabriel, C. (2015). 'Stomach infrastructure: The newest vocabulary in Nigeria's political dictionary'. www.vanguardngr.com/2015/03/stomach-infrastructure-the-newest-vocabulary-in-nigerias-political-dictionary/ (accessed 5 March 2018).

Gaestel, A. (2018). 'Things fall apart'. https://magazine.atavist.com/things-fall-apart-makoko-floating-school/ (accessed 1 August 2018).

Gyekye, K. (2011). 'African ethics'. http://plato.stanford.edu/entries/african-ethics (accessed 29 May 2018).

Hern, M. (2010). *Common Ground in a Liquid City: Essays in Defense of an Urban Future*. Edinburgh/Oakland/Baltimore: AK Press.

Hou, J. (2010). *Insurgent Public Space: Guerrilla Urbanism and the Remaking of Contemporary Cities*. New York: Routledge.

Howard, E. (1902). *Garden Cities of Tomorrow*, 2nd edition. London: Swan Sonnenschein and Co., Ltd.

Ibelema, M. (2000). 'Nigeria: The politics of marginalization'. *Current History* 99, 211–14.

Joseph, R. (2016). 'Dilemmas of democracy and state power in Africa'. www.brookings. edu/opinions/dilemmas-of-democracy-and-state-power-in-africa/ (accessed 23 December 2017).

Kimmelman, M. (2013). 'Who rules the street in Cairo? The residents who build it'. *New York Times* 28 (April), A1.

Lefebre, H. (1996). *Writings on Cities* [E. Kofma and E. Lebas (eds. and trans.)]. Cambridge, MA: Wiley-Blackwell.

Lynch, G. and Crawford, G. (2011). 'Democratization in Africa 1990–2010: An assessment'. *Democratization* 18(2), 275–310.

McDonough, T. (2010). *The Situationists and the City*. New York City: Verso.

Neighbourhood Review (2017). 'A comprehensive review of graceland estate'. www. neighbourhoodreview.com/a-comprehensive-review-of-graceland-estate/ (accessed 4 June 2018).

New Garden City Movement (2013). 'New garden city movement'. www. newgardencitymovement.org.uk (accessed 18 December 2019).

van Nierk, J. (2013). 'Ubuntu and Moral Values'. PhD dissertation. University of Witwatersrand.

Nworgu, J. A. and Ijirshar, V. U. (2016). 'The impact of corruption on economic growth and cultural values in Nigeria: A need for value-orientation'. https://www.researchgate. net/publication/313817474_The_Impact_of_Corruption_on_Economic_Growth_and_ Cultural_Values_in_Nigeria_A_Need_for_Value_Re-orientation (accessed 27 June 2018).

Odalonu, H. B. (2015). 'Challenges confronting local government administration in efficient social service delivery and effective social service delivery: The Nigerian experience'. *International Journal of Public Administration and Management Research (IJPAMR)*, 2(5), 12–22.

Okeke, F. and Chukwuali, C. (2019). 'Environmentally-responsive design'. *A Study of Makoko Floating School Building* 8, 476–87.

Olowolaju, P. S., Ajibola, O., Ishola, A. R. and Falayi, I. (2014). 'Federal government statutory fund allocation to states in Nigeria, West Africa: Any reasonable story to tell?'. *American International Journal of Social Science* 3, 152–64.

Olowoopejo, M. (2013). *Lagos Outlaws Makoko Ultra Modern Floating School*. www. vanguardngr.com/2013/04/lagos-outlaws-makoko-ultra-modern-floating-school/ (accessed 1 October 2017).

Olukoshi, A. (2004). 'Changing patterns of politics in Africa'. *Cadernos de Estudos Africanos* 1 (June), 15–38.

Pagano, C. (2013). 'DIY urbanism: Property and process in grassroots city building'. *Marquette Law Review* 97(2).

Pieterse, E. (2011). 'Rethinking African urbanism from the slum'. https://lsecities.net/wp-content/uploads/2011/11/2011_chw_5060_Pieterse.pdf (accessed 1 October 2018).

Premium Times (2017). 'Abuja flood deaths: Lokogoma residents protest'. www.premiumtimesng.com/regional/north-central/241650-abuja-flood-deaths-lokogoma-residents-protests.html (accessed 4 November 2017).

Punch Editorial (2017). 'Poor implementation of 2017 Budget'. http://sunnewsonline.com/poor-implementation-of-2017-budget/ (accessed 1 December 2017).

Shepard, B. (2014). 'DIY urbanism as an environmental justice strategy: The case study of Time's Up! 1987–2012'. *Theory in Action* 7(2), 42–73.

Sunday Guardian (2016). 'Abuja $470m CCTV camera project lies in ruins'. http://t.guardian.ng/sunday-magazine/cityfile/abuja-470m-cctv-camera-project-lies-in-ruins/ (accessed 1 December 2017).

Tschaepe, M. (2013). 'A humanist ethic of Ubuntu: Understanding moral obligation and community'. *Essays in Philosophy of Humanism* 21(2), 47–61.

van Zeijl, F. (2016). 'The rise and fall of the floating school'. www.zammagazine.com/chronicle/chronicle-26/436-the-rise-and-fall-of-the-floating-school (accessed 27 June 2018).

Chapter 5

Adeniran, T. (2002). 'The Vigilante and Nigeria's internal security'. In *Eminent Persons' Seminar Series*. Ibadan: Development Policy Centre.

Ake, C. (1997). 'Why humanitarian emergency occur: Insight from the interface of state, democracy and civil society'. *United Nations University/World Institute for Development Economic Research, Research for Action* 31.

Andhoga, W. O. and Johnson, M. (2017). 'Influence of Nyumba Kumi community policing initiative on social cohesion among cosmopolitan-sub-locations in Nakuru County'. *International Journal of Social and Development Concerns* 1, 65–76.

Ayiera, E A. M. (2017). 'Community-led security mechanisms: The case of Mlango Kubwa and Kawangware in Nairob'. *The African Review* 44(1), 2–61.

Baker, B. (2010). *Security in Post Conflict Africa: The Role of Nonstate Policing*. Boca Raton: CRC Press.

Barihuta, P. (2017). 'Effectiveness of Irondo as a community-led security mechanism in Kigali'. *African Review* 44(1), 62–98.

Berg, J. (2007). 'The accountability of South Africa's private security industry: Mechanisms of control and challenges to effective oversight'. Occasional Paper Series, Criminal Justice Initiative, 2. Newlands: Open Society Foundation of South Africa.

Berg, J., Akinyele, R., Fourchard, L., Waal, van der and William, N. (2013). 'Contested social orders: Negotiating urban security in Nigeria and South Africa'. In Laurent Fourchard (eds.), *Governing Cities in Africa*. Cape Town: Human Sciences Council (HSRC) Press.

Bjerk, P. (2015). *Building a Peaceful Nation: Julius Nyerere and the Establishment of Sovereignty in Tanzania, 1960–1964*. Rochester, NY: University of Rochester Press.

Boege, V., Brown, M. A, Clements, K. and Nolan, A. (2008). 'On hybrid political orders and emerging states: State formation in the context of "Fragility"'. Berghof Handbook Dialogue 8 (Online version). Berlin: Berghof Research Center for Constructive Conflict Management. www.berghof-handbook.net/uploads/download/boege_etal_handbook.pdf (accessed 30 March 2019).

Boutellier, H. and Van Steden, R. (2011). 'Governing nodal governance: The "anchoring" of local security networks'. In Crawford, A. (ed.), *International and Comparative Criminal Justice and Urban Governance. Convergence and Divergence in Global, National and Local Settings*, 61–82. Cambridge: Cambridge University Press.

Burris, S., Drahos, P. and Shearing, C. (2005). 'Nodal governance'. *Australian Journal of Legal Philosophy* 30, 30–58.

Buur, L. (2006). 'Reordering society: Vigilantism and expressions of sovereignty in Port Elizabeth's townships'. *Development and Change* 37(4), 735–57.

Chabal, P. and Daloz, J. (1999). *Africa Works: Disorder as Political Instrument*. Oxford: International African Institute in association with James Currey/Bloomington: Indiana University Press.

Collier, P. (2007). *The Bottom Billion: Why the Poorest Countries Are Failing and What Can Be Done about It*. Oxford: Oxford University Press.

Dawha, M.K.E. (1996). *Yan Daba, Yan banga and Yan Dauka Amarya : A Study of Criminal Gangs in Northern Nigeria*. Ibadan: French Institute for Research in Africa, IFRA.

Diphoorn, T. and Kyed, H. M. (2016). 'Entanglements of private security and community policing in South Africa and Swaziland'. *African Affairs* 115(461), 710–32.

Ekeh, P. (1992). 'The constitution of civil society in African history and politics'. In Baron, B. et al. (eds.), *Democratic Transition in Africa*. Ibadan: Centre de Recherché d'Documentation Universitaire, Institute of African Studies, University of Ibadan.

Godfrey, A. B. and Dixon, K. (2017). 'Community security initiatives in low-income areas of Kampala'. *African Review* 44(1), 138–60.

Gratz, T. (2010). 'Devi & his men: The rise and fall of a vigilante movement in Benin'. In Kirsch, Thomas G. and Gratz, T. (eds.), *Domesticating Vigilantism in Africa*, 79–97. Woodbridge/Rochester: James Curry/Boydell and Brewer.

Hagberg, S. (2010). 'Vigilantes in war: Boundaries crossing of hunters in Burkina Faso and Cote d' Ivoire'. In Kirsch, Thomas G. and Gratz, T. (eds.), *Domesticating Vigilantism in Africa*. Woodbridge/Rochester: James Curry/Boydell and Brewer.

Hendriks, M. and Buscher, K. (2019). *Insecurity in Goma: Experiences, Actors and Responses*. London/Nairobi: Rift Valley Institute.

Kyed, H. M. (2009). 'Community policing in post-war Mozambique'. *Policing and Society* 19(4), 354–71.

Lal, P. (2015). *African Socialism in Postcolonial Tanzania: Between the Village and the World*. New York: Cambridge University Press.

Landinfo Country of Origin Information Centre (2010). 'Kenya: Mungiki – Abusers or abused?' www.landinfo.no/asset/1123/1/1123_1.pdf (accessed 16 January 2020).

Mamdani, M. (1995). 'Introduction'. In Mamdani, M. and Wamba-dia-Wamba (eds.), *African Studies in Social Movements and Democracy*. Dakar: CODESRIA.

Maza, K. D., Koldas, U. and Aksit, S. (2020). 'Challenges of countering terrorist recruitment in the Lake Chad region: The case of Boko Haram'. *Religions* 11(96), 1–26.

Menkhaus, Ken (2007). 'Governance without government in Somalia: Spoilers, state building, and the politics of coping'. *International Security* 31(3), 74–106.

Mkutu, K. and Sabala, K. (2007). 'Private security companies in Kenya and dilemmas for security'. *Journal of Contemporary African Studies* 25(3), 391–416.

Ndono, P. W., Nzioka, J. M. and Kariuki, M. (2019). 'Effectiveness of the Nyumba Kumi community policing initiative in Kenya'. *Journal of Sustainability, Environment and Peace* 1, 63–7.

Okonta, I. (2012). 'The fire next time: Youth, violence, and democratisation in Northern Nigeria'. Fredrich Ebert Stiftung Discussion Paper 3.

Proctor, J. H. (ed.) (1971). *The Cell System of the Tanganyika African National Union.* Dar es Salam: Tanzania Publishing House.

Raeymaekers, Timothy, Menkhaus, Ken and Vlassenroot, Koen (2008). 'State and non-state regulation in protracted African crises: governance without government?' *Afrika focus* 21(2), 7–21.

Robinson, M. and White, G. (1997). 'The role of civic organisations in the provision of social services: Towards Synergy'. In *Research for Action 37.* Helsinki: UNU/World Institute for Development Economics Research (WIDER).

Ruteere, M. (2009). *Dilemmas of Crime, Human Rights and the Politics of Mungiki Violence in Kenya.* Nairobi: Kenya Human Rights Institute.

Sambaiga, R. F. (2018). 'Changing images of Nyumba Kumbi in Tanzania: Implications for youth engagement in countering violence at the community level'. *The African Review* 453, 4–74.

Sana, O. and Okombo, O. (2012). 'Taking stock of socio-economic challenges in the Nairobi Slums'. In *Community-Led Security Mechanisms in Nairobi 61.* Nairobi: Friedrich-Ebert-Stiftung. http://library.fes.de/pdf-files/bueros/kenia/09860.pdf (accessed 7 November 2019).

Servant, J. (2007). 'Kikuyus muscle in on security and politics: Kenya righteous youth militia'. *Review of African Political Economy* 34(113), 521–6.

Shearing Clifford, Shearing and Jan, Froestad (2010). 'Nodal Governance and the Zwelethemba Model'. In Quirk, H., Seddon, T. and Smith, G. (eds.), *Regulation and Criminal Justice: Innovations in Policy and Research.* Cambridge: Cambridge University Press, 103–33.

Tamuno, T. N. (1970). *The Police in Modern Nigeria, 1861–1965.* Ibadan: Ibadan University Press.

Trefon, T. (2009). 'Public service provision in a failed state: Looking beyond predation in the Democratic Republic of Congo'. *Review of African Political Economy* 36(119), 9–21.

Wisler, D. and Onwudiwe, I. (2007). 'Community policing: A comparative view'. Working Paper 6. Geneva Centre for the Democratic Control of Armed Forces, International Police Executive Symposium.

Ya'u, Y. (2000). 'The youth, economic crisis, and identity transformations: The case of Yandaba in Kano'. In Attahiru, Jega (ed.), *Identity Transformation and Identity Politics Under Structural Adjustment in Nigeria*, 161–80. Uppsala: Nordic African Institute.

Chapter 6

Adebanwi, Wale and Obadare, Ebenezer (eds.) (2013). *Democracy and Prebendalism in Nigeria: Critical Interpretations.* New York: Palgrave Macmillan.

Akinyele, R. T. (2001). 'Ethnic militancy and national stability in Nigeria: A case study of the Oodua People's Congress'. *African Affairs* 100(401), 623–40. DOI: 10.1093/afraf/100.401.623.

Anderson, David M. (2002). 'Vigilantes, violence and the politics of public order in Kenya'. *African Affairs* 101(405), 531–55. DOI: 10.1093/afraf/101.405.531.

Bagayoko, Niagale, Hutchful, Eboe and Luckham, Robin (2016). 'Hybrid security governance in Africa: Rethinking the foundations of security, justice and legitimate public authority'. *Conflict, Security & Development* 16(1), 1–32. DOI: 10.1080/14678802.2016.1136137.

Baker, Bruce (2009). 'Introduction: Policing post-conflict societies: Helping out the state'. *Policing & Society* 19(4), 329–32.

Bekker, Simon and Fourchard, Laurent (eds.) (2013). *Governing Cities in Africa*. Cape Town: HSRC Press.

Brogden, M. (2004). 'Commentary: Community policing: A panacea from the West'. *African Affairs* 103(413), 635–50.

Cheeseman, Nic and de Gramont, Diane (2017). 'Managing a mega-city: Learning the lessons from Lagos'. *Oxford Review of Economic Policy* 33(3), 457–77. DOI: 10.1093/oxrep/grx033.

Daily Post (2018). 'Lagos APC primaries: Why Ambode is not a good party man – Tinubu' (2 October). http://dailypost.ng/2018/10/02/lagos-apc-primaries-ambode-not-good-party-man-tinubu/.

Di Nunzio, Marco (2014). 'Thugs, spies and vigilantes: Community policing and street politics in inner city of Addis Ababa'. *Africa* 84(3), 444–65.

Ferguson, James (2006). *Global Shadows: Africa in the Neoliberal World Order*. Durham, NC: Duke University Press.

Financial Times (2018). 'Nigerian economy: Why Lagos works' (24 March). www.ft.com/content/ff0595e4-26de-11e8-b27e-cc62a39d57a0

Fourchard, Laurent (2008). 'A new name for an old practice: Vigilantes in South-Western Nigeria'. *Africa* 78(01), 16–40. DOI: 10.3366/E000197200800003X.

Gandy, Matthew (2006). 'Planning, anti-planning, and the infrastructure crisis facing metropolitan Lagos'. In Murray, Martin J. and Myers, Garth A. (eds.), *Cities in Contemporary Africa*. New York: Palgrave Macmillan.

de Gramont, Diane (2015). *Governing Lagos: Unlocking the Politics of Reform*. Washington: Carnegie Endowment for International Peace.

Guardian (Lagos) (2018). 'Tinubu reaffirms control in Lagos as Ambode bows' (4 October). https://guardian.ng/politics/tinubu-reaffirms-control-in-lagos-as-ambode-bows/.

Hagmann, Tobias and Péclard, Didier (2010). 'Negotiating statehood: Dynamics of power and domination in Africa'. *Development and Change* 41(4), 539–62.

Helmke, Gretchen and Levitsky, Steven (2004). 'Informal institutions and comparative politics: A research agenda'. *Perspectives on Politics* 2(4), 725–40. DOI: 10.1017/S1537592704040472

Hills, Alice (2008). 'The dialectic of police reform in Nigeria'. *The Journal of Modern African Studies* 46(2), 215–34.

Howden, Daniel (2010). 'Lagos: Inside the ultimate mega-city'. *Independent* (London) (15 April). www.independent.co.uk/news/world/africa/lagos-inside-the-ultimate-mega-city-1945246.html

Ibrahim, Jibrin (2017). 'Politics and the institutional disconnect in Nigeria'. *Daily Trust* (12 January). www.dailytrust.com.ng/politics-and-the-institutional-disconnect-in-nigeria.html (accessed 6 December 2018).

Ismail, Olawale (2009). 'The dialectic of "Junctions" and "Bases": Youth, "Securo-Commerce" and the crises of order in downtown lagos'. *Security Dialogue* 40(4–5), 463–87. DOI: 10.1177/0967010609343302.

Jackson, Paul, Kassaye, Demelash and Shearon, Edward (2019). '"I fought the law and the law won": Evidence on policing communities in Dire Dawa, Ethiopia'. *The British Journal of Criminology* 59(1), 126–43.

Joseph, Richard A. (1987). *Democracy and Prebendal Politics in Nigeria*. Cambridge: Cambridge University Press.

Kyed, Helene Maria (2018). 'Street authorities: Community policing in Mozambique and Swaziland'. *Political and Legal Anthropology Review* 41(S1), 19–34.

LeBas, Adrienne (2013). 'Violence and urban order in Nairobi, Kenya and Lagos, Nigeria'. *Studies in Comparative International Development* 48(3), 240–62. DOI: 10.1007/s12116-013-9134-y.

Lund, Christian (2006). 'Twilight institutions: Public authority and local politics in Africa'. *Development and Change* 37(4), 685–705.

Marr, Stephen (2016). 'Worlding and wilding: Lagos and Detroit as global cities'. *Race & Class* 57(4), 3–21. DOI: 10.1177/0306396815624863.

Menkhaus, Ken (2007). 'Governance without government in Somalia spoilers, state building, and the politics of coping'. *International Security* 31(3), 74–106.

Momoh, Abubakar (2000). 'Youth culture and area boys in Lagos'. In Jega, Attahiru (ed.), *Identity Transformation and Identity Politics Under Structural Adjustment in Nigeria*, 181–203. Uppsala/Kano: Nordic Africa Institute/Centre for Research and Documentation.

Momoh, Abubakar (2003). 'The political dimension of urban youth crisis: The case of the Area Boys in Lagos'. In Fourchard, Laurent and Albert, Isaac O. (eds.), *Security, Crime and Segregation in West African Cities since the 19th Century*. Paris/Ibadan: Karthala/IFRA.

Nolte, Insa (2007). 'Ethnic vigilantes and the state: The Oodua People's Congress in South-Western Nigeria'. *International Relations* 21(2), 217–35. DOI: 10.1177/0047117807077005.

Obi, Cyril (2011). 'Taking back our democracy? The trials and travails of Nigerian elections since 1999'. *Democratization* 18(2), 366–87. DOI: 10.1080/13510347.2011.553359.

Omotola, J. Shola (2010). 'Elections and democratic transition in Nigeria under the Fourth Republic'. *African Affairs* 109(437), 535–53.

Onuzo, Chibundu (2017). *Welcome to Lagos*. London: Faber & Faber.

Owumi, B. and Ajayi, J. O. (2013). 'Traditional values, beliefs and reliance on indigenous resources for crime control in modern Southwest Nigeria'. *African Research Review*, 7(1), 73–94.

Packer, George (2006). 'The megacity: Decoding the chaos of Lagos'. *The New Yorker*, 13 November.

Peck, Jamie, Theodore, Nik and Brenner, Neil (2009). 'Neoliberal urbanism: Models, moments, mutations'. *SAIS Review of International Affairs* 29(1), 49–66. DOI: 10.1353/sais.0.0028.

Pieterse, Edgar (2010). 'Cityness and African urban development'. *Urban Forum* 21(3), 205–19. DOI: 10.1007/s12132-010-9092-7.

Pratten, David (2008). 'Introduction. The politics of protection: Perspectives on vigilantism in Nigeria'. *Africa* 78(1), 1–15.

Premium Times (2017). 'Lagos council polls – Fear of violence, heavy rainfall, others cause low turnout' (23 July). https://allafrica.com/stories/201707230016.html.

Punch (2017). 'Official Lagos LG election results as released by LASIEC' (24 July). https://punchng.com/official-lagos-lg-election-results-as-released-by-lasiec/

Raeymaekers, Timothy, Menkhaus, Ken and Vlassenroot, Koen (2008). 'State and non-state regulation in African protracted crises: Governance without government?' *Afrika Focus* 21(2), 7–21.

Reno, William (2005). 'The politics of insurgency in collapsing states'. *Development & Change* 33(5), 837–58. DOI: 10.1111/1467-7660.t01-1-00251.

Sklar, Richard L., Onwudiwe, Ebere and Kew, Darren (2006). 'Nigeria: Completing Obasanjo's legacy'. *Journal of democracy* 17(3), 100–15.

Tilly, Charles (2003). *The Politics of Collective Violence*. Cambridge: Cambridge University Press.

Vanguard (2018). 'Security of lives, property my biggest achievement in three years – Ambode' (29 May). www.vanguardngr.com/2018/05/997410/

Chapter 7

Abourahme, N. (2018). 'Of monsters and boomerangs: Colonial returns in the late liberal city'. *City* 22(1).

Acquah, I. (1958). *Accra Survey: A Social Survey of the Capital of Ghana, Formerly Called the Gold Coast, Undertaken for the West African Institute of Social and Economic Research, 1953–1958*. London: University of London Press.

Ahlman, J. (2012). 'A new type of citizen: Youth, gender, and generation in the Ghanaian Builders Brigade'. *Journal of African History* 53.

Austin, D. (1964). *Politics in Ghana, 1946–1960*. London and New York: Oxford University Press.

Barrett, W. H. (1958). 'Preface'. In Town and Country Planning Division of the Ministry of Housing, 'Accra: A Plan for the Town: The Report for the Minister of Housing'.

Benzoni, S. (n.d.).'Accra, Ghana'. Informal City Dialogues. https://nextcity.org/informalcity/city/accra (accessed 2 April 2018).

Bissell, W. (2011). *Urban Design, Chaos, and Colonial Power in Zanzibar*. Bloomington, IN: Indiana University Press.

De Boeck, F. (2011). 'The modern Titanic: Urban planning and everyday life in Kinshasa'. *The Salon* 4.

Byerley, A. (2011). 'Displacements in the name of (re-)development: The contested rise and Contested Demise of Colonial "African" housing estates in Kampala and Jinja'. *Planning Perspectives* 38(4).

Clark, G. (1995). *Onions Are My Husband: Survival and Accumulation among West African Market Women*. Chicago, IL: University of Chicago Press.

Cooper, F. (2002). *Africa since 1940: The Past of the Present*. Cambridge: Cambridge University Press.

Enwezor, O. (2002). 'Introduction'. In Enwezor, O., Basualdo, C., Bauer, U. M., Ghez, S., Maharaj, S., Nash, M. and Zaya, M. (eds.), *Under Siege, Four African Cities: Freetown, Johannesburg, Kinshasa, Lagos: Documenta 11, Platform 4*. Ostfildern-Ruit: Hatje Cantz.

GhanaStar (2018). 'Filth collapsing Kaneshie Market' (17 March). http://archive.today/VTIeD (archived 13 January 2023).

GhanaWeb (2010). 'Accra Declared Millennium City' (15 January). www.ghanaweb.com/GhanaHomePage/NewsArchive/Accra-declared-millennium-city-175219

Gittlen, A. (2016). 'As collectors look to African Art, Accra emerges as a creative hub'. Artsy (20 June). www.artsy.net/article/artsy-editorial-ghana-s-capital-is-undergoing-an-artistic-renaissance

Government of Ghana (Ministry of Local Government and Rural Development) (2012). 'Ghana National urban policy and action plan'. www.ghanaiandiaspora.com/wp/wp-content/uploads/2014/05/ghana-national-urban-policy-action-plan-2012.pdf

Hart, K. (1973). 'Informal income opportunities and urban employment in Ghana'. *Journal of Modern African Studies* 11(1).

Hart, J. (2013). '"One man, no chop": Licit wealth, good citizens, and the criminalization of drivers in postcolonial Ghana'. *The International Journal of African Historical Studies* 46(3).

Hart, J. (2016). *Ghana on the Go: African Mobility in the Age of Motor Transportation.* Bloomington, IN: Indiana University Press.

Hart, J. (2020). Of pirate drivers and honking horns: Mobility, authority, and urban planning in late-colonial Accra. *Technology and Culture, 61(2),* S49-S76.

Her Majesty's Stationary Office (1887). *Gold Coast: Annual Report for 1895.* http://libsysdigi.library.illinois.edu/ilharvest/africana/books2011-05/5530214/5530214_1 895/5530214_1895_opt.pdf.

Hirt, S. A. (2009). 'Premodern, modern, postmodern? Placing new urbanism into a historical perspective'. *Journal of Planning History* 8(3).

His Majesty's Stationary Office (1912). *Gold Coast: Report for 1911.* http://libsysdigi.library.illinois.edu/ilharvest/africana/books2011-05/5530214/5530214_1911/5530214_1911_opt.pdf

Holston, J. (1989). *The Modernist City: An Anthropological Critique of Brasilia.* Chicago, IL: University of Chicago Press.

Inkumsah (1958). 'Introduction'. In Town and Country Planning Division of the Ministry of Housing, 'Accra: A Plan for the Town: The Report for the Minister of Housing'.

Larnyoh, M. T. (2018). '"Accra is the new London; everywhere is neat" – Zoomlion CEO'. *Pulse.com.gh* (9 March). www.pulse.com.gh/news/business/accra-is-the-new-london-everywhere-is-neat-zoomlion-ceo-id8094215.html (accessed 2 April 2018).

Lobrano, A. (2016). 'Africa''s capital of cool'. *New York Times Style Magazine* (12 July). www.nytimes.com/2016/07/08/t-magazine/travel/accra-ghana-travel.html (accessed 2 April 2018).

Mayne, A. (2017). *Slums: The History of a Global Injustice.* London: Reaktion Books.

McCaskie, T. C. (2001). *Asante Identities: History and Memory in an African Village, 1850–1950.* Bloomington, IN: Indiana University Press.

Miescher, S. (2012). 'Building the city of the future: Visions and experiences of modernity in Ghana's Akosombo Township'. *Journal of African History* 53(3), 367–90.

Murillo, B. (2012). '"The modern shopping experience": Kingsway department store and consumer politics in Ghana'. *Africa* 82(3).

Murillo, B. (2017). *Market Encounters: Consumer Cultures in Twentieth-Century Ghana.* Athens, OH: Ohio University Press.

Nightingale, C. (2012). *Segregation: A Global History of Divided Cities.* Chicago, IL: University of Chicago Press.

Nkrumah, K. (1958). 'Foreword'. In Town and Country Planning Division of the Ministry of Housing, 'Accra: A Plan for the Town: The Report for the Minister of Housing'.

Osei-Boateng, C. and Ampratwum, E. (2011). 'The informal sector in Ghana'. Friedrich Ebert Stiftung. http://library.fes.de/pdf-files/bueros/ghana/10496.pdf

Parker, J. (2000). *Making the Town: Ga State and Society in Early Colonial Accra.* Portsmouth, NH: Heinemann.

Pellow, D. (1991). 'The power of space in the evolution of an Accra Zongo'. *Ethnohistory* 38(4).

Pellow, D. (2001). 'Cultural differences and urban spatial forms: Elements of boundedness in an Accra community'. *American Anthropologist* 103(1).

Plageman, N. (2010). '"Accra is changing isn't it?": Urban infrastructure, independence, and nation in the Gold Coast's "Daily Graphic", 1954–1957'. *The International Journal of African Historical Studies* 43(1).

Plageman, N. (2013). *Highlife Saturday Night: Popular Music and Social Change in Urban Ghana*. Bloomington, IN: Indiana University Press.

Quayson, A. (2014). *Oxford Street, Accra: City Life and the Itineraries of Transnationalism*. Durham, NC: Duke University Press.

Robertson, C. (1983). 'The death of Makola and other tragedies'. *The Canadian Journal of African Studies* 17(3).

Sackeyfio, N. (2008) 'The stool owns the City: Ga Chieftaincy and the politics of land in Colonial Accra, 1920–1950'. Phd dissertation, University of Wisconsin-Madison.

Schauert, P. (2015). *Staging Ghana: Artistry and Nationalism in State Dance Ensembles*. Bloomington, IN: Indiana University Press.

Simone, A. (2019). *Improvised Lives*. Cambridge: Polity.

Skinner, K. (2011). 'Who knew the minds of the people? Specialist knowledge and developmentalist authoritarianism in postcolonial Ghana'. *The Journal of Imperial and Commonwealth History* 39(2).

UNDP (United Nations Development Programme) (2014). 'Inequality in Ghana: A fundamental national challenge'. Briefing Paper. www.undp.org/content/dam/ghana/docs/Doc/Inclgro/Ghana-unicef%20Inequality%20Briefing%20Paper%20FINAL%20DRAFT%20Apr%202014.pdf

Vanderbeek, M. and Irazabal, C. (2007). 'New urbanism as a new modernist movement: A comparative look at modernism and new urbanism'. *Traditional Dwellings and Settlements Review* 19(1).

Watson, V. (2013). 'African urban fantasies: Dreams or nightmares?'. *Environment & Urbanization* 26(1).

Winterhalter, S. M. (2015). 'Building a new nation: The modern architecture of Ghana'. MA thesis, University of Georgia.

Yeboah, I. (2018) '"Ghana First" demo hits Accra over US military deal'. *Graphic Online* (28 March). www.graphic.com.gh/news/general-news/ghana-first-demo-hits-accra-over-us-military-deal.html (accessed 2 April 2018).

Chapter 8

Addo, N. O. (2010). 'Harnessing Potential in Heritage Sites: The Adaptive Reuse of Old Buildings in Old Accra'. Masters Thesis. Kumasi, Ghana: Kwame Nkrumah University of Science and Technology.

Agyei-Mensah, S. and Owusu, G. (2010). 'Segregated by neighbourhoods? A portrait of ethnic diversity in the neighbourhoods of the Accra Metropolitan Area, Ghana'. *Population, Space and Place* 16, 499–516.

Amarteifio, N. N. (2015). 'The definitive story of James Town British Accra'. The Ade Sawyer Blog. https://adesawyerr.wordpress.com/2015/11/10/the-definitive-story-of-james-town-accra-by-nat-nuno-amarteifio/ (accessed 1 December 2017).

Anyidoho, N. A. (2013). 'Informal Economy Monitoring Study: Street Vendors in Accra, Ghana'. Manchester: Women in Informal Employment: Globalizing and Organizing (WIEGO).

Asiedu, A. B. and Agyei-Mensah, S. (2008). 'Traders on the run: Activities of street vendors in the Accra, metropolitan area, Ghana'. *Norwegian Journal of Geography* 62(3), 191–202.

Ayitio, J. and Sarfoh, O. K. (2014). 'Ebb and flow: Reconfiguring contemporary open spaces in Accra'. UrbanAfrica.net. https://www.urbanafrica.net/urban-voices/ebb-flow-reconfiguring-contemporary-open-spaces-accra/ (accessed 20 November 2017).

Chen, M. with Harvey, J., Kihato, C. W. and Skinner, S. (2018). '*Inclusive Public Spaces for Informal Livelihoods: A Discussion Paper for Urban Planners and Policy Makers*'. Manchester: WIEGO.

Falt, L. (2016). 'From shacks to skyscrapers: Spatial rationalities and the urban transformation of Accra, Ghana'. *Urban Forum* 27(4), 1–22.

Fanon, F. (2001). *Wretched of the Earth [1963]*. London: Penguin Books Limited.

Fieuw, Walter and Mwau, Baraka (2017). 'Creating "urban common's': Towards a sustainable informal settlement upgrading paradigm in South Africa'. In Cirolia, Liza Rose, Görgens, Tristan, van Donk, Mirjan, Smit, Warren and Drimie, Scott (eds.), *Upgrading Informal Settlements in South Africa: Pursuing a Partnership-Based Approach*, 181–98. Cape Town: Juta and Company (Pty) Ltd.

Gillespie, T. (2015). 'Accumulation by urban dispossession: Struggles over urban space in Accra, Ghana'. *Transactions of the Institute of Geographers* 41, 66–77.

Harvey, D. (2012). *Rebel Cities: From the Right to the City to the Urban Revolution*. London and New York: Verso.

Hunter, M. A., Pattillo, M., Robinson, Z. F. and Taylor, K. (2016). 'Black placemaking: Celebration, play, and poetry'. *Theory, Culture & Society* 33(7–8), 31–56.

Jackson, I. (2019). *Sharing Stories from Jamestown: The Creation of Mercantile Accra*. Liverpool: Liverpool School of Architecture.

Kip et al. (2015). 'Seizing the (Every)Day: Welcome to the urban commons!' In Dellenbaugh, M. Kip, M., Bieniok, M., Müller, A. and Schwegmann, M. (eds.), *Urban Commons: Moving beyond State and Market*. Berlin: Bauverlag.

Kuttler, T. and Jain, A. (2015). 'Defending space in a changing urban landscape – A study on urban commons in Hyderabad, India'. In Dellenbaugh, M. Kip, M. Bieniok, M., Müller, A. and Schwegmann, M. (eds.), *Urban Commons: Moving beyond State and Market*. Berlin: Bauverlag.

Mbembe, A. (2003). 'Necropolitics'. *Public Culture* 15(1), 11–40.

Mensah, P. (2014). 'Home-based enterprises as an informal economic activity: A case of Ga Mashie in Accra, Ghana'. Masters Thesis. University of Ghana, Legon.

Murillo, B. (2012). 'The modern shopping experience: Kingsway department store and consumer politics in Ghana'. *Africa* 82(3), 368–92.

Njoh, Ambe J. (2009). 'Urban planning as a tool of power and social control in colonial Africa'. *Planning Perspectives* 24(3), 301–17.

Nunbogu, A. M. and Korah, P. I. (2016). 'Self-organisation in urban spatial planning: Evidence from the Greater Accra Metropolitan Area, Ghana'. *Urban Research & Practice* 10(4), 423–41.

Obeng-Odoom, F. (2018). 'Enclosing the urban commons: Crises for the commons and commoners'. *Sustainable Cities and Society* 40, 648–56.

Osei-Tutu, J. K. (2000/2001). '"Space", and the marking of "space" in Ga history, culture, and politics.' *Transactions of the Historical Society of Ghana* 4/5, 55–81.

Paller, J. (2019). *Democracy in Ghana: Everyday Politics in Urban Africa*. Cambridge: Cambridge University Press.

Pierre, J. (2012). *The Predicament of Blackness: Postcolonial Ghana and the Politics of Race*. Chicago/London: University of Chicago Press.

Porter, L. (2011). 'Informality, the commons, and the paradoxes for planning: Concepts and debates for informality and planning'. *Planning Theory & Practice* 12(1), 115–20.

Quayson, A. (2014). *Oxford Street, Accra: City Life and the Itineraries of Transnationalism*. Durham/London: Duke University Press.

Sackeyfio, N. (2012). 'The politics of land and urban space in colonial Accra'. *History in Africa* 39, 293–329.

Simone, A. (2004). 'People as infrastructure: Intersecting fragments from Johannesburg'. *Public Culture* 16(3), 407–29.

Simone, A. (2012). 'Screen'. In Lury, Celia and Wakeford, Nina (eds.), *Inventive Methods: The Happening of the Social*. London/New York: Routledge.

Simone, A. (2019). *Improvised Lives: Rhythms of Endurance in an Urban South*. Cambridge: Polity Press.

Steel, W. F., Ujoranyi, T. D. and Owusu, G. (2014). 'Why evictions do not deter street traders: Case study in Accra, Ghana'. *Ghana Social Science Journal* 11(2), 52–76.

Town and Country Planning Division of the Ministry of Housing (1958). 'Accra: A plan for the town'. The Report for the Minister of Housing. Prepared by B. A.W. Trevallion and Alan G. Hood under the direction of W. H. Barrett. Accra, Ghana.

Vasudevan, A. (2015). 'The autonomous city: Towards a critical geography of occupation'. *Progress in Human Geography* 39(3), 316–37.

Watson, V. (2009). 'Seeing from the south: Refocusing urban planning on the globe"s central urban issues'. *Urban Studies* 46(11), 2259–75.

Chapter 9

Alie, J. D. (1990). *A New History of Sierra Leone*. London: Macmillan.

AlSayyad, N. (2004). 'Urban informality as a "new" way of life'. In Roy, A. and AlSayyad, N. (eds.), *Urban Informality: Transnational perspectives fom the Middle East, South Asia and Latin America*. Lanham: Lexington Books.

Appadurai, A. (2012). 'Why enumeration counts'. *Environment and Urbanization* 24(2).

Bairoch, P. (1985). *De Jèricho à Mexico. Villes et économie dans l'histoire*. Paris: Gallimard.

Balbo, M. (1999). *L'intreccio urbano. La gestione della città nei Paesi in via di Sviluppo*. Milano: Franco Angeli.

Butt-Thompson, F. W. (1926). *Sierra Leone in History and Tradition*. London: Witherby.

Choplin, A. (2017). 'African urban subalternity: Hegemonic planning, subaltern practices and neoliberal citizenship'. In Gusman, A. and Pennacini, C. (eds.), *L'africa delle città – Urban Africa*, 103–16. Torino: Accademia University Press.

CODOSHAPA and FEDURP (2011). 'Community-led enumeration and profiling: The state of 11 coastal slums in Freetown' [online]. Freetown: Shack Slum Dwellers International.

Davis, M. (2006). *Planet of Slums*. New York: Verso.

Floris, F. (2007). *Eccessi di città. Baraccopoli, campi profughi e periferie psichedeliche*. Torino: Paoline Editoriale Libri.

Freund, B. (2007). *The African City: A History*. Cambridge: Cambridge University Press.

Fyfe, C. and Jones, E. (1968). *Freetown: A Symposium*. Freetown: Sierra Leone University Press.

Holston, J. (2009). 'Insurgent citizenship in an era of global urban peripheries'. *City* 21(2), 245–67.

Johnson, M. (2009). *An Assessment of the Urban Conditions Contributing to Slum Development in Freetown*. Freetown: SLURC.

Johnson, O. E. G. (2011). 'Reforming the customary land tenure system in Sierra Leone'. IGC Working Paper 11/0558. London: London School of Economics and Political Science.

Kandè, S. (1998). *Terres, urbanisme et architecture creoles en Sierra Leone*. Paris: L'Harmattan.

Monica, F. (2014). 'Scrap Cities, Strategie e strumenti per l'automiglioramento degli slum di Freetown'. PhD thesis. Università di Parma.

Monica, F. (2017). 'Dinamiche di auto-organizzazione dello spazio urbano e di autocostruzione negli slum di Freetown'. In Gusman, A. and Pennacini, C. (eds.), *L'africa delle città – Urban Africa*. Torino: Accademia University Press.

Monica, F. (2018). 'Slums as opportunities? Spatial organization, microeconomy and self-made infrastructures in Freetown informal settlements'. Paper presented to 'Through Local Eyes' conference, Addis Ababa, October 2018.

Montero, G.M. (2016). *Analytic Framework: Resettlement vs Upgrading. The Case of Colbot in Freetown, Sierra Leone*. London: Bartlett Development Planning Unit, University College.

Pushak, N. and Foster, V. (2011). 'Sierra Leone''s infrastructure. A continental perspective'. *Policy Research Working Paper* 571, 31–5.

Robert, A. C. (2004). *L'Afrique au secours de l'Occident*. Paris: Les èditions de l'Atelier.

Roy, A. (2011). 'Slumdog cities: Rethinking subaltern urbanism'. *International Journal of Urban and Regional Research* 35(2), 223–38.

Simone, A. (2006). 'Pirate towns: Reworking social and symbolic infrastructures in Johannesburg and Douala'. *Urban Studies* 43(2), 357–70.

Simone, A. (2011). 'No longer the subaltern: Refiguring cities in the Global South'. In Edensor, T. and Jayne, M. (eds.), *A World of Cities: Urban Theory beyond 'The West'*. London: Routledge.

Simone, A. (2014). 'Infrastructures, real economy and social transformation: Assembling the components for regional urban development in Africa'. In Parnell, S. and Pieterse, E. (eds.), *Africa's Urban Revolution*, 221–36. London: Zed Books.

Statistics Sierra, Leone. (2016). 'Population and housing census 2015 – Summary of final results'. Freetown: Statistics Sierra Leone.

Tranberg Hansen, K. and Vaa, M. (2004). *Reconsidering Informality: Perspectives from Urban Africa*. Uppsala: Nordiska Afrikainstitutet.

UN-Habitat (2012). *State of the World's Cities Report 2012/2013: Prosperity of Cities*.

Chapter 10

Alexander, P. (2010). 'Rebellion of the poor: South Africa's service delivery protests: A preliminary analysis'. *Review of African Political Economy* 37(23), 25–40.

Andreas, M. (2015). *Vom Neuen Guten Leben*. Bielefeld: transcript.

Ballard, R., Habib, A. and Valodia, I. (2006). *Voices of Protest. Social Movements in Post-Apartheid South Africa*. Scottsville: University of KwaZulu-Natal Press.

Beall, J. (2013). 'Invention and intervention in African cities'. In Obrist, B., Veit. A. and E. Macamo (eds.), *Living the City in Africa*, 24–44. Basel: Schweizerische Afrikastudien.

Bickford-Smith, V. (2016). *The Emergence of the South African Metropolis. Cities and Identities in the Twentieth Century*. Cambridge: Cambridge University Press.

Bloch, E. (1985[1959]). *Das Prinzip Hoffnung*. Frankfurt am Main: Suhrkamp.

Colland, R. (2016). *Make or Break: How the Next Three Years Will Shape South Africa's Next Three Decades*. Cape Town: Zebra Press.

Cook, J. (2006). 'Connecting the Red, Brown and Green. The Environmental Justice Movement in South Africa'. In Ballard, R., Habib, A. and Valodia Scottsville, I. (eds.), *Voices of Protest. Social Movements in Post-Apartheid South Africa*. Durban: University of KwaZulu-Natal Press.

Daniel, A. (2016). *Organisation-Vernetzung-Bewegung. Frauenbewegungen in Kenia und Brasilien*. Münster: LIT Verlag.

Daniel, A. (2022). 'Practicing Ecotopia in Urban Africa'. *Journal of Utopian Studies* 33(2), 274–90.

Daniel, A. and Exner, A. (2020). 'Kartographie gelebter Ökotopien'. *Forschungsjournal Soziale Bewegungen* 33(4), 785–800. DOI: 10.1515/fjsb-2020-0070.

Daniel, A. and Platzky Miller, J. (2022). 'Imagination, decolonization, and intersectionality: the #RhodesMustFall student ccupations in Cape Town, South Africa'. *Social Movement Studies*, 1-22. DOI: 10.1080/14742837.2022.2079120.

Daniel, A., Müller, S., Stoll, F. and Öhlschläger, R. (eds.) (2016). *Mittelklasse, Mittelschichten oder Milieus in Afrika. Gesellschaften im Wandel?* Baden-Baden: Nomos.

Douglas, G. (2014). 'Do-it-yourself urban design: The social practice of informal "'improvement" through unauthorized alteration'. *City & Community* 13(1), 5–25.

Förster, T. (2013). 'On urbanity: Creativity and emancipation in African urban life'. In Obrist, B., Veit. A. and Macamo, E. (eds.), *Living the City in Africa*, 235–51. Basel: Schweizerische Afrikastudien.

Friedman, S. (2018). 'Dignity and equality at centre of South Africa's land debate'. *The Conservation* (6 March). www.iol.co.za/news/opinion/dignity-and-equality-at-centre-of-south-africas-land-debate-13627480 (accessed 11 February 2018).

Gazette Weekly (2016). 'Urban garden uplifts community'. *The Gazette Weekly* (24 November). www.gazetteweekly.com/ (accessed 3 March 2018).

Goldstone, B. and Obrarrio, J. (eds.) (2016). *African Futures. Essays on Crisis, Emergence, and Possibility*. Chicago: University of Chicago Press.

Green Camp Gallery Project (Green Camp) (2016, 15.03.2016). Organic X at Green Camp [YouTube Video]. https://www.youtube.com/watch?v=oojNjff5rgk (23.10.2022).

Green Camp Gallery Project (2017). *ID: Green Camp Gallery Project – Fusing Nature into the Architecture of Urban Structure*. Film. www.youtube.com/watch?v=kBzIZnP9d4s (accessed 3 March 2018).

Haferburg, C. and Huchzermeyer, M. (2014). 'An introduction to the governing in post-apartheid cities'. In Haferburg, C. and Huchzermeyer, M. (eds.), *Urban Governance in Post-Apartheid Cities. Modes of Engagement in South African Metropoles*, 1–35. Stuttgart: Borntraeger Science Publishers.

Hart, G. (2013). *Rethinking South African Crisis*. Athens/London: University of Georgia Press.

Iveson, K. (2013). 'Cities within the city: Do-it-yourself urbanism and the right to the city'. *International Journal of Urban and Regional Research* 37(3), 941–56.

Jamerson, F. (2005). *Archaeologies of the Future: The Desire Called Utopia and Other Science Fictions*. London: Verso.

Lefebvre, H. (1972). *Revolution der Städte*. München: List Verlag.

Levitas, R. (2011). *The Concept of Utopia*. Oxfordshire: Peter Lang Ltd.

Levitas, R. (2014). *Utopia as a Method*. New York: Palgrave.

Mnyaka, Mluleki and Motlhabi, Mokgethi (2005). 'The African concept of Ubuntu/ Botho and its socio-moral significance'. *Black Theology* 3(2), 215–37. DOI: 10.1558/ blth.3.2.215.65725.

More, T. (2011[1516]). *Utopia*. Hamburg: Nikol.

Mottiar, S. and Bond, P. (2012). 'The politics of discontent and social protest in Durban'. *Politikon* 39(39), 309–30.

Müller, M. (2017). *Auswirkungen internationaler Klimakonferenzen auf soziale Bewegungen. Das Fallbeispiel der Klimakonferenz in Südafrika*. Wiesbaden: Springer.

van Niekerk, S. (2016). 'Green Camp Gallery: An urban oasis'. *The Independent* (26 November).

Obrist, B. (2013). 'Introduction to living the city in Africa'. In Obrist, B., Veit, A. and Macamo, E. (eds.), *Living the City in Africa*. Basel: Schweizerische Afrikastudien.

Praeg, L. (2014). *A Report on Ubuntu*. Pietermaritzburg, South Africa: University of KwaZulu-Natal Press.

Rosa, H. and Henning, C. (2018). *A Good Life beyond Growth*. London/New York: Routledge.

Runciman, C. (2017). 'Is democracy working only for the rich?' *The Citizen* (20 May). https://citizen.co.za/talking-point/1519813/democracy-working-rich/ (accessed 11 February 2018).

Samara, T. R., He, S. and Chen, G. (2013). 'Introduction. Locating rights to the city in the Global South'. In Samara, T. R., He, S. and Chen, G. (eds.), *Locating Rights to the City in the Global South*. London/New York: Routledge.

Schölderle, T. (2012). *Geschichte der Utopie. Eine Einführung*. Köln: UBT.

Seekings, J. and Nattrass, N. (2005). *Class, Race and Inequality in South Africa*. New Haven/London: Yale University Press.

Sosibom, K. (2018). 'The green mind: Xolani Hlongwa'. *Mail & Guardian* (2 March). https://mg.co.za/article/2018-03-02-00-the-green-mind-xolani-hlongwa (accessed 3 March 2018).

Talen, E. (2015). 'Do-it-yourself urbanism: A history'. *Journal of Planning History* 14(2), 135–48.

Vusi, G. (2015). *Political Economy of Post-Apartheid South Africa*. Dakar: Council for the Development of Social Science Research in Africa.

van der Walt, T. (2016). 'Rehabilitation among the ruins'. *Sunday Tribune* (14 August). www.pressreader.com/south-africa/sunday-tribune/20160814/281840053066308 (accessed 3 March 2018).

Wegner, P. E. (2002). *Imaginary Communities: Utopia, the nation, and the spatial histories of modernity*. University of California Press.

Wegner, P. E. (2012). *Imaginary Communities*. Berkley: University of California Press.

Williams, C. (2004). 'Evaluating the motives of do-it-yourself (DIY) consumers'. *International Journal of Retail & Distribution Management* 32(4), 270–8.

Wright, E. O. (2010). *Envisioning Real Utopia*. London: Verso.

Chapter 11

Adler, R. P. and Goggin, J. (2005). 'What do we mean by "civic engagement"?'. *Journal of Transformative Education* 3(3), 236–53.

Agbo, M. and Makuwira, J. J. (2019). 'Cruelty by design: How African cities discriminate against people with disabilities'. In *Nordic Africa Institute Policy Note No 5:2018*. Uppsala: Nordic Africa Institute. http://www.diva-portal.org/smash/get/diva2:1344875/FULLTEXT01.pdf.

Braathen, S. H. and Kvan, M. H. (2008). '"Can anything good come out of this mouth?" Female experiences of disability in Malawi'. *Disability and Society* 23(5), 451–74.

Chivers, S. and Markotić, N. (eds.) (2010). *The Problem Body: Projecting Disability on Film*. Columbus: Ohio University Press.

Chouliaraki, L. (2006). *Spectatorship of Suffering*. London: Sage Publications.

Diller, E. C. (2001). 'Citizens in service: The challenge of delivering civic engagement training to national service programs'. Corporation for National and Community Service: Washington, DC.

Douglas, G. C. C. (2013). 'Do-it-yourself urban design: The social practice of informal "improvement" through unauthorized alteration'. *City and Community* 13(1), 5–25.

FEDOMA (2006). 'National policy on equalisation of opportunities for person with disabilities'. MSDPWD: Lilongwe. http://www.ilo.org/dyn/natlex/docs/ELECTRONIC/104037/126732/F438753255/MWI104037.pdf

Gilbert, J. (2008). 'Against the commodification of everything: Anti-consumerist cultural studies in the age of ecological crisis'. *Cultural Studies* 22(5), 551–66.

Government of Malawi (2006). *National Policy on Equalization of Opportunities for Person with Disabilities*. Lilongwe: Ministry of Persons with Disabilities and the Elderly. http://ilo.org/dyn/natlex/docs/ELECTRONIC/104037/126732/F438753255/MWI104037.pdf.

Government of Malawi (2012). 'Act No. 8 of 2012'. Lilongwe: Government of Malawi.

Groce, N. (2015). 'The Disability and Development Gap'. Working Paper 21. London: Leonard Cheshire Disability and Inclusive Development Centre.

Jones, H. (2009). 'Equity in development: Why it is important and how to achieve it'. ODI Working Paper 311. www.odi.org.uk/resources/download/3480.pdf (accessed 15 April 2018).

Lang, R., Schneider, M., Cole, E., Kett, M. and Groce, N. (2017), 'Disability inclusion in African regional policies: Policy review findings from the ESRC/DFID Bridging the Gap disability and development in four African countries project'. London: University College London and Leonard Chesire Disability.

Leob, M. E. and Eide, A. H. (eds.) (2004). *Living Conditions among People with Activity Limitations in Malawi: A National Representative Study*. Oslo: SINTEF.

Maart, S., Eide, A. H., Jelsma, J., Loeb, M. E. and Ka Toni, M. (2007). 'Environmental barriers experienced by urban and rural disabled people in South Africa'. *Disability and Society* 22(4), 357–69.

Makuwira, J. J. (2010). 'Urbanisation, urban poverty and non-governmental development organisations' intervention mechanisms in Malawi: A review of the literature'. *Australasian Review of African Studies* 31(2), 8–29.

Makuwira, J. J. (2013). 'People with disabilities and civic engagement in Malawi'. *Development Bulletin* 75, 66–71. https://crawford.anu.edu.au/rmap/devnet/dev-bulletin.php.

Makuwira, J. J. (n.d.). 'Spectatorship of suffering and the commodification of disability in Malawi: Issues and perspectives for disability-inclusive development'. Unpublished paper (written 2014).

Makuwira, J. J. and Kamanga, G. (n.d.). 'Enabling or disabling? People with disabilities and the policy context in Malawi'. Unpublished paper (written 2011).

Manda, M. A. Z. (2013). *Situation of Urbanisation in Malawi Report*. Lilongwe: Ministry of Lands and Housing.

Munthali, A. (2011). 'A situation analysis of persons with disabilities in Malawi'. Zomba: Centre for Social Research. https://www.unicef.org/malawi/reports/situation-analysis-children-disabilities-malawi (accessed 20 April 2022).

Munthali, A. C., Swartz, L., Mannan, H., MacLachlan, M., Chilimampunga, C. and Makupe, C. (2017). '"This one will delay us": barriers to accessing health care services among persons with disabilities in Malawi', *Disability and Rehabilitation*, 41(6), 683–90.

Munthali, A., Tsoka, M., Milner, J. and Mvula, P. (2013). 'From exclusion to inclusion: Promoting the rights of children with disabilities in Malawi'. Lilongwe: Government of Malawi and UNICEF. www.unicef.org/malawi/MLW_resources_cwdreportfull.pdf (accessed 20 April 2018).

National Statistical Office (NSO) (2008). *2008 Malawi Population and Housing Census*. Zomba: Government Print.

National Statistical Office (2008). *2008 Population and Housing Census Report*. Zomba: NSO Publications.

Rugoho, T. and Siziba, B. (2014). 'Rejected people: Beggars with disabilities in the city of Harare, Zimbabwe'. *Developing Country Studies* 4(26), 51–7.

Sow, M. (2015). 'Foresight Africa 2016: Urbanisation in the African context'. Africa in Focus (30 December). www.brookings.edu/blog/africa-in-focus/2015/12/30/foresight-africa-2016-urbanization-in-the-african-context/

Swift, T., Sweeting, D. and Magee, L. (2016). 'Design in the '"hybrid city": DIY meets platform urbanism in Dhaka's informal settlement's'. *The Conversation* (20 October). https://theconversation.com/design-in-the-hybrid-city-diy-meets-platform-urbanism-in-dhakas-informal-settlements-61661.

United Nations (2015) *Transforming our world: The 2030 Agenda for Sustainable Development*. Geneva: United Nations. https://documents-dds-ny.un.org/doc/UNDOC/GEN/N15/291/89/PDF/N1529189.pdf?OpenElement.

United Nations (2016). 'New urban agenda: Key comments'. www.un.org/sustainabledevelopment/blog/2016/10/newurbanagenda/

Wazikili, M., Chataika, T., Mji, G., Dube, A. K. and MacLachlan, M. (2011). 'Social inclusion of people with disabilities in poverty reduction policies and instruments: Initial impressions from Malawi and Uganda'. In Eide, A. H. and Ingstad, B. (eds.), *Disability and Poverty: A Global Challenge*, 15–29. Bristol: The Policy Press.

White, S. C. (2010). 'Analysing wellbeing: A framework for development practice'. *Development in Practice* 20(2), 158–72.

World Health Organization (2011). 'World report on disability'. www.who.int/disabilities/world_report/2011/en/

Worldometers (2020). Population of Malawi (2020 and historical) https://www.worldometers.info/world-population/malawi-population/.

Chapter 12

Amin, A. (2013). 'Surviving the turbulent future'. *Environment and Planning D: Society and Space* 31(1), 140–56.

Banda, R. K., Mubita, P., Moonga, G. and Meki, C. D. (2021). 'Bacteriological quality and heavy metal analysis of packaged water produced in Lusaka, Zambia and associated quality control measures'. *Frontiers in Public Health* 9.

Beito, D. T., Gordon, P., Tabarrok, A. and Gordon, D. (eds.) (2002). *The Voluntary City: Choice, Community, and Civil Society*. Ann Arbor, Michigan: University of Michigan Press.

Bujra, J. M. and Baylies, C. (2012). 'Solidarity and stress: Gender and local mobilization in Tanzania and Zambia'. In Aggleton, P., Davies, P. and Hart, G. (eds.), *Families and Communities Responding to AIDS*. London: Routledge.

Chauncey Jr, G. (1981). 'The locus of reproduction: Women's labour in the Zambian Copperbelt, 1927–1953'. *Journal of Southern African Studies* 7(2), 135–64.

Chileshe, P. (August 2005). *Hydropolitical Situational Analysis: Water Resources and Their Uses Second Order Water Scarcity In Southern Africa: Zambia Case Study*. DFID [online]. https://assets.publishing.service.gov.uk/media/57a08c8de5274a27b2001295/R8158-SituationalStage.pdf.

Chishimbi, L. (2010). 'Visit strengthens Zambian dairy and technology'. *Dairy Mail Africa: Publication for the Dairy Industry in Africa* 5(3).

CSO (Central Statistical Survey) (2018). *Zambia Demographic Health Survey 2018*. Lusaka: Central Statistical Office.

Duarte, R. (2016). 'DIY urbanism and top-down planning'. *Planetizen* (24 February). www.planetizen.com/node/84500/diy-urbanism-and-top-down-planning

Ferguson, J. (1992). 'The country and the city on the Copperbelt'. *Cultural Anthropology* 7(1), 80–92.

Ferguson, J. (1999). *Expectations of Modernity*. Berkeley: University of California Press.

Fraser, A. and Larmer, M. (eds.) (2010). *Zambia, Mining, and Neoliberalism: Boom and Bust on the Globalized Copperbelt*. New York: Palgrave Macmillan.

Glennie, C. (1982). *A Model for the Development of a Self-Help Water Supply Program*. Washington, DC: World Bank, Technology Advisory Group.

Gould, J. (2010). *Left Behind: Rural Zambia in the Third Republic*. Lusaka: African Books Collective.

Hansen, K. T. (1997). *Keeping House in Lusaka*. New York: Columbia University Press.

Hansen, K. T. (2000). *Salaula: The World of Second-hand Clothing and Zambia*. Chicago: University of Chicago Press.

Hansen, K. T. and Vaa, M. (eds.) (2004). *Reconsidering Informality: Perspectives from Urban Africa*. Uppsala: Nordic Africa Institute.

Hart, K. (1985). 'The informal economy'. *The Cambridge Journal of Anthropology* 10(2), 54–8.

Hart, K. (2013). 'Manifesto for a human economy'. *The Memory Bank*. https://thememorybank.co.uk/object-methods-and-principles-of-human-economy/

Hayek, F. A. (1948). *Individualism and Economic Order*. Chicago: University of Chicago Press.

Heim LaFrombois, M. (2017). 'Blind spots and pop-up spots: A feminist exploration into the discourses of do-it-yourself (DIY) urbanism'. *Urban Studies* 54(2), 421–36.

von der Heyden, C. J. and New, M. G. (2004). 'Groundwater pollution on the Zambian Copperbelt: Deciphering the source and the risk'. *Science of the Total Environment* 327(1–3), 17–30.

Hunleth, J. (2017). *Children as Caregivers: The Global Fight Against Tuberculosis and HIV in Zambia*. Newark NJ: Rutgers University Press.

Jenkins, P. (2004). 'Beyond the formal/informal dichotomy: Access to land in Maputo, Mozambique'. In Karen Hansen, T. and Vaa, M. (eds.), *Reconsidering Informality: Perspectives from Urban Africa*. Uppsala: Nordic Africa Institute.

Kazimbaya-Senkwe, B. M. and Guy, S. C. (2007). 'Back to the future? Privatisation and the domestication of water in the Copperbelt Province of Zambia, 1900–2000'. *Geoforum* 38(5), 869–85.

Lindell, I. (2010). 'Informality and collective organising: Identities, alliances and transnational activism in Africa'. *Third World Quarterly* 31(2), 207–22.

Lungu, J. (2008). 'Socio-economic change and natural resource exploitation: A case study of the Zambian copper mining industry'. *Development Southern Africa* 25(5), 543–60.

Manje, L. and Churchill, C. (2002). 'The demand for risk-managing financial services in low-income communities: Evidence from Zambia'. ILO Social Finance Working Paper 31.

Martin, A. (1972). *Minding Their Own Business: Zambia's Struggle Against Western Control*. London: Hutchinson.

Moen, E. (2003). 'Private sector involvement in policy making in a poverty-stricken liberal democracy'. Working Paper 2003/04. Centre for development and environment, University of Oslo.

Mouli, C. et. al. (1992). *All Against AIDS: The Copperbelt Health Education Project, Zambia*. London: ActionAid.

Murray, M. J. (2009). 'Fire and ice: Unnatural disasters and the disposable urban poor in post-apartheid Johannesburg'. *International Journal of Urban and Regional Research* 33(1), 165–92.

Musaba, E. and Bwacha, I. (2014). 'Technical efficiency of small scale maize production in Masaiti district, Zambia: A stochastic frontier approach'. *Journal of Economics and Sustainable Development* 5(4), 104–11.

Mususa, P. (2012). 'Topping up: Life amidst hardship and death on the Copperbelt'. *African Studies* 71(2), 304–22.

Mususa, P. (2021). *There Used to be Order: Life on the Copperbelt After the Privatisation of the Zambia Consolidated Copper Mines*. Ann Arbor: University of Michigan Press.

Nyamnjoh, F. B. (2002). '"A child is one person"s only in the womb": Domestication, Agency and Subjectivity in the Cameroonian Grassfields'. *Cell* 267, 71655649.

Nyamnjoh, F. B. (2015). *C est l homme qui fait l homme: Cul-de-Sac Ubuntu-ism in Cote d Ivoire*. Bamenda: African Books Collective.

Schumacher, E. F. (1973). *Small is Beautiful: Economics as if People Mattered*. London: Blond & Briggs.

Scott, E. P. (1985). 'Development through self-reliance in Zambia'. *Journal of Geography* 84(6), 282–90.

Showers, K. B. (2002). 'Water scarcity and urban Africa: An overview of urban–rural water linkages'. *World Development* 30(4), 621–48.

Simone, A. (2001). 'Straddling the divides: Remaking associational life in the informal African city'. *International Journal of Urban and Regional Research* 25(1), 102–17.

Simutanyi, N. (1996). 'The politics of structural adjustment in Zambia'. *Third World Quarterly* 17(4), 825–39.

Smart, J. (2015). 'Urban agriculture and economic change in the Zambia Copperbelt: The cases of Ndola, Kitwe and Luanshya'. Doctoral dissertation, University of Otago.

de Soto, H. (2001). 'Dead capital and the poor'. *SAIS Review* 21(1), 13–44.

Straube, C. (2021). *After Corporate Paternalism: Material Renovation and Social Change in Times of Ruination*. New York & Oxford: Berghahn Books.

Turner, J. F. (1976). *Housing By People: Towards Autonomy in Building Environments*. Marion Boyars.

Vidal, J. (2015). 'I drank the water and ate the fish. We all did. The acid has damaged me permanently'. *The Guardian*, 1 August. www.theguardian.com/global-development/2015/aug/01/zambia-vedanta-pollution-village-copper-mine (accessed 20 January 2022).

World Bank (1981). *Accelerated Development in Sub-Saharan Africa: An Agenda for Action*. Washington, DC: World Bank.

Conclusion

Appadurai, Arjun (2001). 'Deep democracy: Urban governmentality and the horizon of politics'. *Environment and Urbanization* 13(2), 23–43.

Arendt, Hannah (1953). *The Origins of Totalitarianism*. New York: Houghton Mifflin Harcourt.

Arendt, Hannah (1960). 'Freedom and politics: A lecture'. *Chicago Review* 14(1), 28–46.

Arendt, Hannah (1971). *The Life of the Mind*. New York: Houghton Mifflin Harcourt.

Arendt, Hannah (1989). *Lectures on Kant's Political Philosophy*. Chicago: University of Chicago Press.

Arendt, Hannah (2006). *Between Past and Future*. New York: Penguin.

Arendt, Hannah (1998 [1958]). *The Human Condition*, 2nd edition. Chicago: University of Chicago Press.

Bayart, Jean-François (2009). *The State in Africa: The Politics of the Belly*. Cambridge: Polity.

Beltrán, Cristina (2009). 'Going public: Hannah Arendt, immigrant action, and the space of appearance'. *Political Theory* 37(5), 595–622.

Beveridge, Ross and Koch, Philippe (2017). 'The post-political trap? Reflections on politics, agency and the city'. *Urban Studies* 54(1), 31–43.

Bloch, Ernst and Ritter, Mark (1977). 'Nonsynchronism and the obligation to its dialectics'. *New German Critique* 11, 22–38.

Canovan, Margaret (1998). 'Introduction'. In Arendt, Hannah, *The Human Condition*. 2nd edition. Chicago: University of Chicago Press.

Caldeira, Teresa P. R. (2017). 'Peripheral urbanization: Autoconstruction, transversal logics, and politics in cities of the global south'. *Environment and Planning D: Society and Space* 35(1), 3–20.

Chalfin, Brenda (2014). 'Public things, excremental politics, and the infrastructure of bare life in Ghana's city of Tema'. *American Ethnologist* 41(1), 92–109.

Chalfin, Brenda (2017). '"Wastelandia": Infrastructure and the commonwealth of waste in urban Ghana'. *Ethnos* 82(4), 648–71.

Cooper, Frederick (2002). *Africa Since 1940: The Past of the Present*, vol. 1. Cambridge: Cambridge University Press.

Chatterjee, Partha (2004). *The Politics of the Governed: Reflections on Popular Politics in Most of the World*. New York: Columbia University Press.

De Boeck, Filip (2015). '"Divining" the city: Rhythm, amalgamation and knotting as forms of "urbanity"'. *Social Dynamics* 41(1), 47–58.

De Boeck, Filip and Plissart, Marie-Françoise (2014). *Kinshasa: Tales of the Invisible City*. Leuven Belgium: Leuven University Press.

De Boeck, Filip and Baloji, Sammy (2016). *Suturing the City: Living Together in Congo's Urban Worlds*. London: Autograph ABP.

Drexler, Jane M. (2007). 'Politics improper: Iris Marion Young, Hannah Arendt, and the power of performativity'. *Hypatia* 22(4), 1–15.

Dikeç, Mustafa (2013). 'Beginners and equals: Political subjectivity in Arendt and Rancière'. *Transactions of the Institute of British Geographers* 38(1), 78–90.

Ekeh, Peter P. (1975). 'Colonialism and the two publics in Africa: A theoretical statement'. *Comparative Studies in Society and History* 17(1), 91–112.

Gaventa, John (1982). *Power and Powerlessness: Quiescence and Rebellion in an Appalachian Valley*. Champaign-Urbana, Illinois: University of Illinois Press.

Geschiere, Peter (2009). *The Perils of Belonging: Autochthony, Citizenship, and Exclusion in Africa and Europe*. Chicago: University of Chicago Press.

Hart, Keith (1973). 'Informal income opportunities and urban employment in Ghana'. *The Journal of Modern African Studies* 11(1), 61–89.

Honig, Bonnie (1988). 'III. Arendt, identity, and difference'. *Political Theory* 16(1), 77–98.

Hyden, Goran (1980). *Beyond Ujamaa in Tanzania: Underdevelopment and an Uncaptured Peasantry*. Berkeley, California: University of California Press.

Keck, Margaret E. and Sikkink, Kathryn (1998). *Activists beyond Borders: Advocacy Networks in International Politics*. Ithaca, New York: Cornell University Press.

Kohn, Jerome (2006). 'Introduction'. In Arendt, Hannah. *Between Past and Future*. New York: Penguin.

Kulin, Joakim, Sevä, Ingemar Johansson and Dunlap, Riley E. (2021). 'Nationalist ideology, rightwing populism, and public views about climate change in Europe'. *Environmental Politics* 30(7), 1–24.

Lockwood, Matthew (2018). 'Right-wing populism and the climate change agenda: Exploring the linkages'. *Environmental Politics* 27(4), 712–32.

Lührmann, Anna and Lindberg, Staffan I. (2019). 'A third wave of autocratization is here: What is new about it?'. *Democratization* 26(7), 1095–113.

Lund, Christian (2006). 'Twilight institutions: Public authority and local politics in Africa'. *Development and Change* 37(4), 685–705.

Marr, Stephen and Mususa, Patience (2020). 'Can marginalised urban communities face Covid-19 without state support?'. *Corona Times Blog*. www.coronatimes.net/marginalised-urban-communities-covid-19/

Meagher, Kate (2012). 'The strength of weak states? Non-state security forces and hybrid governance in Africa'. *Development and Change* 43(5), 1073–101.

Parnell, Susan and Robinson, Jennifer (2012). '(Re) theorizing cities from the Global South: Looking beyond neoliberalism'. *Urban Geography* 33(4), 593–617.

Ring, Jennifer (1991). 'The pariah as hero: Hannah Arendt's political actor'. *Political Theory* 19(3), 433–52.

Robinson, Jennifer (2002). 'Global and world cities: A view from off the map'. *International Journal of Urban and Regional Research* 26(3), 531–54.

Roy, Ananya and Ong, Aihwa (eds.) (2011). *Worlding Cities: Asian Experiments and the Art of Being Global*, vol. 42. London: John Wiley & Sons.

Scheper-Hughes, Nancy (1992). *Death without Weeping: The Violence of Everyday Life in Brazil*. Berkeley California: University of California Press.

Schindler, Seth and Silver, Jonathan (2019). 'Florida in the Global South: How Eurocentrism obscures global urban challenges—and what we can do about it'. *International Journal of Urban and Regional Research* 43(4), 794–805.

Scott, James C. (1977). *The Moral Economy of the Peasant*. New Haven, Connecticut: Yale University Press.

Scott, James C. (1985). *Weapons of the Weak: Everyday Forms of Peasant Resistance*. New Haven, Connecticut: Yale University Press.

Simone, AbdouMaliq (2003). 'Moving towards uncertainty: Migration and the turbulence of African urban life'. In *Conference on African Migration in Comparative Perspective, Johannesburg, South Africa*, 4–7.

Simone, AbdouMaliq (2004). 'People as infrastructure: Intersecting fragments in Johannesburg'. *Public Culture* 16(3), 407–29.

Simone, AbdouMaliq (2006). 'Pirate towns: Reworking social and symbolic infrastructures in Johannesburg and Douala'. *Urban Studies* 43(2), 357–70.

Simone, AbdouMaliq (2010). *City Life from Jakarta to Dakar: Movements at the Crossroads*. London: Routledge.

Simone, AbdouMaliq (2018). *Improvised Lives: Rhythms of Endurance in an Urban South*. London: John Wiley & Sons.

de Souza, Marcelo Lopes (2006). 'Social movements as "critical urban planning" agents'. *City* 10(3), 327–42.

Swyngedouw, Erik (2009). 'The antinomies of the postpolitical city: In search of a democratic politics of environmental production'. *International Journal of Urban and Regional Research* 33(3), 601–20.

Swyngedouw, Erik (2017). 'Unlocking the mind-trap: Politicising urban theory and practice'. *Urban Studies* 54(1), 55–61.

Thompson, Edward P. (1971). 'The moral economy of the English crowd in the eighteenth century'. *Past & Present* 50, 76–136.

Wolin, Sheldon S. (1983). 'Hannah Arendt: Democracy and the political'. *Salmagundi* 60, 3–19.

Young, Crawford (1994). *The African Colonial State in Comparative Perspective*. New Haven, CT: Yale University Press.

INDEX

The City in History (Mumford) 14
cityness 76–7
civic engagement 5, 27, 161–2
Civilian Joint Task Force (Civilian-JTF) 67
civil society 3, 35, 59, 63, 70, 79, 186,
    198–9
civil war 128
climate change 128, 139–40, 144, 191,
    196–8
colonialism 1, 8, 50, 89, 93, 96, 100, 102,
    109, 115, 128
commodification 163–6
Community Development Association
    (CDA) 81
community-led security 58, 61–4, 67,
    69–71
community policing 6, 62–3, 71–2, 76,
    81–4
Congres d'Internationaux Architecture
    Moderne (CIAM) 110 n.7
conventional urban planning approach
    26, 49
Convention People's Party (CPP) 96, 100
Cooper, F. 198
Copperbelt. *See* Zambian Copperbelt
    (Ferguson)
Copperbelt Health Education Project
    (CHEP) 181
co-presence 13, 17
Cote d'Ivoire 66
Covid-19 pandemic 197–9

Daily Graphic 97, 111 n.15
Danish International Development
    Agency (DANIDA) 176
Dar es Salaam 71
De Boeck, F. 7, 19, 109, 194
decentralization 131
Demetz, P. 16
Democratic People's Party (DPP) 85 n.1
Democratic Republic of Congo (DRC)
    63–4, 66
deprivation 36, 143, 157
Devisch, R. 16, 19
Devtraco Plus, Ltd. 104–5
Dhaka 156
diamond war 128
Di Nunzio, M. 84
Diouf, M. 18–19

disability 155
    in Africa 156–7
    commodification of 163–6
    defined 158
    in Malawi 158–9
    overview 157–8
disabled people's organizations (DPOs)
    155, 157, 160–1, 163, 165
Disciplinary Brigade 66
divining 6
DIY paradigm 34–5, 40
DIY urbanism 2–4, 37, 138–9
    ambiguity 28–30
    engagement with 4–5
    everyday urban life 18–23
    faces of 26–8
    health provisioning 179–82
    in Nigeria 42–4
    organizational structures 7–9
    planning and infrastructure 139
    politics of 185–9, 193–6
    progression 5–7
    scope and breadth 25–6
    socio-cultural context 51–3
    socio-political context 50–1
    tenure rights and land use policies
        140
    and urban living 34–41
    utopia 145–7
    water provisioning 176–9
Douglas, G. 2
DPOs. *See* disabled people's organizations
    (DPOs)
Drew, J. 110 n.7
Drexler, J. M. 192
Duarte, R. 171
Duncombe, S. 48
Durban 5, 144, 147–8, 150
Durkheim 33–5
Dworzak Farm 138

East Cantonments 104
ecotopian community 146–7, 153
Egbesu Boys 67
Ekeh, P. 59–60
Eko Atlantic City 85
Enwezor, O. 89, 109
equality 161, 186
equity 160–1

Milton Keynes UK
Ingram Content Group UK Ltd.
UKHW020256221223
434767UK00003B/80